THOMAS HARRISON is Professor of Ancient History at the University of St Andrews. He is the author of *Writing Ancient Persia* (2011) and editor of *The Edinburgh Companion to Ancient Greece and Rome* (2006) (with Ed Bispham and Brian Sparkes) and *Herodotus in the Long Nineteenth Century* (2020) (with Joseph Skinner).

# THE GREAT EMPIRES
## OF THE
# ANCIENT WORLD

EDITED BY

THOMAS HARRISON

**With 38 illustrations**

On the cover: Jan Brueghel the Elder, *View of a Harbour City
(The Continence of Scipio)*, c. 1600–9 (detail).
Photo akg-images/Alte Pinakothek, Munich.

First published in the United Kingdom in 2009 by
Thames & Hudson Ltd, 181A High Holborn,
London WC1V 7QX

First published in the United States of America in 2021 by
Thames & Hudson Inc., 500 Fifth Avenue, New York,
New York 10110

This paperback edition 2021
Reprinted 2023

*The Great Empires of the Ancient World* © 2009 and 2021
Thames & Hudson Ltd, London

Edited by Thomas Harrison

British Library Cataloguing-in-Publication Data
A catalogue record for this book is available from
the British Library

Library of Congress Control Number 2021943685

ISBN 978-0-500-29588-5

Printed and bound in the UK by CPI Group (UK) Ltd

Be the first to know about our new releases,
exclusive content and author events by visiting
**thamesandhudson.com**
**thamesandhudsonusa.com**
**thamesandhudson.com.au**

# CONTENTS

# INTRODUCTION

## New Visions of Ancient Empires

THOMAS HARRISON

*The Great Empires of the Ancient World* offers accessible and authoritative accounts of all the major early imperial powers, from the empires of the Hittites and New Kingdom Egypt in the 2nd millennium BC through to the early Sasanian Persian empire concluding in around AD 300, from the Mediterranean empire of Rome to the (no less vast) dominions of Qin and Han China.

These empires are united not only by the time period in which broadly they emerged and fell. The relationship between them, geographically and chronologically scattered as they were, is an immensely complex one of rivalry, succession and assimilation. Just as the Han empire of China evolved from the Qin (and indeed itself had more than a single phase), so the Mauryan, Kushan and Gupta empires of South Asia all developed in a complex relationship to their predecessors. The Parthian and Sasanian empires, which grew out of one of the successor states which emerged from the chaos of Alexander the Great's death, both looked back to the Achaemenid Persian empire of the 6th to 4th centuries BC as a model, terming their rulers (as Indian rulers did) 'king of kings' in imitation of the Achaemenids. Both clashed violently with Rome, just as the Achaemenids had with the Greeks; and in both cases the eastern empire then suffered from having its history written by its rivals.

Why study ancient empires now? With the possible exception of the late 19th and early 20th centuries, the history of ancient empires has perhaps never been so timely or generated so much popular interest. This is evidenced, for example, by more or less successful films focused on Roman, Macedonian or Persian empires (*Gladiator* or *Alexander*), or the enormous success of museum exhibitions reappraising ancient empires such as that of the Qin terracotta warriors or the 'forgotten empire' of the Achaemenid Persians. If we are to seek the reasons for the prominence of ancient empires in the popular consciousness, however, we should look not to Hollywood or the world of museums (both, in any event, perhaps trend-followers rather than leaders), but instead at the jostling for power among modern nations.

On the one hand, the great former imperial powers – the United Kingdom, France, Germany, Russia, among others – have all in different ways been forced to come to new understandings of their imperial pasts, all seeking to accommodate (in strikingly different ways) grand ideas of their national destinies to changed environments. Scholarship on empire has moved on in parallel: in particular, the 'postcolonial' trend in modern writing has encouraged an understanding that empires exist as much in people's minds as in external structures of control. The end of empire is no longer seen as a simple matter of the physical withdrawal from a distant colony; rather, it is now understood, empires shape people's understanding of their position in the world, long after the colonizer's flag has been packed away and the brass band departed. Increasingly, attention has focused on the personal experience of empire, on how – both among the imperial subjects and among 'imperialists' – daily life was imbued with the experience of empire.

This recognition of the indirect and personal ways in which empire may manifest itself has led also to the identification of new empires. Just as previous empires – Russia, Ottoman Turkey, as well as western Europe – have claimed to be the successors of Rome, so now the modern United States has taken its turn. The parallel – real or imagined – between America and Rome has been exploited in numerous different ways, more or less positively and more or less convincingly, by journalists, bloggers, cartoonists, as well as by the employees of neoconservative thinktanks. In a positive assessment, two of the latter, Bill Kristol and Robert Kagan, described the United States in the wake

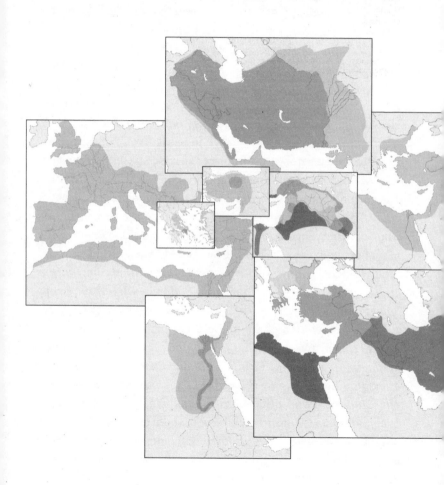

**1** Egyptian
1539–1069 BC

**2** Hittite
1650–1200 BC

**3** Assyrian and
Babylonian
900–539 BC

1600 BC  1500 BC  1400 BC  1300 BC  1200 BC  1100 BC  1000 BC  900 BC  800 BC  700 BC  600

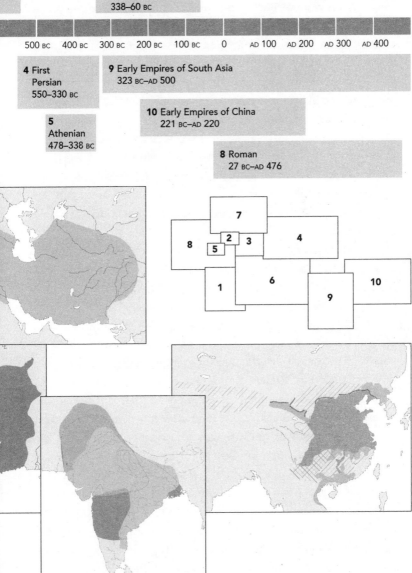

**7** Parthian and Early Sasanian
c. 247 BC–AD 300

**6** Alexander
and Successors
338–60 BC

500 BC   400 BC   300 BC   200 BC   100 BC   0   AD 100   AD 200   AD 300   AD 400

**4** First
Persian
550–330 BC

**9** Early Empires of South Asia
323 BC–AD 500

**5**
Athenian
478–338 BC

**10** Early Empires of China
221 BC–AD 220

**8** Roman
27 BC–AD 476

of the first Iraq war as '[holding] a position unmatched since Rome dominated the Mediterranean world'. From a critical perspective, Presidents George W. Bush and Donald Trump have been compared to (among other Roman emperors) Commodus, Caligula and Nero. In a speech in Italy in 2019, Trump himself referred to a 'shared cultural and political heritage dating back thousands of years, to ancient Rome'.

How should we respond to these parallels? Clearly, the modern appropriation of ancient empires for particular political motives can distort our understanding of ancient empires. All of the chapters in this book reflect and make accessible a vast industry of scholarly reconstruction of ancient empires. Readers can rightly turn to *The Great Empires of the Ancient World* for authoritative accounts independent of passing political currents. On the other hand, there are significant ways in which the history of ancient empires cannot be divorced from modern distortions and appropriations.

The harnessing of ancient history to modern ends is not, first, a new phenomenon. The analogy of ancient and modern empires has been expressed through any number of ways: through imitative architecture, through the heroizing dress of imperial heroes, or (very occasionally) through direct comparison: the conscious search in ancient history for answers to the problems of how to manage an empire in the modern world, how for example to deal with a racially diverse population. Modern empires have looked to a multiplicity of ancient empires for inspiration, rarely just one 'ancestor'. The founders of the American republic (an odd kind of empire admittedly) looked to Carthage as well as to Carthage's historical enemy, Rome. The British found inspiration for their own imperial rule in the Persian empire just as in the Roman. The Germans, like the British, looked to heroes from the resistance to Roman rule – Arminius/Hermann or Boudicca – as well as to the Romans themselves. Just as with the ancient *translatio imperii*, or succession of empires, the implication is that the latest empire is the summation of its predecessors, taking on their best aspects while tempering or avoiding the worst.

It was in this kind of imperial context, crucially, that the modern understanding of ancient empires was forged. This is true in a number of ways. First, of course, the archaeological excavations which unearthed much of the evidence for the empires discussed in this book were frequently carried out under the auspices, more or less direct, of one or other imperial power. The decipherment of cuneiform – the work of a number of European scholars working simultaneously – opened the floodgates to new ways of looking at the empires of the ancient Near East (Assyrian, Babylonian, Persian among others), and so ultimately led to the undoing of 19th-century narratives, usually derived from classical sources, of decadent eastern powers. But at the same time, these modern empires clearly provided – and arguably still provide – a powerful framework for thinking about the reality of the ancient cultures being uncovered. It is hard, for example, in reflecting on the early empires of South Asia not to be influenced by pervasive images of the British Raj, to be tempted to the conclusion that they were precursors of the British unification of India – itself a much more complex phenomenon – under a single rule.

What anyway is an empire? No single term, in reality, encompasses all the empires discussed in this volume: the Athenians' short-lived naval confederacy-turned-empire was termed *archê* or simply 'rule'; the Latin *imperium*, which has given rise to our term empire (imperialism, significantly, is a modern coinage), was a term used to describe any manner of types of formal authority. Moving beyond this narrow issue of terminology, the modern term 'empire' is used arguably to describe a complete menagerie of different beasts. Some are vast and others small-scale. Some exercised rule over distant colonies, while others simply claimed hegemony over the territory of their neighbours. Some were governed by democratic governments, others by monarchies. Some were heavily bureaucratized, others seem to have possessed scant central control. Some took pains to assimilate their subjects, while others kept those they ruled at arms' length, ruling through an ethnically distinct elite. And all had different means of control at their disposal, dictated not only by technology, but also by the size and terrain of their territory. Whether indeed the term empire should rightly be applied, except by way of analogy, to all those contained in this volume is debatable. If we indeed include the contemporary United States in this list of empires, then this definition is stretched even further. Though recent years have seen some US political commentators use the term 'empire' without embarrassment, Americans have tended to style themselves as anti-imperial. Clearly, we would have to accept that the forms of control by which such an empire is maintained are also ingeniously veiled by comparison with historical empires. But then the Roman empire also was cloaked around in republican language.

One other way in which the modern experience of empire has informed the way we look at the empires of the ancient world concerns the moral judgments we make about them. This is true in two ways. A number of chapters in this volume point to the manner in which the empires in question, those of the ancient Near East, have persistently been characterized as morally flawed or decadent, while other empires have had a more positive colouring in scholarship. This is explicable partly by the 'orientalist' assumptions of the first narratives, partly by a historical dependence on ancient sources written from other perspectives: our portrayal of the Persian king Xerxes, for example, has been formed by the account of the Greek-Persian wars of (the Greek) Herodotus, just as the Babylonian Nebuchadnezzar's image has been formed through biblical accounts of the Babylonian exile of the Jews that he initiated.

This kind of unthinking moralism inherited from ancient sources is mostly a thing of the past. In broader terms, however, moralism cannot be escaped so easily. It is still tempting in looking at ancient empires (or indeed any empires) to seek to weigh them on moral scales: to deem, for example, that a degree of financial exploitation was comfortably outweighed by the protection afforded to the imperial subjects, or by the 'civilizing mission' of the imperial power. It is perhaps not an accident, however, that this kind of approach – that of the moral balance-sheet – was one commonly adopted in the context of modern empires, born out of a (more or less) self-conscious desire to vindicate empire. Persisting with these moral scales in mind then might unwittingly reflect the perspective of the imperial power rather than of the subjects of empire – a difference that one can see clearly if one looks at potential modern parallels. One British journalist, Jonathan Freedland, has compared the attractions of togas and central heating in the Roman world with what the US offers the people of the world today: 'It's not togas or gladiatorial games… but Starbucks, Coca-Cola, McDonald's and Disney, all paid for in the contemporary equivalent of Roman coinage… the dollar.' Ingesting Coca-Cola, however, does not involve ingesting American cultural values, still less a commitment to US foreign policy goals. Would the subjects of ancient empires have been any less ambivalent in their response to others' attempts to 'civilize' them?

So how in the final analysis should we look at ancient empires? The Greek historian Thucydides, one of the first theorists of empire (more recently described as the 'favourite neoconservative text on foreign affairs'), strikingly made the Athenians say in justification of their rule over their Greek neighbours that 'It has always been a rule that the weak should be subject to the strong.' Empire (broadly defined now to include any attempt by one political organization systematically to dominate others) is simply a fact of life then, and what we can learn from ancient empires is limited by the different conditions in which they operated. Thucydides adds, however, an Athenian afterthought: 'Besides we consider that we are worthy of our power'. What distinguishes one 'empire' from another is partly the means of control at its disposal, but also perhaps the unique way in which it imagines and seeks to justify itself: brazenly insisting that its rule is justified by past achievements; claiming the mantle (like the Achaemenid Persian empire) of the benign global policeman putting squabbling nations in order, or that the limits of one's empire are the limits of civilization (as with Rome or Qin China); or somehow projecting a sense of timelessness and inevitability, of the universal nature of one set of values (as with the modern USA).

In the Athenians' case also, the inevitability of empire is just another plank of their self-justification. When we focus on this ideological aspect of empires, their ability to recreate themselves endlessly, the differences between ancient and modern empires strip away. It is this complex relationship between past and present, between modern interpreter and ancient empire, that *The Great Empires of the Ancient World* seeks to describe.

# THE EMPIRE OF NEW KINGDOM EGYPT

## 1539–1069 BC

BILL MANLEY

For a moment in history, which we now call the New Kingdom, Egypt was the richest, most powerful and most influential nation on Earth. The moment lasted for 400 years, from the reign of Thutmose III (c. 1479–1425 BC) until the death of the 11th king named Ramesses (c. 1099–1069 BC). During those centuries, a nation with a history stretching back, so it believed, to the very beginning of time, matured to become a populous, multi-ethnic powerhouse of surpassing wealth and intellectual conviction, harnessed to a traditional system of government and a proven military tradition. The gold-mines of Nubia underwrote Egypt's position as the world's richest economy; and far-flung trading networks were founded on brotherhood with nations across northeast Africa, the Near East and the Mediterranean Sea.

The government, religion and art of New Kingdom Egypt were firmly rooted after 1,500 years of rule by god-kings, who from this time would be known as pharaohs. For Thutmose III (54 years as pharaoh) or Ramesses II (67 years), sacred sites such as the Great Sphinx and pyramids at Giza were already ancient and had stood through the ages as proof of the validity of Egypt's most fundamental beliefs. They inspired the pharaohs to rebuild the temples of gods and the monuments of their forefathers, or to 'build anew' and 'increase what was bequeathed to me'. This last sentiment – equating success with family, obligation and expansion – was integral to kingship. Reflecting on his own success as king, in the words of a monument at his southernmost frontier, Thutmose III concedes:

> '*My father, Amun-Ra, was the one who did it, it was not an act of man.*'

Accordingly, grateful pharaohs rewarded the temples of Amun-Ra and the other gods ever more lavishly with land and labour, with tax revenues and commercial privileges, and with festivals. In so doing, the rulers of the New Kingdom built and bequeathed the Ancient Egypt of our modern imagination.

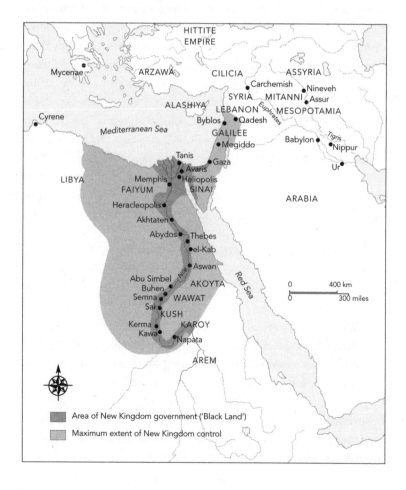

## Belief in Black Land

Historians during the New Kingdom recognized an ebb and flow of power within Egypt. The land, stretching more than 1,000 km (620 miles) along the Nile from the Mediterranean coast to Nubia, had first become a nation with one king and one palace by about 3000 BC. However, in the century preceding the New Kingdom, the land had been carved into three, with kings based at Avaris in the Nile delta, at Thebes in the Nile valley, and at Kerma in Nubia. The kings who ruled Avaris for 108 years styled themselves as Hyksos, 'rulers of foreign lands', a title that has been taken to indicate that they were themselves foreigners, not conquerors of foreign lands. Certainly their towns shared strong cultural, commercial and, presumably, political links with towns in Palestine and Syria as well as with those of the Nile valley. Avaris itself straddled important trade-routes to the Near East and was a major port for the Mediterranean world. In Nubia, a confederation of chiefs recognized at their head a Ruler of Kush, the southern part of Nubia, whose culture, as revealed in archaeology, was distinctly un-Egyptian but whose economic and military clout was considerable. Throughout these two kingdoms a cosmopolitan mix of ethnic groups and languages had developed over centuries, including ethnic Egyptians living and working in Nubia.

The kings of Thebes, unlike many of their countrymen, saw this state of affairs as a travesty of good order. On one stela erected in the temple of Amun-Ra at Karnak, King Kamose (c. 1541–1539 BC) laments:

'Why do I contemplate my might, when there is a Chief in
Avaris and another in Kush? I sit joined to an Asiatic and
a Nubian, each man holding his slice of this Black Land,
dividing the land with me?'

Believing that the rich soil of the Nile-lands formed a single Black Land (kõme), Kamose vowed to 'seek out Asiatics, to crush their places, because east and west are covered with their grease'. So, as the 16th

**KEY DATES**

| | |
|---|---|
| 1530s BC | Ahmose defeats Hyksos kingdom |
| 1480s BC | Thutmose I invades Kush, then takes army to Byblos and Mitanni |
| 1470 BC | Hatshepsut's expedition to Punt |
| 1457 BC | Thutmose III leads army at battle of Megiddo |
| 1340 BC | Akhenaten suppresses major rebellion near Nubian goldmines |
| 1320s BC | Tutankhamun's troops clash with Hittites |
| 1292 BC | New dynasty (19th), from the family of Ramesses I |
| 1274 BC | Ramesses II clashes with Hittites at battle of Qadesh |
| 1209 BC | Merenptah drives away Libyan invaders |
| 1190 BC | New dynasty (20th), from the family of Sethnakhte |
| 1180s BC | Ramesses III drives away Libyan invaders and 'Sea-peoples' |
| 1088 BC | Troops of (viceroy) Panehsī occupy Thebes |
| 1082 BC | Campaign of (general) Piankh against Panehsī ends in division of Egypt |

century unfolded, the Theban dynasty was honing its weapons for an orgy of ethnic cleansing.

Kamose's first attack, on Kush, is mentioned only obliquely in sources, but monuments of his at the old fortress of Buhen confirm that he began by taking control of Wawat, the northern part of Nubia. In contrast, the assault on the kingdom of Avaris is described in some detail in the temple of Amun-Ra. First, the population of Nefrusy is slaughtered because it had made 'a nest for Asiatics'. Later his troops intercept a letter from the king of Avaris, Apōp, begging help from Kush. Apōp seems not only afraid but impotent, and soon Kamose has flown with his falcon-fleet to Avaris itself. The city is massively fortified so the Theban marines cannot capture it, but they ravage its estates and orchards, and loot chariot-teams, battle-axes, oils, foreign timber, precious metals and stones from the shipyards. Kamose returns home to streets brimming with excitement and delight, but grim events had been set in motion.

Kamose died suddenly and his successor, Ahmose I (c. 1539–1514 BC), was just a child, so a stalemate between Thebes and Avaris prevailed for at least a decade. Nevertheless, the dogma of Black Land held sway within the Theban regime, and Ahmose's eventual campaigns against his Hyksos enemy are well documented in tomb inscriptions, such as those of Ahmose-Saibana and Ahmose-Pennekhbet. Both were marines from the town of el-Kab, keen to record the decorations, slaves and grants of land that they earned from the pharaoh. Ahmose took control of the ancient capital, Memphis; then came as many as five campaigns against Avaris, with savage fighting throughout the rivers and canals of the Nile delta. Ahmose-Saibana relates the outcome starkly:

> 'Avaris was plundered, and I took plunder away from it – one
> man, three women, i.e. four heads – and the king gave me
> them for slaves.'

Finally, Theban forces set upon Sharuhen, a fortified town near Gaza in Palestine, at the end of the Horus-roads that crossed the Sinai desert. Once again, Ahmose's marines were hobbled by the need for siege warfare but, after three campaigns, its population also lay slaughtered. Ahmose I had stripped Avaris of its independence, brought the caravans from Palestine under his control and asserted a boundary between Black Land and the lands beyond Sinai that had been obscured in the activities of the Hyksos.

Ahmose's usurpation of control throughout Egypt and Wawat was complete by the end of his reign, although he did face two uprisings against the new order. One was led by 'Aata, probably a Nubian chieftain, 'whose fate hastened his doom', according to Ahmose-Saibana. The second was in Egypt, perhaps in the newly conquered delta. Ahmose's regime was not without opponents but the Theban vision of Black Land prevailed, and in time his son succeeded as Amenhotep I. A generation later, Amenhotep died without a surviving son, but the throne passed unchallenged to a courtier, Thutmose I

(c. 1493–1481 BC), who fathered a dynasty that ruled Black Land until the death of Tutankhamun, some 175 years later.

## Swallowing Nubia

Nubian opposition to Egyptian control was expected. Any expansion, whether along the river or into the surrounding deserts, was bound to be at the expense of Kush, so the annexation of Nubia entailed decades of war. From the reign of Kamose, a new office, 'King's Son', was used to govern the occupied lands; it was never held by an actual son of the king, but his title indicated the elevated status of a viceroy. Kamose had annexed Wawat as far as Buhen, and Amenhotep I as far as the fortified island of Sai, but the troops of Thutmose I campaigned into Kush itself, to Tombos, just 30 km (19 miles) from Kerma. Thutmose also divided Wawat into five districts to negate opposition from within the land's traditional tribal structure. Indigenous chiefs were accorded the status of Egyptian courtiers and encouraged to prosper from the subjugation of their own countrymen. A rebellion instigated by Kush was suppressed by Thutmose II in c. 1481 BC, once again with great ferocity, at which point the annexation of Wawat was effectively complete.

In broad terms, New Kingdom policy towards Nubia was shaped by two considerations. On the one hand, Wawat and Kush were evidently part of Black Land, and likewise any ruler of Kush was a blatant pretender to pharaoh's hegemony. On the other hand, the vast mineral wealth of Nubia was to become the foundation for a formidable economy. These two considerations had different strategic implications: the conquest of Black Land entailed expansion along the Nile, but the quest for gold required mining-expeditions trekking ever deeper into the deserts. Most mines presented huge difficulties, not least for safety in deserts whose climate and nomadic inhabitants could be equally hostile to Egyptians. Nevertheless, the pharaohs now began to exploit Nubia's mineral wealth on a scale previously unimagined. One inscription of Thutmose I marks the spot where a mining expedition had crossed the desert and found itself back at the Nile, far to the south of Kerma. Its broken words still resound:

> 'If any Nubian encroaches the mandate that my father, Amun,
> has given to me, [his head?] shall be lopped off… and he
> shall have no heirs.'

The reign of Thutmose's grandson, Thutmose III (c. 1479–1425 BC), partly shared with the old king's daughter, Hatshepsut (c. 1473–1458 BC), was the decisive moment when Kush, surrounded and crushed, simply capitulated. The government of Black Land was reorganized so that Nubia was swallowed up, and the viceroy (now styled 'King's Son of Kush') was afforded the same powers in Nubia that a pair of viziers held in Upper Egypt and Lower Egypt. A system of control modelled exactly on Egypt's was put in place by founding and developing temple-towns, trading-towns and forts. In Year 32 of Thutmose's reign, more than a century after Kamose's initial attack, Wawat and Kush began to pay 'taxes' (*bãk*) to pharaoh's palace, the same as any district of Black Land.

At the death of Thutmose III, Black Land had attained what would be its essential form for the next four centuries. The remains of the temple of Amun-Ra at Gebel Barkal, near what would become the fortress of Napata, probably represent the southernmost limit of Egyptian control at any period of history. Beyond there, the arid land of Karoy formed a natural frontier. Nubian chiefs now grew wealthy from trade between Black Land and other African nations, such as Ãrem, Nmãy and Punt. In Wawat they were typically buried in Egyptian-style tombs, and the material culture of the Nubian population took on Egyptian characteristics. Mining expanded so far that expeditions to the gold-laden desert of Akõyta could be supported by ships on the Red Sea. Of course, uprisings against Egyptian control did recur and were not insignificant: an uprising in Akõyta as late as c. 1341 BC, in the reign of Akhenaten, required intervention under the command of the King's Son of Kush himself, and some 225 Nubians were slain or impaled as a result. Nevertheless, the area was still being mined by Egyptians 150 years later.

## The Extent of Black Land

Black Land's most exotic trading partner was Punt. Modern historians disagree whether Punt was on the coast of Africa or Arabia, but for the ancients it was simply at the edge of the world. Here was God's Land, a garden of Amun-Ra's pleasure with the goddess Hathor and an emporium for the gods' own luxuries, especially the heavenly incense called *antŏ* as well as fragrant woods, spices and exotic hides. Egyptians had first reached Punt a thousand years earlier but contact had long since been lost. So Hatshepsut dispatched a naval expedition 'to open the way', and her temple at Deir el-Bahri in Thebes includes detailed depictions of that fabulous and bizarre land and of ships laden with 'its wonders'. Trade between the nations continued for at least three centuries, and children of Punt's chiefs were among the foreigners raised in the Egyptian palace. However, most wonders from Punt arrived not by sea but with caravans travelling via Ārem and Nmãy in modern Sudan. The edge of the world, in other words, was just a donkey-trip from the frontiers of Black Land, which now spanned 'the four corner-poles of the sky'.

At the far edge of the world, God's Land was discovered in the snow-covered mountains of Lebanon (*Libnãn*). Here were terraces of tall, straight timber (the one resource Black Land conspicuously lacked) rising high over the valley of the Euphrates, 'that upside-down water which goes upstream in going downstream'. From the Nile, Lebanon was most easily reached by sea, via Egypt's traditional ally, the magnificent port of Byblos, whose mayor governed a hinterland crisscrossed by trade-routes linking the Levantine ports to great kingdoms in Anatolia and Mesopotamia. Byblos was Egypt's ancient partner in ideas and values as well as trade, and would now be central to a new episode of Egyptian expansion.

## Mastering the Near East

No ideology spurred the New Kingdom into conquering lands beyond the Nile: the credo of Black Land involved only Egypt and Nubia. Therefore, the regime's long entanglement with the Near East, one that would sporadically entail war on the grandest scale, was shaped by political self-interest. Moreover, there is no compelling evidence that Egypt's armies were active in neighbouring Palestine until the 22nd Year of Thutmose III, more than 60 years after Ahmose overran Sharuhen and opened up the roads into the Near East. It is no coincidence that Kush's capitulation was by then complete and the southern frontier of Black Land was no longer at war. Our understanding of the subjugation of Nubia is based on Egyptian monuments, in which Nubian voices or dissenting opinions are barely heard. However, for Egypt's activity in the Near East we have not only royal monuments but also diplomatic correspondence – texts both from Egypt and from other nations. The words of friend and foe alike reveal a consistent policy of defending Egypt's interests assertively but with the minimum of military intervention. The pharaohs were interested in the ports that handled commerce on the Mediterranean Sea and the towns that managed caravans across the Near East.

On the other hand, the treacherous hills of Palestine were best avoided. Archaeological indications that fortresses from Ashkelon to Jericho were burned or abandoned across several decades at the beginning of the New Kingdom are the calling-cards not of Egyptians but of ruthless local chiefs. Egypt's armies recognized the value of urban communities, and rarely destroyed towns or the lands on which they subsisted. Instead they measured success in terms of plunder fetched for temples or prisoners transported as slaves. To eliminate an important town risked breaking the chain of commerce. Troublesome chiefs were sometimes deposed in favour of more amenable characters but generally the pharaohs left towns in the hands of chiefs with some native wit, albeit after extracting an oath of loyalty. Ironically it takes a stela of Thutmose III to get these quarrelsome chiefs to speak with one voice:

> 'We will not return in our allotted lives to evil-doing against
> Menkheperra [Thutmose III], our lord, because we have seen
> his power, and he has allowed us breath only so far as he is
> pleased to.'

Egypt's policy towards the Near East became discernible during the 1480s BC, when Thutmose I led an army to Nahrãn, the 'land of the Twin Rivers', the Orontes and Euphrates. A list of towns in his monumental account suggests that Thutmose avoided Palestine altogether and moved his troops by sea to Byblos, going from there up the coast to Sumur, then through the mountains inland. His purpose is uncertain: perhaps he simply wished to reassert Egypt's presence in the port and its hinterland, and highlight the premium he attached to the timber-terraces. However, he also had a stela carved on the far bank of the Euphrates, marking his boundary on the doorstep of the kingdom of Mitanni. No doubt the king of Mitanni had viewed Nahrãn as his own business until then, but his reaction is not recorded.

Three decades later, freed from the exhausting war in Nubia, his grandson, Thutmose III, undertook 17 campaigns in Palestine and Syria in just 21 years. The first of these in c. 1458 BC was decisive: he marched his armies from the port of Gaza to besiege the port of Joppa and then fall on the town of Megiddo, which controlled the main trade-routes in the north of Palestine. There he found 'the leaders of all lands standing on their chariots in their tens and hundreds, each one there bringing his own army'. It not clear whether there had been a specific provocation that precipitated the war, but it was a singular event for so many erstwhile rivals to unite on a battlefield. However, Thutmose's armies had long experience of how to wage war proficiently, and soon 'made them as those who had never been, those who wallow in their own blood'. The town was surrounded and taken after seven months. A glimpse of the human cost of this long-ago campaign may be the terracotta cones discovered near Gaza, stamped with the names of Thutmose III and Hatshepsut. Perhaps they formed part of a mass grave for fallen Egyptians, whose individual identities were too numerous to be recorded.

Thutmose III presented his victory at Megiddo as proof that all humanity gathered together would fall before pharaoh, if Amun-Ra so willed. The chiefs of the region had certainly learned what his regime could achieve. In subsequent campaigns, he established bases at Gaza and Byblos, and led armies into the Orontes valley, which was a Syrian highway, and southwards into Galilee to ravage the lands of the chief of Qadesh, who had led the enemy at Megiddo. Qadesh too was a commercial hub, where highways through the mountains of Lebanon met the Orontes valley, so its chief had to be won over for Egyptian ambitions to flourish. Thutmose III also forded the Euphrates to uproot orchards in Mitanni and cut a stela beside that of his grandfather. By the pharaoh's fourth decade, military activity was ongoing but on at least four campaigns his armies contented themselves with displays of arms rather than fighting, while Lebanon, like Wawat and Kush, began paying taxes to the palace. Monuments of Thutmose's son, Amenhotep II (c. 1426–1400 BC), also record the ostentatious display of violence. He had seven 'rebellious' chiefs abducted from Syria, slaughtered them himself, and had their impaled bodies hung from the walls of Thebes and Napata. Six years later he sailed from Memphis to depose Qaqa, a chief based near Megiddo, on a campaign characterized in his monumental account by the immolation of the population of a village called Atōrīn.

## Managing Palestine

After the early years of Amenhotep II, military intervention in the Near East was needed only to punish dissent. The towns of Palestine were not subjects and did not pay taxes, but their chiefs were mindful of the shadow cast by the pharaoh, whose caravans and troops crossed their lands at will. They did well to send him gifts and write regularly to affirm their goodwill, in case their activities might be misconstrued as hostile. The discovery in 1887 of an archive of such correspondence, in the royal palace at Akhtaten (modern Amarna), furnished a uniquely detailed source for studying the region during the New Kingdom. It comprises some 350 letters between the pharaoh and his ruling contemporaries during the last years of Amenhotep III (c. 1390–1353 BC), the reign of his son, Amenhotep IV (c. 1353–1336 BC), and the first years of his son, Tutankhamun (c. 1332–1322 BC), in all 20 years or so around 1350 BC. Their hackneyed phrases are an affected blend of indifference on the part of great kings and impotence on the part of local chiefs. The pharaohs, it seems, were willing to indulge the local chiefs in interminable disputes so long as they learned what was happening straight from the horses' mouths.

Most letters can be divided into two groups. One involves kings whose status equalled that of the pharaoh, in Mesopotamia (Mitanni, Babylonia, Assyria), Anatolia (Hatti, Arzawa) and Cyprus (Alashiya). These letters are filled with elaborate greetings and effusions on brotherhood:

> 'Tell Nimmuariya (Amenhotep III), the king of Egypt, my
> brother. So speaks Tushratta, king of Mitanni, your brother.
> For me all goes well. For you may all go well. For Gilukhepa
> may all go well. For your household, your wives, your sons,
> your chiefs, your warriors, your horses, your chariots, and in
> your country, may all go well.'

Brotherhood demands gifts and the exchange of royal women as brides, hence Tushratta continues, 'my father loved you and you in turn loved my father, and, in keeping with this love, my father gave you my sister (Gilukhepa)'. Trading in and out of Egypt is a royal prerogative, so diplomatic gifts are the basic mechanism for international commerce: the pharaoh exports ebony, linen, oils and, most of all, gold, in exchange for silver, copper, oils, and especially timber and horses. Little is said about politics but Tushratta's letter ends, 'with this I send my chief minister, Keliya, and Tunipibri', so the politics is sorted out face to face by officials.

The second group of letters involves chiefs whose authority is local and who subordinate themselves before the pharaoh. Their words exaggerate their servility but remind him how useful they may be:

> 'To the king, my sun, my lord. Message of Abdiashirta, your
> servant, the dirt under your feet. I fall at the feet of the king, my
> lord, seven times and seven times. As I am a servant of the king,
> and a dog of his house, I guard all Amurru for the king, my lord.'

These 'dogs' outdo one another in claims of loyalty and in demands for gold, troops or other indulgences that only a great king can supply. Likewise, they are ever ready to expose the treachery of their peers, so the political situation is recounted in absurdly chaotic terms. Nevertheless self-serving accounts of their own activities reveal that many risk the pharaoh's wrath in order to gain some political advantage over their peers. Their demands of the pharaoh usually go unheeded, but the culture of brinkmanship does not always benefit Egypt and may engender conflicts that threaten safe passage for the all-important caravans. The raiding of one 'rebel', Labayu, so threatens the roads around Megiddo that Amenhotep IV orders a group of chiefs to set aside their differences and work together to eliminate Labayu in battle.

A quarter of the letters are from Byblos, whose mayor, Ribhadda, is the only lesser chief sufficiently familiar to ask after the pharaoh's health. Ribhadda's concerns are dominated by the aggression of Abdiashirta, chief of the land of Amurru in the mountains of Lebanon:

> 'Anyway, who is Abdiashirta, the dog, that he tries to take all
> the cities of the king, the sun, for himself?'

After Sumur is taken from Ribhadda and Byblos itself besieged, Amenhotep IV is obliged to summon Abdiashirta's successor, Aziru, to Egypt, where he is detained for at least a year. Yet the pharaoh allows even Aziru to return to his homeland, where he then defects to the one power in the region able and willing to accept his allegiance in defiance of the pharaoh. This is the first intimation in Egyptian sources of the aggression of Suppiluliuma I of Hatti and the gathering clash of empires.

Later tradition treated Amenhotep IV (who changed his name to Akhenaten, 'Spirit of the Sun') and his immediate successors as bogus pharaohs, but the controversy they provoked was a matter of religion not politics, and during their lifetimes their authority was unopposed within Black Land. The richness of their monuments and the insights from the archaeology and texts they left mark this as the moment when the New Kingdom's power and influence were at their zenith, and decisive military and diplomatic interventions in Nubia and the Near East by Amenhotep IV reveal his command of the international stage. All the while manpower and wealth flowed uninterrupted into ever more massive royal foundations from Nubia to the Nile delta. When Tutankhamun passed away without an heir, so did the line that had ruled Black Land for nearly two centuries, but any strife was managed within the ruling group and settled so that the family of Ramesses I (c. 1292–1290 BC) became a new dynasty, which, far from breaking with the past, spoke and acted as a bulwark of tradition.

### Asserting strength

From 1500 BC to 1300 BC Black Land's population had probably doubled, perhaps to more than four million. The straggling streets of Memphis were swelled in part by immigrants bringing crucial skills: seamen, merchants, horse-trainers, mercenaries, glassworkers and, of course, translators. Ancient texts reveal names from Babylon to Greece to Libya. However, the traditional structures of Egyptian society held firm, from the domestic level to the king and his palace at the heart of the nation. The king would make an elaborate show of rewarding officials at home and abroad, while the temples of the gods who sponsored his success grew to unprecedented sizes, and were able to organize land and labour on a grand scale. Most folk identified themselves with a temple or a major estate, which helped to build a sense of belonging to something beyond the local community – a sense of nation. Increasingly this was also true of Wawat and Kush, where temples became the main instrument of government.

However, beyond Black Land international relations were in flux. The kingdom of Mitanni was being squeezed into submission by Hatti in the north and Assyria in the south. Suppiluliuma I led an army provocatively along the borders of territory loyal to the pharaoh and clashed with the chief of Qadesh, so doubts clouded the loyalty of chiefs in Lebanon and the Orontes valley. Accordingly Ramesses' son, Sety I (c. 1290–1279 BC), launched a series of campaigns in which disloyal peoples and cities were forced to acknowledge his hegemony, notably the kingdom of Amurru, which had remained defiant since Aziru defected to Suppiluliuma. Sety's success was considerable, and culminated in the defeat of a Hittite army at Qadesh. However, the issue had not been brought to a settlement at his death and became part of the legacy for his own son, Ramesses II (c. 1279–1213 BC).

The new king kept nipping at the fringes of Hittite expansion and then, in his fourth year, led his armies to Byblos and from there into Amurru. The next year he pounced on a Hittite-sponsored coalition at Qadesh, in the most celebrated battle of the ancient world. In the event, the Egyptian army was tricked by spies and strung out approaching the city. Ramesses himself was ambushed and nearly killed leading the vanguard, and credited his survival only to the intervention of Amun-Ra:

> 'I found that Amun came when I called him, and gave me his
> hand, and I rejoiced. He called in support, as if next to me,
> "Forward! I am with you!"'

In the end the king's leadership and the timely arrival of reinforcements let the African army fight out a grim stalemate, in which the Hittite emperor, Muwatalli, lost sons and other key leaders. Ramesses' account of the battle was later set out across the walls of his largest temples, and there is sincere humility in the thanksgiving for his deliverance.

In the inconclusive aftermath, Hatti regained Amurru and conquered Api, but Ramesses then reversed these losses and made his own gains. Both nations came to recognize that the stand-off established at Qadesh was immovable, and indeed that the regime of Shalmaneser I in Assyria now posed a common threat. A diplomatic agreement was desirable, so in c. 1258 BC Ramesses agreed a formal division of control over the Near East with the new Hittite emperor, Hattusili III. The Egyptian version of the treaty was also inscribed on a temple-wall at Karnak, and the god-given peace would endure for the rest of the New Kingdom. Thereafter, a handful of campaigns in Palestine, as late as the reign of Ramesses VII (c. 1137–1129 BC), were set-piece displays of arms more than meaningful military ventures.

## Tensions and pressures

Inevitably a reign such as the 67 years of Ramesses II, by which he outlived a dozen sons and many more grandsons, generated dynastic tensions. These did not affect the succession of his son, Merenptah (c. 1213–1204 BC), but there were brothers, nephews and others with competing claims to the throne. The succession of Sety II (c. 1204–1198 BC) was usurped, at least in Thebes, by his relative, Amenmesse. The resultant unrest lasted more than a decade and was only ended by a new dynasty, probably from within the royal family, headed by Sethnakhte (c. 1190–1187 BC). However, Sethnakhte's son, Ramesses III (c. 1187–1156 BC), was the intended (perhaps actual) victim of an assassination plotted within the palace. There is unequivocal evidence that such dynastic crises affected the nation more generally by creating a climate of anxiety. Equally clearly, however, the major institutions of the regime, including the palace, continued to function effectively throughout the events.

A more constant threat to Black Land in the later New Kingdom was invasion from Libya. Both Sety I and Ramesses II sent armies into areas west of Egypt, and Ramesses constructed forts along the fringes of the Nile delta. However, Mashwash and Libu peoples from the west settled frequently in and around Memphis. They had seemingly been accommodated peacefully until suddenly Merenptah used force to drive away a mass incursion, slaying thousands according to his monumental account. Initially famine had brought refugees flocking to be with kinfolk, but among them were non-Libyan peoples, and the incursion threatened to overwhelm the regime's control in the northwest. Mass incursions were driven away twice more, by Ramesses III, but they do seem to have been exceptional events within a long-standing pattern of settlement, from which Egypt gained skilled workers and commercial contacts.

Around 1180 BC Ramesses III also drove away an invasion from the north, by a confederation historians usually call the 'Sea-peoples', although ancient accounts identify only a minority as being 'of the sea'. The fighting by land and in the creek-waters of the Nile delta has been spun by modern writers into a tale of marauders overthrowing mighty empires. In fact, many of the invaders were women and children, and they should probably be recognized as displaced communities, perhaps victims of the break-up of the Hittite empire during the reign of Suppiluliuma II. This invasion made no lasting impression on Egypt itself, but it seems to have had a lasting impact on the political and cultural make-up of Palestine and, in that sense, held implications for the pharaohs.

The success of Ramesses III in the face of invasions indicates how he still led an effective nation, while the temple-town for Amun-Ra he founded at Medinet Habu remains one of Egypt's greatest monuments. However, the military and building activities of his successors lack lustre. Is this symptomatic of a decline in the pharaohs' authority? In Nubia the infrastructure of government and of gold-mining was long established, so what significant new building was necessary? In the Near East, Hatti's demise left Egypt unchallenged as a superpower. Archaeology has indeed revealed fundamental changes in Palestine's political and cultural landscape following the retreat of Hittite control, but these would have been irrelevant for the pharaohs so long as new rulers accommodated his interests as mindfully as their predecessors. Certainly local chiefs had no other 'great king' to turn to, at least until the re-emergence of Assyria during the 10th century BC. In these circumstances, the absence of military campaigns during the last century of the New Kingdom reflects Black Land's unchallenged mastery. At a local level, there were robberies in the royal cemeteries, especially during the reign of Ramesses IX (c. 1126–1108 BC), but palace officials conducted the prosecutions, so anarchy was not seen to erupt.

Nevertheless, two momentous developments at the beginning of the 11th century BC do seem to mark the end of the New Kingdom. One was the emergence of a city within a city at Thebes, where oracles took over the king's role in running the affairs of Amun-Ra's temples and estates. Around 1088 BC, the armies of the King's Son of Kush, Panehsī, occupied Thebes and chased away the high-priest of Amun-Ra. After seven years, the commander of the Egyptian armies, Hrihor, in turn marched into Thebes, was recognized as the new high-priest, and assumed the titles of a king. Another general, Piankh, chased Panehsī's troops back into Nubia. At the other end of the country, a shadowy figure named Smendes emerged as *de facto* king at Tanis. At face value, this may seem like the collapse of central government but Hrihor, Piankh and Smendes were closely related to one another and also to the pharaoh, Ramesses XI (c. 1099–1069 BC). Ramesses' reign remained unqualified outside Thebes, and documents were ascribed not to competing kings but to a special era of 'repeating births', which may refer to the duplication of kings or to a period of renaissance. As a result, it is unclear how far these events stemmed from genuine shifts in power or how far from dynastic squabbling.

## Black Land interrupted

Events in the south had a second, emphatic, outcome. Panehsī, erstwhile King's Son of Kush, used the pharaoh's own armies to put Nubia out of Egyptian rule. After more than four centuries, Black Land, in Kamose's vision, simply ceased to exist. This was the end of the New Kingdom in ideological terms, but the practical effect on the nations of Egypt and Nubia is harder to substantiate. For Egypt there must have been a dramatic reduction in gold and taxes, but Egypt was still rich in natural resources, steeped in the wealth it had garnered for centuries, and there are strong currents of continuity within the regime. At the death of Ramesses XI, a new royal line was headed by Smendes (c. 1069–1045 BC), and the royal cemetery was moved to Tanis in the Nile delta, but Tanis was the estate of Amun-Ra in the north and the new kings maintained close links with the high-priests at Karnak, often formalized through marriage. In time the high-priest Psusennes even became king, as Psusennes II (c. 950–945 BC). If a major display of arms is sufficient evidence, the New Kingdom out-lasted Ramesses XI by 150 years. In the face of Assyrian politicking, Shoshenq I (c. 945–925 BC) led a powerful army against Assyria's ally, the kingdom of Israel. Shoshenq's account, inscribed beside his majestic new entrance to the temple of Amun-Ra, is strikingly reminiscent of the campaigns of Thutmose III and Amenhotep II. In other words, the campaign can be understood as an attempt to confirm Egypt's long-standing authority in Palestine, largely unquestioned since the demise of Hatti.

However, despite Shoshenq's success, tensions were at work within Egypt itself that would result in the breakdown of pharaonic authority. For example, Libyan immigration in the Nile delta had created a chiefdom of Libu only loosely bound to the palace. Initially the pharaohs checked such divisions by assigning political offices to their family, and loyal officials were rewarded with the right to hold high offices through inheritance rather than royal favour. The outcome was a regime which owed everything to the pharaoh but which was structurally less coherent than it had been in the New Kingdom. As a result, dynastic rivalries threatened the unity of the nation in a way that seemed impossible during the New Kingdom. An inscription of Osorkon II (c. 875–835 BC) bemoans the fact that even his sons were enemies, and another from the temple of Amun-Ra describes the country in terms of 'elemental confusion'. In this sense, the 9th century BC marks the real demise of the New Kingdom.

## Legacy

The story of Nubia after the expulsion of Panehsī's armies from Thebes is notoriously difficult to reconstruct. A loss of centralized control seems to have allowed a number of quasi-pharaonic families to compete for power from places such as Kawa and Semna, once great centres within Black Land. In Wawat, meanwhile, unpredictable patterns of agriculture, perhaps caused partly by political uncertainty, forced most folk to adopt a more nomadic lifestyle on the desert fringes or migrate to more stable areas in Kush. However, Nubia's obscurity ended in a manner as abrupt as it was unforeseen, when a pharaoh from Kush took control of Egypt.

In the middle of the 8th century BC, a line emerged at Napata as the overlords of Kush. Their arts and funerary customs, were essentially those of the New Kingdom, and from the reign of Kashta (c. 770–747 BC) they styled themselves as pharaohs. In religion they recognized the pre-eminence of Amun-Ra, and at Gebel Barkal built an enormous new temple on the site founded by Egyptians seven centuries earlier. Kashta's successor, Piye (c. 747–715 BC), resolved to celebrate the festivals of Amun-Ra in Thebes itself, and in c. 728 BC a Nubian army used force to impose his will on Upper Egypt. Within months this Nubian pharaoh had travelled to Memphis and Heliopolis to receive homage from the rulers of Egypt, including no less than four other kings. In victory Piye founded a tradition of kingship in Kush that would be an authority in Africa for a millennium. Yet the well-spring for every aspect of Kush's ruling culture was Black Land and the centuries when Egypt and Nubia had been one nation.

So in Nubia, as in Egypt, the splitting of Black Land was just the latest of many transformations of the kingdoms along the Nile. The pharaohs' monuments still loom large in our imagination, perhaps because their magnificence makes us recognize how shallow the roots of our own culture may be in the scheme of history. Or perhaps we get an inkling that our roots reach into Black Land, as the Bible and the classical historians suggest. A wonderfully comic adventure, *The Tale of Wenamun*, was composed at the end of the reign of Ramesses XI, even as Hrihor, Smendes and Panehsī were playing out the final act of the New Kingdom. In the tale, Egypt's fondest ally, the mayor of Byblos, reflects on history:

> 'So, Amun founded all lands, but he founded them after he had
> founded the land of Egypt, where you've just come from. Thus,
> Art started there and has reached where I am, while Learning
> started there and has reached where I am.'

If so, then it was the New Kingdom which brought the Egyptian, and indeed African, values of Black Land to a wider world. Under the pharaohs, Egypt's gods held sway to the ends of the earth, while their neighbours in Nubia, Libya and Palestine gained affluence and security, at the cost of acknowledging their inferiority. Around the Red Sea and the Mediterranean Sea, through Anatolia and the Near East, many others grew in wealth and status by embracing, emulating or challenging the pharaohs. Along with gold, ivory and incense, Egyptian caravans and boats transported art, ideas and even poems whose words made their way into the Biblical psalms. Centuries later the land of the pharaohs cast a spell over Cambyses, Alexander, Caesar and Hadrian. There is no reason to suppose that the great civilizing influence of the New Kingdom simply expired one day in the 11th century BC.

# THE HITTITE EMPIRE

## 1650–1200 BC

TREVOR BRYCE

At its greatest extent in the 14th and 13th centuries BC, the kingdom ruled by the Hittites stretched westwards to the Aegean coast of Anatolia and southeastwards across northern Syria to the western fringes of Mesopotamia. How appropriate is it to refer to Hatti, the kingdom of the Hittites, as an empire? There is no doubt that it lacked many of the attributes commonly associated with later empires, like those of Persia, Rome and 19th-century Europe. But if in a broad sense the term 'empire' is applicable to any widespread dominion that contains states and territories subject to a central authority, then Hatti at the peak of its development clearly displayed some of the fundamental characteristics of empire. We shall consider these below, as we investigate the rise of the Hittite kingdom to the status of a major power in the Near Eastern world, and the means which its kings used to maintain its influence in this world through a period of almost 500 years.

## The origins and growth of the kingdom

In the early 17th century BC, an eastern Anatolian king called Labarna went to war against his neighbours. One state after another fell before him, until he had seized control of the entire region extending through Cappadocia southwards to the Mediterranean Sea:

> 'His country was small. But on whatever campaign he went,
> he held the enemy lands in subjection by his might. He kept
> devastating the lands and deprived them of power, and he
> made them the boundaries of the sea.'

Labarna is generally regarded as the founder of the Hittite ruling dynasty, a line of kings that held power for almost half a millennium until the end of the Late Bronze Age (early 12th century BC), despite several crises in its history that almost destroyed it. The dynasty almost certainly represented one of several Indo-European population groups that arrived in Anatolia some time during the Early Bronze Age (3rd millennium BC). Its ancestral seat was a city called Kussara, probably located in the region near the modern city Sar (classical Comana in Cappadocia). Labarna's reign was marred by rebellions and by power struggles within his own family, until the royal succession passed to his grandson Hattusili (c. 1650 BC). The new king honoured his grandfather's achievements by adding the name Labarna (sometimes written Tabarna) to the royal titulary. But his kingship took a fresh direction when he established a new royal capital on a ruined, abandoned site in north-central Anatolia, in the Land of Hatti. The city was called Hattusa. A century earlier, Hattusa had been destroyed, and its site declared accursed, by a king called Anitta, whose dynasty had also originated in Kussara. The city's re-foundation by Hattusili (though some scholars argue that it had been rebuilt by one of Hattusili's predecessors) effectively marked the beginning of the Late Bronze Age kingdom of Hatti.

Hattusili set about asserting his control over a number of eastern Anatolian lands, including those that had rebelled against his grandfather. But his military ambitions extended much further afield. Early in his reign, he embarked on an aggressive new programme of military conquest, taking his forces into northern Syria. Here he attacked the lands subject to the king of Yamhad, and destroyed a number of their cities, such as Alalah on the Amuq plain and Hahhum on the Euphrates. He may also have penetrated deep into northern Mesopotamian territory, in a campaign directed particularly against the kingdom of Tikunani, whose capital likely lay in the region of modern Diyarbakır. Hattusili's eastern campaigns ended mostly in victory. But his successes were tempered by one major failure. Despite repeated attempts, the king never succeeded in breaching the defences of Aleppo, the royal capital of Yamhad. That task was accomplished by his grandson and successor, Mursili I, who captured and sacked the city. Mursili then marched his troops to the Euphrates river, and south along the river to Babylon. This city was also captured, looted and torched by the Hittites, thus bringing to an end the royal line of the Babylonian king Hammurabi.

The assassination of Mursili within a few years of his return from Babylon sparked off a series of power struggles within Hatti between rival branches of the royal family. These continued through the reigns of the first four of Mursili's successors, whose violent occupation of the throne always ended with their forcible removal from it. Mursili's fifth successor, Telipinu, also seized the throne in a coup (c. 1525 BC). However, he then sought to stabilize the monarchy by laying down regulations governing the royal succession, and empowering a broadly based council called the *panku* to ensure that these regulations were adhered to. He also attempted to win back some of the subject territories lost to the kingdom during the reigns of his predecessors, whose squabbles had prompted uprisings among his subjects and exposed its core territory to enemy invasion.

## The era of the New Kingdom

While Telipinu succeeded in both halting his kingdom's slide towards extinction and regaining a number of its lost territories, he failed to restore to it the status and the influence it had achieved in the Near Eastern world during the reigns of Hattusili I and Mursili I. In the century following his death in c. 1500 BC, Hatti was ruled by a succession of apparently inconsequential kings, at the same time as Egypt and the Hurrian kingdom of Mitanni were emerging as the dominant powers of the Near Eastern world. Under its 15th-century BC pharaohs Thutmose I and Thutmose III, Egypt had carried out extensive conquests in Syria-Palestine, and established permanent Egyptian sovereignty over many cities and states in the region. And from its

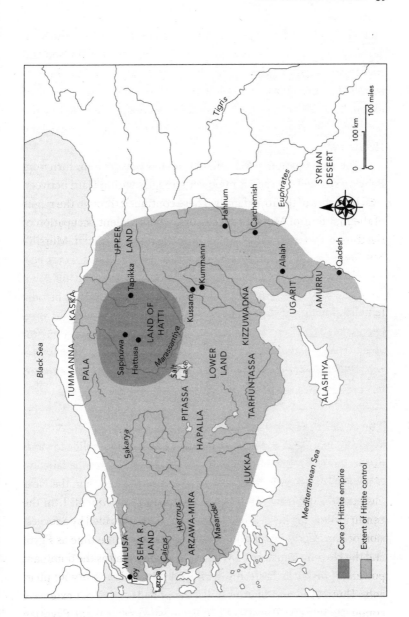

**KEY DATES**

| | |
|---|---|
| Early 17th century BC | |
| | Foundation of Hittite kingdom |
| 1595 BC | Sack of Babylon |
| 1525 BC | King Telipinu establishes laws of royal succession |
| 1400 BC | Beginning of New Kingdom and development of an empire |
| Early–mid 14th century BC | |
| | Hittite kingdom almost destroyed in massive invasions |
| 1327 BC | Destruction of Carchemish, last Mitannian stronghold |
| 1274 BC | Battle of Qadesh, fought with Egypt |
| 1258 BC | Peace Treaty with Egypt |
| 1228 BC | Battle of Nihriya, fought with Assyrians |
| Early 12th century BC | |
| | Fall of Hattusa and collapse of kingdom |

homeland in northern Mesopotamia, Mitanni had extended its sway over large parts of northern Syria and eastern Anatolia. The kingdom of Hatti re-emerged, eventually, as a major player in the international scene when, after many decades of relative insignificance, its fortunes had taken a turn for the better with the accession of a king called Tudhaliya in c. 1400 BC. (He is often referred to as Tudhaliya I/II since we cannot be sure whether the events attributed to him belong to one or to two kings so named.) Tudhaliya's occupation of the Hittite throne marks the beginning of a new era in Hittite history, sometimes referred to as the New Kingdom.

Tudhaliya conducted extensive campaigns of conquest both in western Anatolia and in Syria. In the wake of one of his Anatolian campaigns, which resulted in the defeat of an alliance of 22 states called the 'Assuwan Confederacy', he brought back to Hattusa as prisoners of war 10,000 foot-soldiers and an elite chariot contingent, 'lords of the bridle', along with 600 teams of horses. Transportation of conquered populations back to Hatti was to become a regular feature of campaigns conducted by later Hittite kings in enemy and rebel lands. In Syria, Tudhaliya allegedly destroyed the lands of the kings of Aleppo and Mitanni. But this claim, made by a later Hittite king, is probably exaggerated. Mitanni in particular was far from a spent force. Its final showdown with Hatti was yet to come.

For many of his military enterprises, Tudhaliya was partnered by his son-in-law, who was also his adopted son and co-regent Arnuwanda I. From the records of the latter's reign, it is clear that Hittite victories in this early New Kingdom period were offset by instability in a number of the subject territories and ominous developments in enemy territories beyond Hatti's frontiers. These reached their peak in the reign of Arnuwanda's successor (or successor-but-one) Tudhaliya III, during the first half of the 14th century BC. The kingdom suffered its most serious crisis to date when massed enemy forces invaded its homeland territory from all directions, and the Hittite capital was captured and destroyed. Tudhaliya had before then removed his royal court to a residence-in-exile in the city of Samuha, perhaps located on the upper course of the Marassantiya river (the classical Halys river, known today as the Kızıl Irmak river). From here he planned the recovery of his kingdom, and with the support of his son Suppiluliuma drove the enemies from all his territories. Suppiluliuma, who was very likely the chief architect of the Hittite recovery, succeeded his father on the Hittite throne in c. 1350 BC, and embarked without delay on the greatest project of his reign – the destruction of the kingdom of Mitanni. This objective was largely achieved in a brilliant one-year campaign in northern Syria and northern Mesopotamia in c. 1344 BC, but the kingdom lingered on until the siege and capture of its final stronghold, Carchemish on the Euphrates, in 1327 BC.

Suppiluliuma imposed his sovereignty upon many of the northern Syrian states formerly subject to Mitanni, and the yearly military campaigns conducted by his son and (second) successor Mursili II (c. 1321–1295 BC) re-established and consolidated Hittite rule over many parts of Anatolia. In Syria, mounting tensions between Hatti and Egypt over disputed subject territories culminated in a major military showdown between the Hittite king Muwatalli II and the pharaoh Ramesses II near the city of Qadesh on the Orontes river in 1274 BC. Although the outcome of the battle itself was essentially a stalemate, Hatti was clearly the long-term victor in terms of its territorial acquisitions at Egypt's expense. After Qadesh, a border between Hittite and Egyptian territory just north of Damascus seems to have been tacitly acknowledged by both kings. In 1269 BC, a treaty drawn up between Ramesses and Muwatalli's second successor Hattusili III formalized friendly relations between the two powers; the peace between them, consolidated by two royal marriage alliances, held firm until the fall of the Hittite kingdom early the following century.

Hatti was now entering the final decades of its existence, and by the early regnal years of Hattusili's son and successor Tudhaliya IV (c. 1237–1209 BC), there is evidence that the kingdom was already in irreversible decline. Tudhaliya was not only faced with increasing unrest and uprisings in his subject territories, but also suffered a major military defeat at the hands of the Assyrian king Tukulti-Ninurta I in northern Mesopotamia, and very likely was confronted by plots against him and an open challenge to his authority by members of collateral branches of his own family. Food shortages within Hatti may also have added to the increasing instability of the Hittite kingdom. In the reign of the last Hittite king Suppiluliuma II (1207–?), Hattusa was abandoned by the royal court, and the city gradually fell into ruin. With its abandonment, or even before it, the kingdom over which it held sway collapsed.

Relics of the culture and civilization of Late Bronze Age Hatti survived in the so-called Neo-Hittite kingdoms which arose in parts of eastern and southern Anatolia and northern Syria during the early centuries of the Iron Age. Indeed there is evidence that in several of the Neo-Hittite kingdoms, descendants of the Late Bronze Age Hittite dynasty survived and continued to hold power for generations after the Late Bronze Age kingdom which the dynasty had ruled came to an end.

### The structure of the kingdom

The core territory of Hatti, commonly referred to by scholars as the Hittite homeland, lay in north-central Anatolia within the region bounded by the Halys river, called the Marassantiya in Hittite texts. By far the largest of its cities was the royal capital Hattusa, the administrative and religious centre of the kingdom. Regional centres within the homeland, such as Sapinuwa (modern Ortaköy) and Tapikka (modern Maşat) where tablet archives have been found, were under the immediate authority of local officials appointed by the king. Of these the most important held the office of BEL MADGALTI (literally 'lord of the watchtower'), which took responsibility for the security of their region, the maintenance of its roads and irrigation channels, the collection of taxes and the administration of justice on the king's behalf. Adjacent to the homeland on its northeastern and southern frontiers were regions known respectively as the Upper and Lower Lands, which served as buffers against enemy incursions. New Kingdom texts refer to the installation of Hittite military governors in them, and the provision of garrisons of Hittite infantry and chariotry. Beyond the homeland and its buffer zones, the kingdom consisted of two viceregal centres, located at Aleppo and Carchemish, and an array of vassal states extending over large parts of Anatolia and northern Syria. Hittite territory in Syria extended to the region north of Damascus, where the frontier with Egypt lay.

The viceregal kingdoms were established at Aleppo and Carchemish by Suppiluliuma I, during the final stages of the king's destruction of Mitanni. The first two viceroys were his sons Telipinu and Piyassili (Sharri-Kushuh). They exercised within their regions all the powers – administrative, military, judicial, religious – of the Great King himself, and sometimes conducted diplomatic negotiations with local Syrian rulers on his behalf. Henceforth, every viceroy until the fall of the kingdom was either the son of the Hittite king or a high-ranking member of his family. The vassal states were ruled by local kings who were bound by oaths of allegiance to the Great King. Their obligations

as vassals required them to provide military support to their overlord
when called upon, and to act as his local intelligence agents, giving
him early warning of anti-Hittite activities in their region. The treaty
sometimes stipulated an annual tribute payable by the vassal. A small
number of subject-rulers were granted *kuirwana*, or 'protectorate',
status. This gave them a few ceremonial privileges, and occasionally
the right to annex enemy territory which they had conquered on the
Hittite king's behalf. But in practice, their apparently privileged status
was little more than a diplomatic fiction. Very much the same obligations, and the same restrictions, were imposed upon the *kuirwana* as
upon the vassal rulers. Provided they fulfilled their treaty obligations,
both types of rulers were allowed to govern their states as they saw fit.
It was only in rare circumstances that a Hittite garrison was imposed
upon a subject state, and then only if the state had proved particularly
troublesome and a military presence was deemed necessary to restore
order and support the Hittite-appointed or endorsed local ruler.

## The kingdom in its broader context

The Near Eastern world was made up of a large array of kingdoms,
the majority of which were no more than small city-states, which
had an urban centre and a few square kilometres of peripheral territory, normally used for farming or grazing purposes. Many of the
Syro-Palestinian kingdoms conquered by the 15th-century BC pharaoh
Thutmose III belonged to this category. Larger kingdoms extended
over greater expanses of territory and included, in addition to the main
urban centre, a number of smaller towns and villages, and sometimes
fortified settlements along their frontiers. The five Middle Bronze Age
kingdoms of eastern Anatolia, attested as MATU (literally 'lands') in
Assyrian colony texts, fell into this category, as did the Late Bronze
Age kingdoms of Arzawa in western Anatolia, attested in Hittite texts.
Ranking well above both categories, in size, political importance and
military might, were the superpowers of the Late Bronze Age Near
East. There were four of these – the kingdoms of Hatti, Egypt, Babylon

and Mitanni, with Mitanni being replaced after its destruction in the mid-14th century BC by a renascent kingdom of Assyria.

The superior status of these kingdoms was officially recognized in diplomatic texts by the designation of their rulers as 'Great Kings'. This term (commonly represented by the Sumerogram GAL.LUGAL) was used precisely and exclusively of the four rulers, by themselves in their royal titulary, by their subject rulers and by their foreign counterparts. The Great Kings' acknowledgment of one another as peers is further indicated by their addressing one another as 'My Brother', a form of address used only, in diplomatic protocol, by persons of equal status. One of the Hittite kings, probably Urhi-Teshub, sternly rebuked the 'upstart' Assyrian king Adad-nirari I for addressing him as 'My Brother' before he had been acknowledged, apparently, as a member of the elite group:

> *'As my grandfather and my father did not write to the King of Assyria about brotherhood, you shall not keep writing to me about brotherhood and Great Kingship. It is not my wish!'*

Collectively, the four Great Kings held sway over almost the entire Near Eastern world, incorporating as subject territories within their realms the numerous petty and medium-sized states which constituted the lesser kingdoms of this world. Babylon and Assyria covered between them the whole of Mesopotamia. New Kingdom Egypt's sway extended from Nubia through the land of the Nile into southern Syria and Palestine. Hatti laid claim at its peak to much of the rest of the Near Eastern world, its authority extending over large parts of northern Syria and Anatolia west of the Euphrates.

We have noted that the core territory of the Hittite kingdom was the region in north-central Anatolia bounded by the Halys/Marassantiya river. This was the essential 'land of Hatti'. Unlike the core populations of many other empires, Hatti's population almost certainly had no strong sense of a common national identity, nor any perception that they had a special status which set them above the peoples of the subject states outside the homeland. In fact, they never used – nor could they have used – a single specific ethnic term to identify themselves. They simply referred to themselves as 'the people of the land of Hatti', adopting a traditional name for the region where they lived which extended back many centuries before Hittite history began. The name 'Hittite' was originally adopted by scholars from the Old Testament, where it is used, in the form *hittî*, to refer to a small Canaanite tribe who dwelt in the hills of Palestine in the early 1st millennium BC. There are, however, five biblical passages in which the plural form *hittîm* refers to 'kings of the Hittites' and 'the land of the Hittites'. These Hittites are to be distinguished from the Canaanite group and can confidently be assigned to the Neo-Hittite kingdoms which arose in northern Syria and southern and eastern Anatolia in the late 2nd millennium BC. Many of their inhabitants, particularly their ruling elites, may well have been descendants of the Late Bronze Age 'Hittites'. The latter were a mixed population, made up of a number of different ethnic groups – Hattians, Luwians, Hurrians prominent among them – speaking a range of languages. Though the Indo-European 'Hittite' language (called Nesite by those who wrote and spoke it) remained the official chancellery language of the kingdom throughout its history, it was very likely spoken by only a minority of the homeland's population. And the population mix was constantly changing, particularly during the 14th century BC when tens of thousands of transportees were brought from conquered territories and resettled in the homeland. We have no sense of a culturally or ethnically coherent core population which saw itself as the most important element in an imperial enterprise.

In references to the Hittite kingdom in foreign texts, the term 'Hatti' became virtually synonymous with the kingdom as a whole, including all its subject territories. But it should be emphasized that far from attempting to impose their civilization on the lands which constituted their 'empire', the Hittites were highly receptive to the cultures of these lands, incorporating many elements of them into the fabric of their own society. This was a natural consequence in part of the transportation system, which brought back to the homeland thousands of booty-people each year, constantly enriching and diversifying both the ethnic and the cultural mix of the population. The Hittites also consciously absorbed the foreign cultures, most clearly seen in the Hittites' practice of incorporating the gods of the conquered territories, along with their cults, into their own pantheon. It was a proud boast of the Hittites that they were the 'people of a thousand gods'. There was no sense in the Hittite kingdom of a core population which saw itself as dominant. The kingdom's ethnic and cultural inclusiveness was one of its most distinctive features. In this respect, it differed from many other political and military powers, both ancient and modern, which have been termed as empires.

## The military dimension

The driving force behind Hittite imperial enterprises were the Hittite Great Kings, members of a royal dynasty which ruled the kingdom throughout its entire history. The king occupied his throne by right of succession through his family line, and with the endorsement of the gods. He ruled in the gods' name:

> 'For the land belongs only to the Storm God; Heaven and
> Earth together with the army belongs only to the Storm God.
> And he made the Labarna, the king, his deputy and he gave
> him the whole land of Hattusa.'

As the gods' deputy on earth, the king was the chief priest of his realm. He was also the kingdom's supreme judicial authority, and the commander-in-chief of its armies. In both text and sculpture, Hittite kings presented themselves in the image of a lion who pounces without mercy upon its prey. The lions which still today flank the main entrance to the Hittite royal capital symbolize both the might of the Hittite king and the empire over which he held sway. Hittite imperial power was also symbolized by the double-headed eagle, as depicted at the entrance to the Hittite city now called Alaca Höyük, one of the most important cult-cities of the Hittite realm.

Like many of his Bronze Age counterparts, the king regularly led his troops on military campaigns, sometimes on an annual basis. Prowess in the field of battle demonstrated a king's fitness to rule. Indeed, demonstration of such prowess was an important element in the ideology of kingship, and almost certainly provided one of the chief incentives for the expansion of the Hittites' subject territories. As one historian of the Hittites has commented: 'Military expansion became an ideology in its own right, a true sport of kings.' But it was more than just a sport. To maintain the respect and support of his subjects, a king had to match his predecessor's achievements in war, and if possible to surpass them. Hattusili's military enterprises far surpassed those of his grandfather Labarna, and in his march across the Euphrates he even challenged comparison with the legendary Akkadian ruler Sargon. Yet Hattusili was outdone by his grandson and successor Mursili, who captured and sacked Aleppo, a prize that had eluded his grandfather, and then went on to destroy Babylon.

Seen in this light, the military campaigns of the early Hittite kings have the appearance not of empire-building enterprises, but rather of personal adventures designed primarily for the king's own aggrandizement. Indeed, there may be some element of truth in this. The Syrian campaigns of Hattusili and Mursili appear to have been little more than large-scale raiding expeditions which brought back substantial plunder to Hatti. No attempt was made to impose any form of Hittite authority over the conquered territories in Syria. After their destruction, the Hittite forces promptly withdrew. But strategic and economic considerations may have played some role in the campaigns. A number of the cities attacked by Hattusili lay on major routes linking Anatolia with Syria and Mesopotamia, and Hattusili may have been concerned to ensure continuing supplies to his land of tin, used in the

I (above) Akhenaten ('Spirit of the Sun'), pharaoh in New Kingdom Egypt in the 14th century BC, was sometimes represented in enigmatic form: masculine and feminine, human and animalistic, figurative and abstract.

II (left) Akhenaten's Great Wife, Nefertiti, and their young daughters form a holy family around him in official scenes from homes as well as temples and palaces.

**III, IV** Hittite libation vessels in the form of a stag and a bull's protome (an adornment consisting of a frontal view of an animal head or bust of a human), from the 13th century BC.

**V** A seated Hittite goddess, in gold, with a child in her lap, from the site now known as Alaca Höyük. *c.* 1300 BC. Aside from reliefs carved onto rock faces, our knowledge of Hittite art is confined largely to figurines and small artifacts.

**VI** (below) Statuettes, in gold and lapis lazuli, of various deities worshipped by the Hittites. Dated to the 13th century BC.

**VII** Shalmaneser III and his predecessor Assurnasirpal II rapidly expanded the Assyrian empire through incessant military campaigning. The so-called Black Obelisk of Shalmaneser III, excavated at Kalhu and dated to *c.* 828 BC, shows the submission of defeated kings and the tribute Shalmaneser collected, which surprisingly includes two-humped camels, more commonly associated with Iran. The cuneiform inscription that covers the obelisk relates the campaigns Shalmaneser mounted over 31 years and the loot he captured.

VIII (above) In wells of
the second citadel of Kalhu,
archaeologists discovered
ivories that originally
decorated furniture looted
by the Assyrians during
their conquests. The pieces
were crafted in various
parts of the empire and
beyond.

IX (right) This wall
painting from Til Barsip
shows in profile the heads
of two Assyrian men.

**X** Achaemenid silver horn-shaped *rhyton* (drinking vessel) with a protome in the shape of a winged griffin with lion's paws. There is a drinking hole in the griffin's chest. The exquisite design of the *rhyton* attests to the quality of tableware enjoyed by the Persian elite throughout the empire.

**XI** A staircase relief from the palace of Darius the Great at Persepolis. Servants bring food and livestock into the palace – all of which is bound for the Achaemenid royal dinner table.

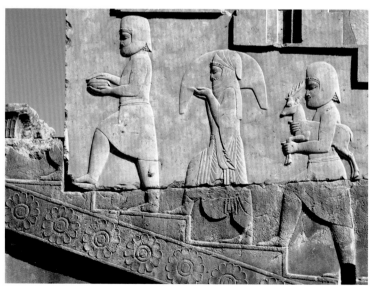

**XII** (left) An Achaemenid gold armlet (one of a pair) showing two leaping griffin lions. Cells used for inlays of glass or semi-precious stones are clear to see.

**XIII** (below) An exquisite model of a chariot, depicting a charioteer and a seated Persian nobleman. The front of the chariot is decorated with the head of the Egyptian god Bes, a protective deity whose popularity throughout the Persian empire can be confirmed by the number of amulets of the god's image found across the Achaemenid region.

**XIV** The Laocoön Group, a Hellenistic marble sculpture of two boys and their father, all entangled in a deadly fight against sea snakes. Nero added this sculpture to his collection in the Domus Aurea ('Golden House'), the colossal palace he built for himself in the heart of Rome. It was found there in 1506, almost intact: only Laocoön's right arm was missing. The sculptor Michelangelo amended it, pointing it upward in a gesture of defiance. The original arm was found in 1957; it is bent. A little less heroic than Michelangelo's vision of him, the 'real' Laocoön may be even more touching in his hopeless struggle against divine fate.

manufacture of bronze, along the routes used by Assyrian merchant caravans to Anatolia during the Assyrian Colony period (20th–18th centuries BC). None of the surviving texts refer to such a motive, which is not surprising since those texts that do survive are devoted to extolling the king's military exploits. But plunder and personal glory may well have been the prime incentive for the Hittite kings' first ventures into Syrian territory. We should remember too that though the king was an absolute monarch, he needed the support of his military officers and other high-ranking officials with whom he shared the spoils of battle. Plundering expeditions conducted against wealthy cities provided a valuable source of income for the kingdom, and must have contributed much to the goodwill of the king's subjects towards him.

Constant military campaigning was also necessary to ensure the kingdom's survival. Hatti's core territory was landlocked, had no effective natural defences and was surrounded by enemy forces – most notably the Kaskan tribes in the Pontic region to the north, and the Hurrians in the southeast. The homeland's frontiers could be secured only by regular campaigns beyond them, led personally, whenever possible, by the king. The Hittite state needed a ruler at its helm whose paramount quality was that of a war leader. Even so, military victories provided no more than temporary respite from the constant threats posed by Hatti's enemies to the security of the homeland. There were also resource considerations. A far from unlimited supply of manpower meant that major campaigns conducted by the Hittites in distant regions seriously depleted the defence forces of the homeland, making it vulnerable to enemy attack. On a number of occasions, military victories abroad were offset by incursions into the homeland during the army's absence.

### The diplomatic alternative

Matters came to a head when, in the period following Mursili I's assassination, the kingdom lost many of its subject territories through rebellion, and the homeland fell prey to invaders. While Telipinu succeeded in winning back some of these territories, the strategically important state of Kizzuwadna in southern Anatolia remained independent. Rather than commit his troops to a costly and probably inconclusive conflict, Telipinu decided to come to terms with Kizzuwadna's ruler, a man called Isputahsu, by concluding a treaty with him. In effect, this marked a turning-point in the history of the Hittite kingdom. Although the treaty with Isputahsu seems to have been essentially in the nature of a compromise (it survives only in fragmentary form), it demonstrated that diplomacy could be at least as effective an instrument in maintaining the security of the Hittite kingdom and extending its influence as military force.

As we have noted, the greatest period in the expansion of Hittite power and influence came in the 14th century BC, during the period of the New Kingdom, in the reigns of Suppiluliuma I and his son Mursili II. Both kings carried out extensive conquests in Anatolia and northern Syria, and followed up their victories by reducing or restoring the conquered territories to subject status. But apart from Suppiluliuma's establishment of viceregal seats at Aleppo and Carchemish, the New Kingdom rulers never imposed direct rule upon their subject territories. Rather, they sought to maintain their authority over them through local vassal rulers and the treaties they drew up with them like that between Telipinu and Isputahsu. An important aspect of them was that they were personal compacts, drawn up between the Hittite king and his vassal. The vassal swore allegiance only to his overlord. He was thus bound to a person, not to the Hittite state, and was absolved of all his treaty obligations if the Hittite throne were seized by a usurper, unless he was called upon to help restore to the throne its legitimate occupant – i.e. his treaty-partner. As we have also noted, the king interfered in the internal affairs of a vassal state only in rare instances – for example, to help prop up a loyal vassal who had been removed from his throne by an anti-Hittite faction in the state, or on one occasion to threaten subjects in a certain vassal state with capital punishment for practising incest. Clearly, the Hittite policy of allowing almost complete autonomy to the subject states was pragmatically based. Hatti's kings simply did not have the resources to establish their own administrations in these states, or to ensure that they remained submissive to Hittite authority by installing permanent garrisons of Hittite troops in them.

Despite the largely 'hands-off' policy of Hittite kings towards the vassal states, anti-Hittite uprisings, especially in western Anatolia, were far from rare. And vassal rulers themselves frequently proved unreliable, or treacherous, sometimes consorting with foreign powers in their attempts to break their kingdom's ties with Hatti. On the positive side, the treaties gave a measure of stability to a number of regions where Hittite vassal rule was established. This provided Hittite kings with some relief, if only for limited periods, from the need for constant campaigning in these regions, and the substantial commitment of resources which such campaigns entailed. In Syria, where Hatti shared a border with Egypt, the vassal states played an important role in maintaining a balance of power between the two Great Kingdoms. And control of the northern coastal states gave the Hittites direct access to the products brought by trade to the eastern Mediterranean ports.

## A Hittite 'empire'?

Whether or not the kingdom of Hatti warrants being described as an empire depends ultimately on how broadly this term is defined. Hittite kings claimed sovereignty over large expanses of territory throughout Anatolia and northern Syria. But in effect, there were only two regions where the Hittites actually ruled. One was the homeland itself in north-central Anatolia, the other consisted of those parts of northern Syria which were directly subject, from the reign of Suppiluliuma I, to the viceroys at Aleppo and Carchemish. Otherwise, the kingdom over which the Hittites claimed sovereignty was essentially a conglomerate of quasi-autonomous states, whose rulers signed personal contracts with the Hittite king and sometimes provided him with troops, tribute and military intelligence – unless they were rebelling or joining in alliances against him. The kingdom as such remained a fragile, tenuous structure, which fluctuated dramatically in size during the five centuries of its existence, and several times came close to extinction before its final collapse. But there is no doubt that Hatti played a major role in the history of the Late Bronze Age Near East, and at times profoundly influenced the course of events in this world. It was one of the four Great Kingdoms of the age, becoming for a time in the last half of the 14th century BC the most powerful of them all.

# THE EMPIRES OF ASSYRIA AND BABYLONIA

## 900–539 BC

MARC VAN DE MIEROOP

In 722 BC, the Assyrian king Shalmaneser V conquered the city of Samaria and terminated the royal house of Israel; in 587 BC the Babylonian king Nebuchadnezzar II did the same to the city of Jerusalem and the royal house of Judah. These events were not unusual nor of extraordinary interest to the victorious kings and their entourages. But they left a deep mark on the historical consciousness of the region and far beyond, because the victims described them in one of the great works of world literature, the Hebrew Bible. For centuries people read of these conquests and despised their perpetrators, though they knew little more about them than what was written in the biblical text. Other than that, only Greek authors of the 5th century BC and later provided a few garbled accounts and mostly fantastic tales of Assyrian and Babylonian kings and queens. By the early 19th century AD the ancient tales of Assyrian and Babylonian violence and decadence perfectly fitted the then common perception of the Middle East as a dangerous and exotic place. Painters and poets delved into the stories to compose images of grandeur, indolence and cruelty that projected modern stereotypes onto the distant past.

Assyria and Babylonia were thus never forgotten, but it was the victims rather than the creators of the empires who shaped their memories. This situation changed radically in the mid-19th century AD, when archaeologists began to explore the ancient ruins of these cultures. The first great discoveries in ancient Mesopotamia, when the region was part of the Ottoman empire, uncovered the capitals of Assyria (Assur, Kalhu and Nineveh) and Babylonia (Babylon). Monumental buildings came to light, often packed with works of art. Tens of thousands of ancient records, carved in stone or impressed on clay using a script called cuneiform, were excavated. Archaeologists filled newly built museums in London, Paris, Berlin and Istanbul with these objects and texts. Exploration has continued ever since, though political events in the Middle East, particularly in Iraq and Syria, often make work difficult if not impossible. The material available to a historian of the Assyrian and Babylonian empires, however, is now abundant and varied. The decipherment of cuneiform in the mid-19th century allows us to read innumerable texts from the Assyrians and Babylonians themselves. Objects, buildings, cities and numerous other remains provide us with multiple sources to study their empires.

It is remarkable that, despite the abundance of sources that have become available in the last 150 years, these empires still have negative connotations that are often absent in the study of other ancient empires. It is obvious that they were of seminal importance to the history of the Middle East for some 400 years, from around 900 to 539 BC. How we judge them today should probably depend more on how we perceive empires in general – as systems oppressing many people over a wide area or as enabling great projects – than on the negative appraisal of people in the past who suffered from them. The Assyrian and Babylonian empires are examples of a long series of ancient empires, neither worse nor better. Their early date and the rich data available for them make them of special interest in the study of empires in history. While Assyria and Babylonia are mostly investigated independently and as two separate political structures, we shall discuss them here together, both because of the strong continuity in practices between the two and the fact that they ruled the same regions of the ancient world.

## The military dimension

In the 10th century BC the entire Middle East was politically divided into small states. Many of the regions that had flourished in the 2nd

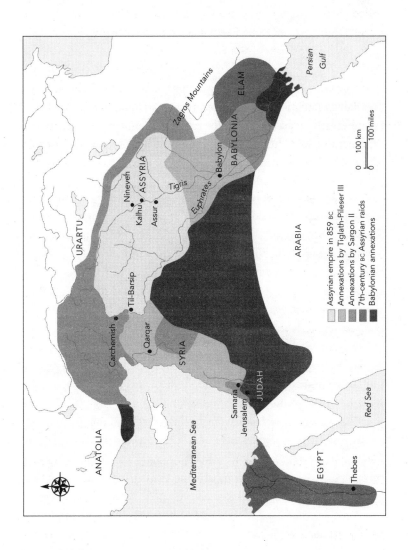

## KEY DATES

| | |
|---|---|
| 858–824 BC | Shalmaneser III mounts major campaigns to extend empire |
| 745–727 BC | Tiglath-Pileser III reforms provincial system and standing army |
| 713–706 BC | Sargon II builds capital of Dur-Sharrukin (Khorsabad) |
| 704–681 BC | Sennacherib moves capital to Nineveh |
| 680–669 BC | Assyrian conquest of Egypt |
| 668–627 BC | Elam ravaged, Babylonian revolt crushed |
| 614–605 BC | Destruction of Assyrian empire |
| 539 BC | Conquest of Babylon by Persian king, Cyrus |

millennium BC were now poor and disorganized, and political power had shifted to newcomers, principally to tribes from northern Syria with a nomadic background, the Arameans. The city-residents feared and loathed these people, but it is clear that the Arameans had increased their influence everywhere and occupied much of the rural land as well as some cities, especially in the western part of the Middle East. It was in the west that they established small states around old urban centres, regularly in concert with other populations. In the east the old kingdoms of Assyria and Babylonia survived, but Babylonia in particular was unstable, with a quick succession of dynasties. In Assyria the same family occupied the throne for many generations, but the regional extent of their power was limited.

The Assyrians fundamentally changed this situation in the mid-9th century BC. Especially two men, Assurnasirpal II (883–859 BC) and Shalmaneser III (858–824 BC) rapidly expanded the kingdom's reach through incessant military campaigning, primarily in the west. Assurnasirpal systematically annexed all territories between the Assyrian heartland on the Upper Tigris in northern Iraq and the Euphrates river in western Syria. Shalmaneser crossed the Euphrates with his troops in order to confront the rich states further west. Opposition to their expansion was fierce. In 853 BC, Shalmaneser fought a battle against a large coalition of western states near a place called Qarqar and seems to have lost – though he never officially acknowledged this. Shalmaneser only recovered several years later, but by 841 he was able to raid numerous states of western and southern Syria and force them to pay tribute.

Assyria's success depended on stability in the centre and that faltered upon Shalmaneser III's death. Although his son Shamshi-Adad V (823–811 BC) managed to take control – with the help of Babylon's king who imposed a humiliating treaty – provincial administrators gained much of their independence, and states across the Euphrates stopped paying tribute. Over the next 80 years Assyria's central power was limited. Theoretically the Assyrian king ruled all of northern Iraq and Syria from the area east of the Tigris to the Euphrates, but in reality local governors paid only lip service to him. At the same time powerful rival states emerged in the north and southeast: Urartu, which controlled eastern Turkey and threatened Assyria's provinces in northern Syria, and Elam in southwestern Iran, which meddled in the affairs of Babylonia to its west.

In 744 BC, Tiglath-Pileser III (744–727 BC) initiated fundamental changes in the running of the Assyrian empire together with a long series of military campaigns. The reforms continued in subsequent reigns and reduced the powers of governors and state officials. The kings restricted their territories in size and forced them to share powers with others. Tiglath-Pileser's successors are the most renowned military men of Assyrian history: Shalmaneser V (726–722 BC), Sargon II (721–705 BC), Sennacherib (704–681 BC), Esarhaddon (680–669 BC) and Assurbanipal (668–627 BC). For about a century they campaigned almost annually in all parts of the Middle East. In the east and north they clashed with the states of Urartu and Elam, in the south they fought Babylonian opposition, in the west they gradually annexed more Syrian and Anatolian states, as well as the state of Israel. The furthest point Assyria reached was when King Assurbanipal sent troops to capture the Egyptian capital of Thebes in the year 664–663 BC.

Assyria's military strength may seem to have been unmatched, but this was the effect of the Assyrian propaganda, rather than reality. In fact, the struggles with major rivals were protracted and not always successful. The greatest challenge the empire faced was the control of its southern neighbour, Babylonia. Throughout the period when Assyria was gaining ascendancy over the Middle East under strong leaders, power in Babylonia was divided. Urban residents and tribal people from the countryside were competing for kingship, which had changed hands numerous times. During Assyria's second phase of expansion started under Tiglath-Pileser III, several of its kings captured Babylon's throne but when their attention was drawn elsewhere, local opposition managed to wrest it away. The solution of making another Assyrian or a faithful Babylonian king also failed. Either the local population removed them or they ended up defying Assyria. In frustration some Assyrian kings reacted with great violence: Sennacherib claims to have wiped Babylon off the face of the earth in 689 BC (an exaggeration, but he did cause much damage) after a tribal leader had seized the throne, and from 652 to 649 BC Assurbanipal ransacked the entire country in a prolonged war against his own brother, who he himself had made king of Babylon.

These efforts to overcome Babylon were to no avail and in 626 BC, when Assurbanipal had just died, a leader of the Chaldean tribes, Nabopolassar, initiated a dynasty in Babylon that would last for almost 90 years, the Neo-Babylonian dynasty. Soon he was able to turn against Assyria, whose capital Nineveh he sacked in 612 BC. In order to replace Assyria as the regional superpower Nabopolassar's troops had to push westward for at least another seven years, mopping up Assyria's last resistance in 610 BC and confronting the Egyptians in a major battle in 605 BC at Carchemish, on the Euphrates river. He and his successors continued Assyria's policy of threats of military action followed by conquest as a last resort only in order to subdue territories at the fringes of the empire. Most notorious today is Nebuchadnezzar II's treatment of Jerusalem and the state of Judah, as the Hebrew Bible describes it in detail. Assyria had left Judah under local rule though it had stripped the country of much of its territory. Nebuchadnezzar first attacked Judah in 597 BC, deporting part of its population. After a rebellion, he laid siege to Jerusalem for two years and finally destroyed the city in 587 BC, deporting yet more people. Even later the assassination of the Babylonian governor in 582 necessitated further military intervention. Nebuchadnezzar II annexed other previously independent Syrian states and his successors extended the empire into southern Anatolia and Arabia. These events are much less clear to us, as the Babylonians did not describe them in detail – unlike the Assyrians whose military actions dominate the official record. Still, there is no doubt that Babylonia was a worthy successor of Assyria.

From 605 to 539 BC the Babylonians were the masters of the Middle East from the Mediterranean Sea to the Zagros mountains. They could not control events in Iran, however, where the Persians from the southwest under King Cyrus II (559–530 BC) rapidly extended their powers northward to Anatolia. For some seven years the Persian and Babylonian states shared a lengthy border from the Persian Gulf to the Mediterranean Sea. In 539 BC, Cyrus directed his troops against Babylon, whose resistance may have been weakened by internal resentment against the current king, Nabonidus. Soon Cyrus captured the city and almost the whole of its empire. The Persian empire was born, ending the 400-year-long dominance of Mesopotamian states in Middle Eastern history.

## Pacifying the empires

Modern accounts of the Assyrian and Babylonian empires tend to focus on the military activity that led to the imposition of these countries' rule over vast areas. We describe conquests. But the greatest task empire-builders face throughout history is to make their successes last without having to maintain a massive military presence. In the study of the Assyrian and Babylonian empires we are confronted with great differences in the sources that these two cultures left behind.

The Assyrians were explicit in their accounts of military actions and this detail enables us to determine how they pacified regions. They also left us correspondence from imperial bureaucrats that allows for the study of the administration of certain areas. The Babylonians, on the other hand, were much vaguer in their accounts of conquest and virtually no actual documents of the imperial bureaucracy exist. Yet, from sources such as the Hebrew Bible and some administrative records we can conclude that there was great continuity in practices between the two empires.

Both Assyria and Babylonia steadily expanded the limits of their empires. However, both seem to have done so reluctantly: their aim was not conquest but rather to gain access to the resources of regions on the periphery with the least direct interference in daily affairs. When encountering new territories they used their substantial military might to scare the inhabitants into voluntarily giving tribute, that is, annual payments of valuable goods. They kept local rulers on the throne as long as they obeyed and paid up. Yet, such arrangements tended to fail when vassals took advantage of the absence of the imperial army and rebelled. After a second conquest the Assyrians and Babylonians selected a member of the local aristocracy who they thought would be more obedient to take on rule as a puppet king. Those men had often been educated in the imperial capital, and the fact that they were imposed on a country made them unpopular at home and more dependent on the empire for their survival. But they also regularly rebelled and thus triggered a final stage of submission, when the empires annexed the region and administered it directly through imperial officials rather than local men.

Both empires had sufficient flexibility to adjust their practices to local circumstances, but the sequence of vassal, puppet ruler and governor – each step triggered by rebellions – seems to have been at the basis of their policies everywhere. The Bible shows how this happened in the cases of Israel and Judah. Early in the reign of Tiglath-Pileser III, which started in 744 BC, the Israelite vassal King Menahem paid his tribute loyally. When an anti-Assyrian rebel, Pekah, seized the throne, Tiglath-Pileser intervened and made a puppet-ruler, Hoshea, king. Hoshea's later unwillingness to pay tribute to Shalmaneser V provoked another campaign, and in 722 BC the Assyrians annexed Israel as a province and destroyed its capital Samaria. Similarly in the case of Judah, the Babylonian Nebuchadnezzar II replaced the local vassal Jehoiachin in 597 BC with the puppet-king Zedekiah. Zedekiah's rebellion in 589 BC forced Nebuchadnezzar's return and in 587 BC he made Judah a province under a Babylonian governor.

The Assyrians and Babylonians employed fear to maintain obedience. Whenever the imperial armies were forced to act they did so with great violence. The Assyrians were careful to broadcast the misery their troops could cause in texts and images, with such success that these messages still shape the perception of their empire today. They narrated and depicted how they killed, flayed and beheaded people; burned and demolished cities, and washed away their ruins into the river; cut down orchards and ploughed fields with salt. While these depictions may have been hyperbolic, they were sufficiently realistic to terrify anyone who saw the Assyrians advance. It is likely that many submitted before a single arrow was shot.

One method of control and punishment that both the Assyrians and Babylonians used had a radical impact on the character of conquered regions and their inhabitants: namely mass deportations. The practice of moving groups of people from one end of the empire to another was common policy in both empires. This was done in different stages, first deporting selected people, mostly political leaders and skilled artisans. When regions remained defiant, large parts of the population ended up living abroad, including entire communities of men, women and children. The practice had several advantages for the empires. The fear of being uprooted probably pushed many to submit rather than fight. Deportation caused the people to end up in foreign lands whose local populations resented them, so they had to rely on the empire for protection. At the same time the empire could use their labour in building projects or to develop new agricultural lands. Moreover, they could resettle other people in the regions the deportees left behind. Scholars estimate that the Assyrians moved around some 4.5 million people over three centuries, a staggering number for these early times. Figures for Babylonia are unavailable.

From around 900 to 539 BC, the Assyrians and Babylonians thus gradually converted the diverse regions of the Middle East into a more unified and homogeneous whole. They mixed populations and created provinces with similar administrative structures. Their policies had a great impact both on the core of the empires and on the peripheries that they annexed.

## The impact of empire on the Assyrian and Babylonian heartlands

The primary aim of the empires' expansion seems to have been to gain access to resources. Although Assyria and Babylonia had a rich agricultural basis, the conquered territories provided goods and materials that were rare or unavailable in the homelands, which naturally varied from region to region. In southern Anatolia, for example, there was metal ore, in the Lebanon mountains there was wood, and in the Zagros mountains there were horses. The conquerors found treasures that people had accumulated everywhere, which caused particular interest. Assyrian accounts detail the materials and craft products they looted from the palaces of defeated kings: silver and gold, semi-precious stones, woven textiles, furniture, statues, vessels, weapons and much more. Some defeated countries were extremely wealthy such as Egypt. When Assurbanipal looted its capital Thebes, he boasted:

> 'My hands captured that city in its entirety with the support
> of the gods Assur and Ishtar. Silver, gold, precious stones,
> as much as there was in the holdings of his palace, brightly
> coloured and linen clothing, large horses, male and female
> residents, and two tall pillars made from pure silver, whose

*weight was 2,500 talents [75,000 kg] and which stood at the*
*gate of the temple, I removed from their position and took to*
*Assyria.'*

All kings listed what they looted. It is clear that the conquests provided
an influx of wealth, while the subsequent systems of annual tribute
and taxation generated a constant stream of assets. At the same time
the deportations supplied the empires with labour forces far beyond
their core populations.

It is no surprise then that the Assyrians and Babylonians – at least
the ruling classes – could shape their environment to reflect their
empires' grandeur. Massive building projects took place whenever
the empires flourished. Kings erected grand palaces with numerous
rooms and large courtyards. They roofed them with cedar beams
brought in from the distant mountains of Syria, decorated them with
stone wall-reliefs and with panels of wood and ivory, furnishing them
with elaborate fittings. They built and restored temples to their gods.
They laid out gardens planted with exotic trees. They expanded and
embellished cities. All these projects were possible only because of
the empires' resources. The ruins of Mesopotamian cities and palaces
today may not be very impressive, as their mud brick architecture
is much decayed, their roofs and gates have disappeared, and their
decorations were taken away. But in ancient times they would have
been magnificent and clear signs of their builders' power and wealth.

Cities were not the only places that received attention. Both
Assyrians and Babylonians developed the countryside and benefited
agriculture through irrigation projects. The Assyrians laid out a system
of canals to bring water from the mountains to cities such as Nineveh.
Irrigation was much more important in Babylonia where rainfall was
so scarce that no one could grow crops without watering them artifi-
cially. The Neo-Babylonian kings expanded and systematized the canal
system to crisscross the entire southern region of Mesopotamia. The
work initiated a long period of agricultural prosperity there that lasted

many centuries after the dynasty's end. We have no documentation on who dug the canals and built other infrastructure, but it seems likely that imported labour played a great role in these massive projects.

The deportations had other effects on the core of the empires as well. The influx of people from regions all over the Middle East made the populations of Assyria and Babylonia more diverse. People from the west in particular seem to have been numerous and influential. Arameans had already started to migrate into Assyria and Babylonia in the early centuries of the 1st millennium BC, but the deportations from Syria increased their numbers by far. The Aramaic language became the commonly spoken tongue in Assyria and Babylonia. Since they mostly wrote on perishable parchment rather than on clay tablets that preserve better (though some tablets inscribed with Aramaic exist), we know little of their actual writings. But representations of scribes in Assyria show men standing side-by-side writing Akkadian on clay tablets and probably Aramaic on parchment scrolls. The written Akkadian language of the mid-1st millennium BC shows influences from Aramaic, which may have been the language of daily use even in the court.

Other deported people likewise had an impact, albeit more limited. Documents from the centre of Babylonia in the 6th century BC show the presence of a large number of people with Hebrew names (Judean deportees), and the existence of villages of Anatolians, Arabs and Phoenicians. The enormous geographical reach of the empires and their dynamic economies probably also encouraged people to gravitate to their cores voluntarily. Phoenician merchants from the Mediterranean coast settled in Assyrian cities to conduct trade, and Egyptians came to Babylon. All these people brought their own languages and customs; they probably looked and dressed differently from the local populations, cooked distinctive foods, and behaved distinctively. Assyrian and Babylonian societies became more diverse.

Despite the great variety of people with different religions, intellectual traditions and habits, it cannot be said that Assyria and Babylonia were multicultural societies. Their high cultures were remarkably traditional and impervious to outside influences. Since the 2nd millennium BC Babylonian culture had been dominant in both countries. People read the same literature, they honoured their gods in similar ways (even if some deities were different), and they adhered to the same intellectual and scholarly traditions. Assyria's access to Babylonian writings increased when it controlled the south, and kings such as Assurbanipal sent out scholars to collect materials that were not yet available, but this was just an extension of the regular absorption of Babylonian culture. The influence was not reciprocal: Babylonia accepted little Assyrian culture in return. Neither country paid much attention to the literatures and intellectual traditions of the regions they conquered, though both adopted the Aramaic language for some of their daily writings. The Assyrians also imitated artistic and architectural styles from conquered regions, but in cultural terms the empires made little difference to the Mesopotamians.

The empires were very large and complex structures, ruled in an autocratic way with the king as the ultimate source of authority for every decision. He needed to rely on a group of officials to govern, however, and the highest of those probably derived primarily from the empires' heartland. Despite the fact that we know many names and titles of Assyrian officials, the available documentation does not reveal clearly what each one did or even how many people were involved. But the numbers must have been large and grew with the empire. The Assyrian hierarchy had seven high officers at the top. The titles do not describe their functions accurately, however, as is the case in most palace organizations throughout history. They included the treasurer, palace herald, chief cupbearer, chief eunuch, chief judge, grand vizier and commander-in-chief. While titles seem to differentiate between civilian and military duties, in reality all were involved in both spheres of activity. These high officials must have spent much time in the capital where they formed the king's cabinet, but they were also governors of strategic border provinces.

The Assyrian king personally chose his high officers. Although he probably selected men from the elites, he was not obliged to keep an office in the hands of one family. On the contrary, kings were careful not to make offices hereditary. Several of the highest officials were castrated men, who could not create dynasties in competition with the royal house. There is virtually no information on how people rose through the ranks. It seems likely that a king would have chosen men with previous experience to fill the highest posts, but the available data does not allow for the reconstruction of anyone's career path. Despite these shortcomings of the evidence, we should imagine that in the heartlands of both Assyria and Babylonia large groups of wealthy officials existed whose careers depended on the empires' success and who benefited from the conquests and the subsequent influx of resources. Their numbers must have risen in parallel with the expansion of the areas Assyria and Babylonia controlled. The growth of imperial elites affected their societies in many ways still invisible to us.

## The impact of empire on the conquered territories

Although Assyria and Babylonia were reluctant to take over the administration of the territories they conquered, increasingly more regions of the Middle East became provinces of the empires. The presence of imperial bureaucrats led to changes in the provincial cultures and economies, partly enforced, partly because local populations willingly adopted the rulers' practices. We know much more about Assyria's impact than Babylonia's in this respect, as the latter empire left little evidence on the subject. The transition of power from one to the other does not seem to have caused drastic changes. Babylonia was less interested in the development of the provinces, however, and this neglect led to a reduction of the empire's impact, it seems, though much remains unclear to us.

When Assyria turned regions into provinces it installed an administration that mirrored the one in the capital. As representative of the king, the governor was surrounded with the same luxuries the court had in Assyria, but on a smaller scale. For example, after Shal-maneser III conquered the Syrian city Til Barsip on the Euphrates in 856 BC, he and his successors gradually turned it into an Assyrian town. Shalmaneser renamed the city Dur-Shalmaneser, 'Fortress of Shalmaneser'. Excavations there revealed a huge 7th-century BC citadel with a throne room. The building was decorated with wall paintings that showed the same scenes as the stone reliefs in Assyrian palaces, which originally were also decorated with paint. In the provinces the imagery was the same, but the materials were less expensive, as a governor did not equal the king. Throughout the city existed houses of rich citizens, who adopted Assyrian customs. The house of one man named Hanni, for example, contained a group of cuneiform tablets in full Assyrian style. Hanni was also wealthy enough to own lavish furniture, which was decorated with the same type of ivories as those discovered in the palace at Kalhu. The decorations were not as varied as those in the capital, however. Til Barsip survived the transition from Assyrian to Babylonian empires intact, and its inhabitants maintained their earlier traditions inspired by Mesopotamia until they abandoned the city, possibly because Babylonia's neglect of the region made their lifestyle unsustainable.

In northern Syria east of the Euphrates river the Assyrians pursued a policy of replacing local traditions with Assyrian ones. For example, they used in their public inscriptions only the cuneiform script and Akkadian language; unlike others in ancient Near Eastern history (such as the Persians) they never displayed a multi-lingual inscription that would be easier to understand for local populations. Before the massive expansion of the empire starting with Tiglath-Pileser III in the mid-8th century BC, there existed a clear differentiation between regions that the Assyrians called 'the land of Assur' and those under 'the yoke of Assur'. The first term referred to areas whose economies and cultures had become fully integrated into the Assyrian, including in religious terms. The inhabitants of these areas gave offerings to the god Assur as if he were their god. The Assyrians interfered much less in the areas under 'the yoke of Assur', which remained under local rule, paid tribute and honoured their own gods.

When the Assyrians rapidly annexed territories after 745 BC, they gave up this clear distinction and may have tried to develop all the empire's assets as much as possible to their advantage. At Ekron in southern Palestine, for example, a region still under vassalage rather than annexed, they reorganized olive oil production, increasing the number of oil presses and standardizing their layout. The oil was no longer for local consumption only but for other parts of the empire as well. The Assyrians had realized that development of resources in the territories they already controlled brought in substantial benefits. The Babylonians, however, were different in that respect. During their conquests they ransacked regions such as Judah and Ekron, but they did not bother to redevelop them. The richer farmlands in the Babylonian heartland, which they actively expanded, may have made them less concerned with agricultural resources from the provinces.

In all their policies the Assyrians displayed great flexibility; political, cultural and military considerations influenced how they behaved. Even in neighbouring regions they varied their level of interference depending on local circumstances. Provinces adjoined vassal states, and the Assyrians left some areas alone because they were not interested in their resources, or because they wanted a buffer zone with enemies beyond. Sometimes a vassal state was closer to the core of the empire than a province because it was beneficial for the Assyrians to leave local structures in place. We cannot look at a map of the Assyrian empire and assume that the impact of the empire was uniform or extended in concentric circles from the core. It was a patchwork of regions that each had specific interactions with the core and consequently different mixtures of local and imperial elements.

## The ideology of the Assyrian and Babylonian empires
Empires are systems of exploitation: a group of people imposes its will on others and forces them to submit. The creators of empires need

to invest much effort into the enterprise, often manpower that only their own populations can provide. Throughout history there always was a need to convince audiences of the correctness of the empire's existence and its behaviour. The audiences are varied both within the empire's core and in the regions it wants to control. Both contain elites – people who make decisions and impel others to act on them – and commoners, who often experience events more directly than the elites. They receive innumerable messages, some ephemeral, such as military parades, others more lasting as they are expressed in writing, images or the shaping of the environment. The study of ideological expressions of support for the Assyrian and Babylonian empires is multifaceted and must work with numerous lines of evidence. We can address only a few examples here to illustrate the riches of the Assyrian and Babylonian material.

In 714 BC, the Assyrian king, Sargon II, defeated in battle King Ursa of Urartu, Assyria's great rival to the north. Upon Sargon's return one or more courtiers composed a long account of the campaign, which was addressed to the people of the city of Assur. We do not know whether it was ever read out to them: written in high literary Akkadian it may have been incomprehensible to most people. It is clear, however, that some in Sargon's entourage devoted much effort to the task of constructing a document that was meant to show the king had been correct in his actions. One of the most remarkable aspects of the account is how it portrays the enemy kings as direct opposites. Ursa disobeys the gods, he is foolish and does not know his limitations; Sargon listens to the gods, he is wise and observes the limits the gods have set him. When the account narrates the battle between the two, it shows Sargon as a valiant warrior who massacres numerous enemies single-handedly. In contrast, Ursa is a coward, who despite his numerous troops runs away on the back of a mare and hides like a woman in the corner of the mountains. The end of the account describes how Ursa loses his mind: he tears off his clothes, pulls his hair, pounds his chest, throws himself on the ground and cries in constant pain. Ursa is not a true king but a madman, while his opposite Sargon is a wise ruler. Should we not agree then that Sargon was right in destroying Ursa?

Slightly more than a century later kings Nabopolassar and Nebuchadnezzar used the wealth of their new empire to redesign their capital Babylon. They built new walls, gates, roads, and palaces. The plan of their city is striking because of its regularity. The inner city is a rectangle enclosed by two walls 7 m (23 ft) apart and respectively 3.7 m (12 ft) and 6.5 m (21 ft) wide. In the inscriptions the builders left behind they portray Babylon as a haven of order in a world of chaos. That order was far-reaching due to Babylon's contacts throughout the land. At every New Year's festival the gods of other cities visited the supreme god Marduk of Babylon and the king led them all into the city in a procession that displayed the war booty of the preceding year. An essential idea to the Assyrian and Babylonian empires was that they were forces of order and brought peace to their inhabitants. The empires were a benefit to the world, if not the entire universe.

## Resistance to empire

Throughout history subjects of empires have defied them and have refused to obey the will of foreign rulers. Resistance can take many forms. It can be violent, including the assassination of imperial representatives; it can be civil disobedience; it can involve an unwillingness to assimilate. It is hard to investigate these actions in the Assyrian and Babylonian records, since the sources give almost exclusively the empires' perspective and non-violent resistance in particular remains hidden. It is clear, however, that both empires had to deal with persistent opposition. The first task of many new rulers was to restore order in provinces that had taken advantage of the previous emperor's death to rebel and withhold taxes.

Consequently kings made efforts to improve relations with conquered people. Some Assyrians, for example, tried hard to placate their Babylonian subjects. Esarhaddon, whose father had devastated Babylon, funded the reconstruction of temples and cults and tried to present himself as a good Babylonian king. His policy was to culminate in the return of the statue of the Babylonian god Marduk to his temple in Babylon, but even the transport was difficult as Babylonians along the way rallied around the statue. We do not know exactly how they expressed their displeasure; they caused much trouble, however, and for a long time frustrated Esarhaddon's plans.

Violent opposition was ubiquitous. We read of the murder of governors and other imperial representatives, and the army had to return repeatedly to particular areas to quell uprisings. Certain regions were especially recalcitrant. For example, Babylonia never accepted Assyrian rule and even when Assurbanipal's brother was king of Babylon he led the country's fight against the Assyrian army. It is no surprise then that such resistance in the end led to Assyria's demise. An independent Babylonia turned against Assyria in the late 7th century BC, gaining the assistance of peoples from the Zagros mountains in the east, the Medes and Scythians (who may have been hired as mercenaries). The victims of imperial oppression took their revenge. Babylonia's end was of a different nature, although not necessarily because it was a less repressive empire. Its territory and riches tempted the Persians of Iran, who had never been under Babylonian rule. The outsiders captured a vast empire in one fell swoop.

## The place of the Assyrian and Babylonian empires in world history

When, in the mid-5th century BC, the Greek historian Herodotus wrote his account of the Persian wars, he contrasted his small country to the vast Persian empire, which could, he claimed, rely on two million soldiers. His investigation led him to search for Persian predecessors which he found in Assyria and Babylonia. But he knew little about them, especially Assyria. Already in the 5th century BC they were distant history. Today, when our knowledge of world history stretches much further down in time than Herodotus', we still see the Assyrian and Babylonian empires as the start of a long sequence of empires in the Middle East: Persian, Alexandrian, Seleucid, Roman, Parthian, Sasanid, Umayyad, Abbasid and Ottoman. All integrated part or the entirety of the regions Assyria and Babylonia controlled in their massive territories.

Yet, many scholars also use the term 'empire' to identify earlier political formations in the region. They speak, for example, of the 'first-world empire' in the mid-3rd millennium BC, or even of an informal trade empire in the late 4th millennium BC. Were Assyria and Babylonia merely imitators of earlier empires? The answer is both yes and no: they took over practices that existed before but also introduced crucial innovations.

Here we may stress these novelties over the continuities. Many times before states had indeed imposed their wills on others, but these structures had been ephemeral and geographically limited. In contrast, Assyria and Babylonia unified vast areas for some 400 years and their actions fundamentally restructured life everywhere. The process had it highs and lows and only from 745 BC on was a fuller integration of the territories involved. The rulers experimented with a new system and had no earlier examples to follow. If the Egyptians and (perhaps) Hittites of the late 2nd millennium BC had created empires previously, this was unknown to the 1st-millennium Assyrians and Babylonians. They showed inexperience in their efforts and learned the hard way that conquest was easier than pacification. Assyria's annual campaigning may be glorified in the official record (what official record does not glorify the empire's actions?), but it was exhausting and had diminishing returns. Empire builders had to learn how to follow up on their aggression, and neither Assyria nor Babylonia seem to have been good at it. Later empires in the region, such as the Persian, may have learned from them, but that is for another chapter.

# THE FIRST PERSIAN EMPIRE

## 550–330 BC

LLOYD LLEWELLYN-JONES

In 2005 the British Museum produced a major exhibition on the history and culture of the first Persian empire, that ruled by the Achaemenid dynasty. Despite boasting such luminaries as Cyrus the Great, Darius the Great and Xerxes, the exhibition was entitled *Forgotten Empire* in an attempt to emphasize the notion that while the Achaemenid empire was the largest and most influential empire in the pre-Alexander period – a true world empire in fact – its impact on later history and scholarship has been (and continues to be) seriously misunderstood and undervalued. It is fair to say that if Persia enters into the historical consciousness at all, then it is usually filtered through the classical or biblical imagination. By and large, the 'authentic voice' of ancient Persia has been either ignored or mistreated and we engage with the ancient Persians as either the champions of the Hebrew nation (the biblical slant), or the oppressors of the free world (the classical tradition). Moreover, today it is difficult to comprehend that the land we now call Iran once lay at the heart of a magnificent empire; its importance as an ancient world power and a cultural axis has been almost completely eclipsed by the Western media's obsession with the changes that have taken place within Iran since the Islamic revolution of 1978.

Thus, in the West, ancient Persia is best remembered for its war with Greece and its later invasion and ultimate defeat by Alexander of Macedon. For the Persians themselves, the Greco-Persian wars were little more than tiresome border skirmishes which took place over 2,000 miles from the heart of the empire in Iran. Yet so much of our understanding of Persian history is filtered through ancient Greek sources, especially the influential 'histories' of Herodotus, Xenophon, Arrian and Ctesias of Cnidus, that we find it difficult to separate the Greek fabrication of Persian history and culture from its reality. The Greek perspective on the history and nature of the Achaemenid empire pits Greek freedom and democracy against 'Oriental' (i.e. Persian) tyranny and despotism.

In modern popular Western culture the image propounded in the ancient Greek sources still dominates. Two 21st-century Hollywood movies exemplify the trend in which the Persian empire is only viewed as a negative stereotype of 'Otherness'. Oliver Stone's movie *Alexander* (2004) displays all the familiar Orientalist notions about the inferiority and picturesqueness of Eastern societies. So much so, indeed, that in terms of its portrayal of East–West relationships, *Alexander* has to be seen as a stale cultural statement and a worn-out reflection of the continuing Western preoccupation with an imaginary exotic Orient. More interesting, however, is *300*, Zack Snyder's 2007 film version of the graphic novel by Frank Miller. Snyder's take on the Thermopylae story and the slaughter of the 300 Spartans at the hands of the Persian army is a fantasy; it is created as the battle would have looked in the minds of the Greeks, as they mythologize the story of the 300's sacrifice. This is not history, and the 'Persians' of the film are a bizarre blend of sadomasochistic, effeminate, ninja-like cartoon villains (as equally bizarre are the Spartans' oiled and pumped porn-star bodies). However, *300* does nothing to promote the quest to locate and understand the real Persian empire.

Achaemenid art was once dismissed as repetitive and uninspired: thus George Curzon, the Viceroy of India, walking through the ruins of Persepolis in 1901 commented that, '1,200 human figures move in solemn reduplication upon the stones – what monotony and fatigue! It's all the same, and the same again, and yet again.' Now scholarship is beginning to reassess Persian art and to recognize not only the aesthetic timeless beauty of the artworks, but also the importance of art for understanding imperial ideology and Persian cultural norms.

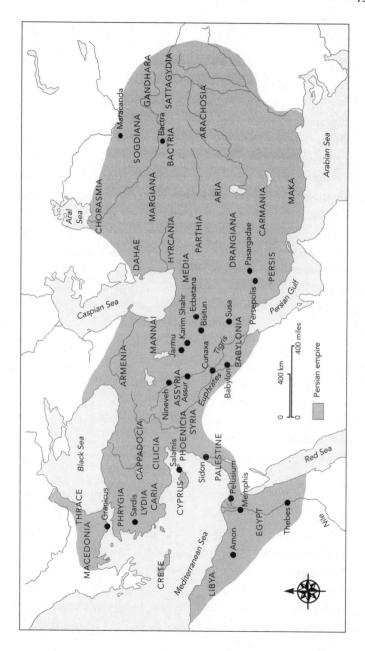

## KEY DATES

| | |
|---|---|
| 539 BC | Conquest of Babylon by Cyrus the Great |
| 530 BC | Cyrus dies in battle |
| 525 BC | Cambyses conquers Egypt |
| 515 BC | Construction of Persepolis Palace begins |
| 500 BC | First coinage; Persian Royal Road built |
| 490 BC | Persians defeated by Greeks at Marathon |
| 480 BC | Xerxes defeats Greeks at Thermopylae, but his fleet is destroyed at Salamis |
| 465/449 BC | Peace of Callias between Persia and Athens |
| 401 BC | Artaxerxes I defeats rebel army led by his brother at Cunaxa |
| 333 BC | Darius III escapes after losing at Issus to Alexander the Great |
| 331 BC | Final defeat for Darius at battle of Gaugamela |
| 330 BC | Darius murdered; Persian capital Persepolis sacked by Alexander |

Achaemenid art drew widely on Egyptian, Assyrian, Babylonian and Elamite motifs, and in turn the Persians exerted a strong influence on the arts of Greece. Achaemenid art is therefore an eclectic mix of styles and motifs drawn from different parts of the empire, but fused together to produce a harmonious look which is distinctly Persian. Egyptian and Assyrian motifs (like winged disks and winged *genii*, pediment shapes and designs, and even the canons for depicting the human figure) are frequently melded together so that Achaemenid art can be said to reflect, in physical form, both the diversity and unity of the empire as a whole.

Recent scholarship – based on a new understanding using ancient textual sources from all parts of the empire, together with analogies of Achaemenid art and archaeology – has recognized that classical authors displayed a heavy bias against Persian culture. We can now determine that in spite of revolts, succession crises and regicide, the vast empire nevertheless held together as a coherent unit for 230 years. It showed no signs of internal weakness or stagnation at the time when the Macedonians took over power from the last Achaemenid king Darius III. It is wrong to think of the first Persian empire as the 'Forgotten Empire', and it is more appropriate to re-label it the 'Misrepresented Empire'.

## Chronology of empire

Made up of 23 lands (including Persia), the Achaemenid empire stretched from Libya to India and from southern Russia to the Indian Ocean. What was the process of acquiring an empire of this scale? It is fair to suggest that, in fact, there was never *one* Persian empire, but multiple empires, since throughout its 230-year history the empire was in a constant state of flux, expanding and contracting and expanding yet again. Provinces and peoples were added to the central government by force or coercion and were lost from Persian control through wars, rebellions and uprisings. Egypt, for example, was lost for almost 60 years before being re-conquered and forced back into the empire. After the reign of Xerxes, however, there was no territorial expansion, although there were still nationalist or localized revolts. A brief overview of the empire's history reveals how quickly the status quo could change.

## Establishing empire

Cyrus II (559–530 BC), 'The Great', was ruler of the small southwestern Iranian kingdom of Persia, located in the modern Iranian province of Fars. He also styled himself 'King of Anshan', referring to an area in the foothills of the Zagros mountains and once ruled by the powerful and culturally sophisticated Elamites. It would seem that the earliest Persian monarchs regarded themselves as the natural inheritors of Elamite lands and perhaps even saw themselves as the custodians of Elamite culture.

Early in the reign of Cyrus, the Persians were one of several Iranian tribes who were vassals to the Medes. The powerful Median kingdom was expanding in the north of Iran to the point where its military might was strong enough to campaign against the wealthy region of Babylonia. Babylon itself was only saved from attack when in 550/549 BC Cyrus, supported by a coalition of south Iranian tribes, marched north to attack the Median king, Astyages. Following the sack of the Median capital, Ecbatana, Cyrus turned his attention towards northern Media, including the ancient kingdom of Urartu in the area of Lake Van. The chronology of this period is hazy, but it is possible that Cyrus also occupied Elam and claimed possession of its capital Susa. Cyrus also undertook a war in Bactria.

Following this a Persian campaign moved against the wealthy and powerful kingdom of Lydia in Asia Minor. Croesus of Lydia had brought the cities of Ionia under his rule and his wealthy capital, Sardis, benefited from extensive trade routes with Mesopotamia. The sack of Sardis meant that Cyrus was able to take other important cities along the Ionian coast, which were placed under the control of Persian satraps (provincial governors) and administrators.

By 540 BC Cyrus was ready to attack Babylon and moved his army into Mesopotamia, marching first on Opis and then on Sippar. He entered Babylon on 29 October 539 BC, having already taken its king, Nabonidus, prisoner. Apparently meeting no military resistance, Cyrus appointed his son, Cambyses, as the city's regent, although he maintained the status quo by allowing Babylonian officials to continue in their governmental and religious offices. Much of our knowledge of the fall of Babylon comes from the so-called Cyrus Cylinder – a clay foundation deposit written in Akkadian discovered near the sanctuary of Marduk in the city. It was presumably composed on Cyrus' orders, although the whole document is written from a Babylonian point of view in traditional Babylonian terms. As a piece of imperial propaganda, the Cylinder attempts to legitimize Cyrus' conquest of Babylon by representing the king as the champion of the god Marduk, who finds in Cyrus the city's saviour. It seems that the Babylonians benefited from Cyrus' capture of their city; certainly the Jews of Babylonia profited from his benevolence and were allowed to return to their homelands. Other peoples did not fare so well under Cyrus: the citizens of Opis were massacred en masse, and, following the fall of Lydia, the population was deported to Nippur in Babylonia, where a community of Lydians is later attested.

In the years following the conquest of Babylonia (538–530 BC) Cyrus was occupied gaining a truly international empire: Aria, Parthia, Sogdiana and Margiana fell to him on the eastern front, while near the Jaxartes river he founded a city which the Greeks called Cyropolis. In the west, Cilicia, Syria and Palestine came under Cyrus' rule and while he never held Egypt, he had clearly marked it out for conquest.

At Pasargadae in the modern Fars province of Iran, Cyrus constructed a tomb and a palace planted with a formal garden irrigated by myriad water-channels. The result was nothing short of a desert paradise – *pairidaêza* (Greek *paradeisos*) – which acted as an empire in miniature, as flora from all across Cyrus' conquered lands were brought together as a physical statement of Persia's ever-growing power.

## Expanding empire

In 530 BC Cyrus died in a war against the Massagetae. He was succeeded by Cambyses (530–522 BC), who having been trained for the succession by his father ascended peacefully to the throne. A Babylonian text dated 31 August 530 BC names Cambyses as 'King of Babylon, King of Lands'. At his accession Cambyses appointed his younger brother, Bardiya, as a governor of Media.

Cambyses' greatest achievement was the conquest of Egypt in 525 BC, following the death of the last native pharaoh, Amasis. He was crowned according to ancient rites at Memphis with the pharaonic throne name Mesuti-Re. Following the conquest of Egypt, the neighbouring countries of Libya and Cyrene offered submission to the Persian forces before Cambyses marched south, down the Nile, stationing a Jewish garrison on the island of Elephantine to protect Persian interests in the south. He then advanced and conquered at least a part of Nubia.

Greek sources tend to portray Cambyses as a mad despot, tyrannically oppressing his subjects and impiously debasing the religious traditions of his conquered nations. Much of this slander emanates from the accounts of Egyptian priests who were opposed to Cambyses' attempts to reduce their power and wealth. Archaeological evidence from Egypt suggests that Cambyses adopted a policy of religious tolerance – inscriptions from the Serapeum in Memphis (524 BC) confirm that he honoured the death of a sacred bull with due rites and rituals. Like Cyrus in Babylon, Cambyses co-opted the support of Egyptian nobles to maintain his sovereignty and was sensitive to Egypt's religious and cultural traditions.

## Rebellious empire

Cambyses' death occurred in Egypt in the summer of 522 BC. His brother, Bardiya, was assassinated after a few months' rule and was replaced on the throne following a violent and bloody palace coup, by Darius I, also 'the Great' (521–486 BC), the governor of Parthia, who solicited the support of six other Persian nobles. Immediately, rebellions broke out across the empire and turmoil quickly spread from province to province. Babylon, Media, Armenia, Scythia and even Parsa itself erupted in chaos as provinces tried to break free of Persian rule. Darius was ruthless in suppressing the revolts and bringing the empire to heel, an act which, amazingly, he accomplished in little more than a year. He captured and executed the rebel leaders and for the rest of his reign he was never threatened with an uprising again.

High above the Royal Road near Ecbatana, Darius had an account of the suppression of the rebellions carved deep into the rock face of Mount Bisitun. A huge raised relief dominates the surface of the stone showing Darius standing at the head of a line of rebellious kings, each one fettered to the next by a rope. Darius is depicted on a larger scale than the other figures on the relief and he places his left foot upon the belly of the prostrate figure of the rebel Gaumata. In his left hand Darius clutches a bow, a symbol of his military authority, which is echoed by the presence of two armed guards standing to his rear. Darius' right hand is raised in adoration of the figure in the winged disk at the centre of the scene: this is probably Ahuramazda, the supreme deity of the Achaemenids; he offers Darius the kingship in the form of a ring.

## Consolidating empire

In 518 BC, after confirming his hold on the empire, Darius I was able to expand its borders as far as the Punjab; in 513 BC he attempted to conquer the Scythians north of the Black Sea too. In Darius' reign the empire reached its zenith and extended from Libya to Bactria.

Darius was particularly concerned with implementing empire-wide building and engineering projects: in Egypt he was responsible for the creation of a canal between the Nile and the Red Sea, and for building temples to Egyptian gods at Hibis in the Fayum. In the Iranian heartland, Ecbatana and Pasargadae were expanded and embellished and he started a mammoth building programme at Persepolis. The Elamite city of Susa was afforded a new lease of life by Darius when he chose it as his administrative capital. An important inscription from Susa records how Darius enlisted workmen from all over the empire to build and decorate his palace in a truly international endeavour.

Late in his reign Darius came into contact with the Greeks, and while he may have had ambitions to incorporate Greece into the empire (and was certainly keen to punish Athens for its interference in Persian affairs), Herodotus' account of Greco-Persian tensions probably exaggerates the Persian response to the Greek resistance. However, before he could launch a Greek campaign Darius died and was buried in a tomb at Naqsh-I Rustam, near Persepolis. It was left to his son Xerxes to punish the Greeks.

## Troubled empire

Xerxes (485–465 BC) took control of the empire, and, in all essentials, he continued his father's policies of expanding and strengthening the empire, although it must be noted that our knowledge of Xerxes' reign is almost totally confined to the western periphery of the empire, due to our complete dependence on Greek sources. Moreover, evidence for the events of the latter years of his reign is sparse and mainly conjectural. Because of his aggressive policy towards the Greek lands, classical sources depict Xerxes as a hubristic megalomaniac, but this is probably far from the truth.

Xerxes' first task was coping with a rebellion in Egypt, which had begun prior to Darius' death. He appointed his brother Achaemenes as satrap of Egypt, a policy frequently adopted by the Achaemenid kings whereby close family members were appointed to important satrapal positions, so much so that the running of the empire became a family concern.

In 481 BC Babylonia erupted in revolt. Again Xerxes drew on his close relatives for aid and the rebels were subdued by Megabyzus, Xerxes' cousin (who afterwards became one of the supreme commanders of the campaign against Greece). Xerxes responded to the revolt by dividing the huge satrapy of Babylonia into two: 'Babylonia', embracing all of modern Iraq and Syria, and 'Beyond the River', including Syria-Palestine and lands west of the Euphrates.

One aim, in which Xerxes ultimately failed, was to force the mainland Greeks to acknowledge Persian power. From the perspective of Persia's long-term Aegean policy, extending a measure of control to European Greece was logical and the importance of this Persian expansion is signalled by the fact that Xerxes himself led the expedition. Xerxes captured Athens in 480 BC, but his navy was then defeated by the Greeks at Salamis (see The Athenian Empire). The city was recaptured a year later, although shortly afterwards the Persian general Mardonius was killed at the battle of Plataea and his army was heavily defeated. In August 479 BC the Greeks again routed the Persians at Mycale, causing the plan for the invasion of Greece to be abandoned. These battles were turning points in relations between the Greeks and Persians as it became clear that the Persian army was not invincible. During the following decades Persia lost much of its territory in Europe and the Greek cities of Asia Minor acquired increasing independence.

As Xerxes was marching his army into Greece in 480 BC, a second revolt in Babylonia broke out (the renewed unrest in Babylon would explain Xerxes' rapid departure from Greece). His rapid intervention in Babylonia was successful, since the province did not revolt again. However, according to Arrian, Xerxes punished the city by razing the temple of Marduk to the ground and removing the god's statue from the city. Is there any truth to this? Certainly the royal titles found in Babylonian texts of the period show a demotion in status of the city in the titulary of the king from 'Xerxes, King of Babylon, King of Lands' in regnal year 3 to just 'Xerxes, King of Lands' in regnal year 5. Yet there is no archaeological evidence to suggest that Xerxes destroyed Babylon's temples. Babylonia was probably not treated generously after two revolts, but exactly what form Xerxes' punishment took we do not know; its sanctuaries and cults suffered no noticeable decline and the New Year Festivals of Marduk went on uninterrupted.

In August 465 BC, Xerxes was murdered in a court coup. The events are obscure, but the plot seems to have been hatched by Xerxes' son, Artaxerxes, in cahoots with powerful eunuchs.

### Later empire

From the death of Xerxes on, and despite badly understood changes and developments in its infrastructure, the Persian empire can be classified as a fully mature and stable entity; far from being a time of stagnation, the late Achaemenid period saw a renewed spate of military activity and the re-conquest of rebellious territories.

When Artaxerxes I (465–425 BC) died he was followed to the throne by three of his sons in quick succession, his youngest reigning as Darius II (424–405 BC). With his wife, Parysatis, he eliminated all potential opposition so that the succession from Darius to his eldest son Artaxerxes II (405–359 BC) passed smoothly. Nevertheless Artaxerxes' younger brother, Cyrus the satrap of Lydia and Phrygia Minor, nursed ambitions for the crown and in this he was encouraged by the powerful queen mother, Parysatis. Royal women sometimes played a key role in the politics of the empire and although they could not rule in their own right, they had access to political agency through their intimate relationships with the Great Kings.

Cyrus gathered together an army of Persian nobles, troops from his satrapy, and a force of Greek mercenaries, including the Athenian soldier Xenophon, who has left us a valuable description of Cyrus' ill-fated revolt (*Anabasis*). The rebellious army met with Artaxerxes' troops at Cunaxa in Babylonia in 401 BC and Cyrus was killed. His bid for the throne had failed to gain more widespread support among the Persian nobility and Artaxerxes II's power remained unshaken.

At the same time Egypt attempted to break free of Persian control and successful campaigning led, between 401 and 399 BC, to the expulsion of the Persians. This was a serious blow to the Great King, and Achaemenid history for the next 56 years is dominated by the continuous efforts to regain control of this important province. The Persians turned their attention to ensuring that Syria-Palestine and Asia Minor remained under firm control and in 387/386 BC, Artaxerxes was able to impose a settlement on the Greeks (the 'King's Peace'), whereby they recognized that the cities of Asia Minor were under Persian control.

Artaxerxes II was succeeded by his son Artaxerxes III (359–338 BC). The major achievement of his reign was the re-conquest of Egypt in 343 BC, after hard and brutal campaigning. This had been preceded by the crushing of a revolt in Phoenicia, headed by the ruler of Sidon, Tennes; Artaxerxes' punishment of Sidon was swift: Tennes was executed, some of the city was destroyed and a part of its population was deported into Babylonia.

Artaxerxes' successor, Artaxerxes IV, reigned for only two years before a member of a collateral branch of the Achaemenid family seized the throne as Darius III (336–330 BC). Darius' reputation has suffered badly since he was fated to be the opponent of Alexander of Macedon, whose brilliant military victories spelled the end of the

Achaemenid dynasty. In reality, Darius was a brave soldier and an able administrator who posed a serious threat to Alexander's dreams of glory. He met Alexander in battle at Issus in 333 BC and again at Gaugamela in 331 BC but was defeated at both encounters. He fled to Ecbatana to try to raise fresh troops and thence to Bactria where he was killed by his satrap, Bessus, in 330 BC.

## Maintaining empire: a *Pax Persiaca*?

The longevity of such a vast empire is testimony to the Achaemenid policy of both tolerance towards its conquered peoples and its ruthlessness in maintaining power. The royal rhetoric recorded in the cuneiform inscriptions and disseminated widely across the empire, emphasized that all conquered nations were united in service to the Great King, whose laws they were required to obey and whose majesty they were obliged to uphold. The king was championed by Ahuramazda, the chief god of the Achaemenids, who granted the monarch the gift of kingship in order to put an end to chaos and bring about world order. The royal texts frequently used the motif that unrest and rebellion were linked to cosmic disorder and the growth of the Lie (*drauga*). The Great King was the champion of Truth (*arta*) and therefore crushed and quelled rebellious subjects so that order (also represented by the word *arta*) could triumph. Rebellion against Persian authority was therefore seen as a revolt against divine authority because the Great King served Ahuramazda's will on earth as the guarantor of justice and the maintainer of the social order.

Darius the Great, a truly brilliant bureaucrat, divided the empire's territories into administrative satrapies (provinces), under the control of satraps (governors), in order to maintain the levy of tribute required from each region. Darius' Bisitun Inscription (*c.* 520 BC) provides the oldest extant list of the constituents of the empire. It begins with two core lands, Persia and Elam. Then the order roughly follows the map of the empire in a clockwise fashion, first referring to the western provinces or satrapies, then those in the northern part, followed by the lands in the east of the empire. The ordering of the provinces of the empire here is interesting, since lands lying closest to the imperial centre (Elam, Babylonia) are privileged in the text over those at the periphery of empire (Ionia, Maka), suggesting an Achaemenid ideology of hierarchy: proximity to Persia signifies a higher level of civilization.

The impression we have of the administration of the Achaemenid empire is that the top posts were in the hands of a tiny group of men drawn exclusively from the highest echelons of the Persian aristocracy, especially from within the royal family. But satraps could come from more humble origins, and even non-Persian satraps are known, such as Metiochus, the son of the Athenian general Miltiades. The king was therefore at liberty to bestow the rank of 'Honorary Persian' on an individual not of pure Persian blood. The satrap enjoyed the privilege of being the Great King's representative. He was required to administer the collection of taxes and tribute and to raise armed forces when occasion required and, at a regional level, the satrap was also required to make all governmental decisions. For matters of international importance, however, he was obliged to consult the king and his chief ministers. As a representative of the king, the satrap kept court and maintained court ceremony based on that at the heart of the empire: he sat in audience, received petitions, observed religious rites and celebrated royal festivals.

Every satrapy covered an extensive area, ruled from a capital (which also acted as an administrative centre) where the satrap had a palace and a court. Thus, the satrapal capital of Media lay in Ecbatana, in Egypt it was Memphis, in Lydia it was Sardis, in Babylonia it was Babylon, in Phrygia it was Daskyleion, and in the satrapy known as Babylonia Beyond the River, it was Damascus. A palace discovered in Samarkand in Uzbekistan was probably the residence of the satrap of Bactria-Sogdiana. The palaces of the satraps, often acquired from local kings or nobles, were frequently set among villages and parks which helped support the feeding of the court and provided space for hunting expeditions. Many members of the royal family had private estates scattered throughout the empire which could be farmed by locals for the profit of the owners or leased out for fees. Satrapal palaces could also be utilized by the king and his court as they progressed across the empire on regular seasonal migrations: Babylon, Susa, Ecbatana and Persepolis in particular were routinely visited by the royal court.

The regional capitals were used to store the taxes that poured in from the satrapies; these taxes were paid in both coin and kind, the latter including foodstuffs used to maintain the vast satrapal court and its dependents. The Persepolis Fortification Texts attest to the fact that workers at the palace of the Great King were paid in food and wine rations, but not in coins or precious metals. However, taxation payments in precious goods and metals (especially silver) were widely used and one of the most important administrative jobs in each satrapy was the *ganazabara*, 'Treasurer'. The treasuries were well guarded by soldiers and a record of goods going into and out of the storerooms was maintained in detail by an army of bureaucrats and scribes. The vast imperial treasury at Persepolis was a symbol of the Great King's power over his empire, and it is no coincidence that, in 330 BC, Alexander selected the treasury to be destroyed as a symbol of his conquest of the empire en masse.

The palaces were also centres for provincial administration; here royal orders were delivered to the satrap from the central authority. Royal decrees, identifiable by the king's seal, have been found as far afield as Nippur, Samaria and Artašat in Armenia, although the biggest hoard of royal seals was discovered at Daskyleion in Anatolia. In his turn, the satrap issued decrees and statements which were disbursed throughout the province. Archives were kept of all royal and satrapal decrees so that they could form future reference. The Old Testament Book of Ezra, for instance, recalls how Darius I ordered that the royal archives of Babylon be searched for a copy of a decree issued by Cyrus the Great. In fact the document, an edict granting the Jews the right to rebuild the Jerusalem temple, was found not in Babylon at all, but in the archives of the palace at Ecbatana.

The satraps relied on a healthy interaction with local elites. In pursuing good inter-regional relationships, the institutions of marriage and concubinage should not be overlooked. Although we have very little information about the wives of satraps (let alone those of lesser-ranking Persian commanders and officials), there certainly were marriages between Persians and local women. Likewise, the marriage of the Paphlagonian prince, Otys, to the daughter of the Persian noble, Spithridates, recorded by Xenophon attests to the reverse practice of elite men taking Persian brides. Such alliances gave the local elite a foothold in the Persian honour system. In addition, both kings and satraps took women from among subject peoples into their harems as concubines. According to Herodotus, 'every man has a number of wives, a much greater number of concubines', and while this scenario of empire-wide polygyny cannot be taken at face value, it may well be representative of privileged members of Iranian society. Persian nobles, especially satraps, certainly imitated the royal polygynous custom: Pharnabazus, satrap of Phrygia, kept a court full of concubines at Sardis. The Great King's 360 concubines were, so to speak, physical manifestations of the Persian realm.

The Persian system depended very much on cooperation with local power-holders and they frequently used well-established regional administrative systems to work for them. Additionally, Persians often employed individuals who were familiar with localized government to work with them. The Egyptian nobleman Udjahorresnet is a case in point; a former naval commander under the last indigenous pharaohs of the Saite dynasty, he was stripped of his military rank under Cambyses but was accorded the privileged title of king's 'friend' along with a high rank in the temple of Neith at Sais. In other words, Udjahorresnet was denied any effective military power, but retained in royal service in a honorific position and could operate as a royal adviser.

The same system can be seen at work with the lesser kings and local dynasts. A good example is the use the satrap Pharnabazus made of the local rulers of Dardanus. When Zenis, the long-serving pro-Persian client-king of Dardanus, died, Pharnabazus had planned to bestow the satrapy to someone else. But Zenis' wife, Mania, petitioned Pharnabazus to bestow the province on her. The satrap took the unusual step of appointing a woman to the post to keep it within Zenis' family. Pharnabazus was delighted to find that Mania paid the tribute into the satrapal treasury just as regularly as her husband had done. These events illustrate the advantage of employing local elites to defend Persian interests. Conversely, dependence of the local dynasts on the satrap, and his power to strip the family of rank, kept them in check.

The smooth-running of the empire was facilitated by an excellent infrastructure. First-rate roads connected the main satrapal centres of the empire with the imperial core. The most important of these highways was the Royal Road which connected Sardis to Persepolis, via Susa and Babylon; an eastern branch led first to Ecbatana and thence onwards to Bactra and on to Pashwar, while another road connected Persepolis to Egypt, via Damascus and Jerusalem. The roads were measured in 6-km (3.7-mile) intervals (*parasangs*) and road-stations were set up around every 28 km (17.4 miles) of the route to accommodate the quick change of fresh horses for any imperial messenger carrying official documents. Herodotus estimated that the distance from Susa to Sardis, 450 *parasangs*, could be covered in 90 days.

The Persians displayed no desire to impose their language or culture upon the conquered nations; the Great Kings utilized local languages for their decrees and employed Aramaic as a form of *lingua franca* throughout the imperial territories to help facilitate effective communication. In the realm of religion, too, the Persian kings were careful to appear as active upholders of local cults, if only to ensure control of the wealthy sanctuaries and the adherence of powerful priesthoods. Even in small administrative regions, like Jerusalem and Magnesia-on-the-Maeander, the Persians granted temple privileges and acknowledged the support their local gods had given them.

However, this seemingly laissez-faire attitude towards cultural autonomy needs to be balanced by the fact that the Persians could prove to be merciless overlords if crossed. Rebellious subjects and states were treated ruthlessly: populations were uprooted and deported across the empire, and their holy shrines were burned and destroyed. Herodotus records the Persian destruction of the sanctuaries of Apollo at Didyma and of Athena in Athens. Artaxerxes III's reputation for harshness and cruelty is perhaps justified by his treatment of Sidon, while his violent re-conquest of Egypt is recorded on the stela of an Egyptian nobleman named Somtutefnakht: 'The Asiatic... slew a million at my sides', he recalls. As the heirs of the great Assyrian empire, the Persians inherited many kinds of savage punishment techniques documented in Assyrian and later neo-Babylonian sources: impaling, decapitation, killing of children, burning, whipping, strangling, stoning, castration, blinding, cutting of a living body in two, cutting off breasts, nose, ears, lips, hands, arms, snipping out the tongue, branding, flaying, crucifixion and skinning alive. Thus in one passage of the Bisitun Inscription, Darius proudly proclaims:

> '[The rebel] Phraortes was seized and led to me. I cut off his nose, ears and tongue, and I put out one of his eyes.'

The empire was founded and maintained by military might. The army consisted of infantry, horse and camel cavalry, and elite charioteers. The Persians also routinely incorporated subject and mercenary Greeks in their army, each of whom received a monthly wage (a gold *Daric* per month in 401 BC). By the time of Alexander, these mercenaries had become a regular part of the army and their leaders had even been incorporated into the Iranian aristocracy. Other areas of the empire sent men to bolster the imperial army: Scythian charioteers and bowmen and Bactrian camel-riders are well attested.

The size of the imperial army was never as large as the Greeks suggested and historians now estimate that Xerxes' forces for the Greek campaign numbered around 70,000 infantry and 9,000 horsemen, while the army of Artaxerxes II at Cunaxa was probably around

40,000 in number. Darius III's troops at Gaugamela amounted to about 34,000 cavalry and some infantry. The army was led by a supreme commander, who was either the Great King himself or a close relative. Next in command was an officer in charge of a division of 1,000 men, subdivided into 10 battalions. The most famous of the army units was the crack fighting team known as the Ten Thousand (or 'Immortals'), a division of which served as the royal bodyguard.

A characteristic of the Achaemenid period is that commanders and dignitaries participated in actual fighting, and many of them died in action. Although imperial royal ideology propounded the peace and unity of the realm, Great Kings also emphasized their ability to rule by force. In order to be an effective ruler, the king had to be a brave soldier first.

## The Persian empire today

There can be no doubt that the first Persian empire was of enormous significance for the development of the idea of 'empire'. It made possible the first significant and continuous contact between East and West, and prepared the ground for Alexander the Great's vision of what an empire could be.

Within Iran itself, the debate on what the Achaemenid empire means in a modern framework is very much alive. Mohammed Reza Shah's obsession with the Achaemenid dynasty during the 1970s led to a backlash against the study of, and engagement with, the Persian past throughout the formative period of the Islamic Revolution. Yet today the monuments of ancient Iran are both studied and enjoyed by the Iranians, who appraise the Achaemenid empire as being at the apex of the history of Iranian civilization. Cyrus the Great is particularly revered as a visionary leader of great moral integrity and brilliance and the Cyrus Cylinder is frequently claimed as the first Bill of Human Rights. In Iran the first Persian empire is remembered with immense pride.

In the West, the study of the Achaemenid empire continues to expand and change, and, despite today's political tensions, the dialogue between Western and Iranian scholars is flourishing as never before. Textual studies of indigenous Persian sources continue to appear, and the archaeology of the empire is still producing unexpected finds which constantly force scholarship to rethink and re-mould their definitions of empire. Are the ancient sources on Persia really as Hellenocentric as they are often presented as being? Can we study the ancient Persian empire without forcing the subject to be viewed through the prism of Orientalism? Achaemenid studies stand at the threshold of new and interesting debates in which the concept of empire will play a key role.

# THE ATHENIAN EMPIRE

## 478–404 BC, 378–338 BC

ALASTAIR BLANSHARD

Greece emerged after the collapse of the Mycenaean civilization (c. 1100 BC) as a patchwork of individual city-states. Yet while these were important – they remained the 'atoms' of the political landscape – the trend from the 9th century BC onwards was for this autonomous isolationism to be gradually ceded to other institutions beyond the city-state. Greece gave itself over to a series of increasingly important and complex networks. Communities bound themselves in ties of mutual obligations through oaths. Cities sent out expeditions to establish independent communities in distant lands. These overseas settlements were often linked to their 'mother cities' through religious, cultural and political bonds. As the wealth of cities increased, elite members of society were not satisfied vying among themselves within the boundaries of their own states. They looked for new arenas where they could compete for honour and status, arenas that promised an international audience and even wider acclaim. Ambitious tyrants extended their influence through the creation of political alliances. Sparta enslaved the neighbouring territory of Messenia and other states likewise unified large sections of the Peloponnese under their leadership. Cities banded together to form religious unions to celebrate common cults or administer shared sanctuaries. This period of Greek history is characterized by an increasing trend towards centralization that unlocked the social, economic and cultural resources of the Greek world. It was a world ripe for empire.

That the agent for empire should be Athens was not, however, a certainty. Before the end of the 6th century BC, there were few signs that Athens would become the dominant power in the Aegean. Indeed, there were other candidates that were much more promising. Sparta dominated the Peloponnese. Corinth was wealthier and had more extensive trade connections; it was mother city to dozens of colonies throughout the Mediterranean and was an influential player in the Peloponnesian region. Corinth also had an ambitious elite who were not averse to the idea of extending their power. Yet these elements never translated into an empire. The story of the rise of Athens then is a story both about the inevitability of empire and the opportunities provided by chance.

## The birth of the Athenian empire

The immediate origins of the Athenian empire lay in the aftermath of the Greek defeat of the Persians after their invasions in 490 BC and 480/479 BC. This victory over Persia was certainly unexpected. Persian expansion in Asia Minor and the surrounding regions had gone largely unchecked for over a century. Persian resources far exceeded those of Greece, and the size of the Persian army dwarfed that of the Greeks.

Within this story of opposition to Persia, Athens played a prominent role. It had responded to a call for assistance when the wealthy Greek cities on the coast of Asia Minor had risen in revolt against Persian rule in 499 BC. In 490 BC, when the Persians invaded mainland Greece under King Darius, they were stopped in their tracks just outside Athens on the coastal plains of Marathon. Athenian soldiers routed the Persian infantry, slaughtering soldiers in the boggy landscape, and driving the enemy into the sea. When Darius' successor, King Xerxes, returned with an even larger army in 480 BC, Athens was one of the leading members of the coalition of 30 or so states that opposed Persia. It even had the possibility of leading this coalition. However, to avoid disagreement and ensure the support of Sparta, it ceded overall command to the Spartans. In the final analysis, it was probably the largely Athenian naval victory at the battle of Salamis that contributed most to the eventual routing of the enemy.

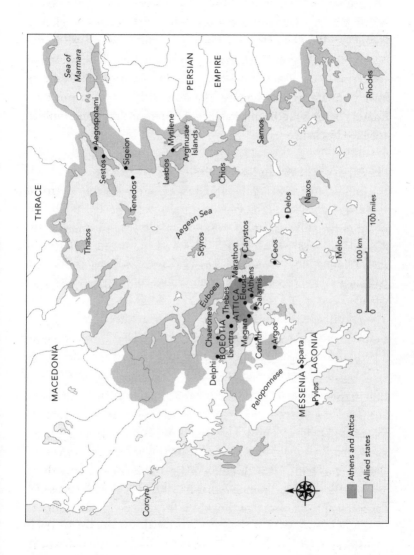

Athens had every reason to oppose the Persians. For one thing, they threatened her newly founded democracy. The reforms of the Athenian statesman Cleisthenes in 509 BC had given Athens a democratic constitution and this democracy had been established in the wake of the expulsion of the previous tyrannical regime, the Peisistratids (c. 546–510 BC). One of the members of this dynasty, the former tyrant Hippias, had found refuge at the Persian court and his restoration was clearly seen by the Persians as an ideal way to further their interests. He even accompanied the Persian forces to Marathon, ready to take over the running of the city following a Persian victory. In the first instance, Athens was fighting to avoid a regime change.

Yet the aim of saving the city and its newly formed democracy is only part of the story of Athenian resistance. This desire for self-preservation coincided with increasing ambition on the part of the state. The Peisistratids, like most tyrants, had been keen to make a mark on the wider Greek stage. Their extensive building works, their patronage of the arts, and their establishment of client tyrants on the island of Naxos and the city of Sigeion, had given Athens a taste of a world outside the borders of Attica. Indeed, there is much that is proto-imperial about the rule of these tyrants. The city was enjoying a period of increased prosperity prior to the Persian invasions. The tyrants had accelerated the unification of Attica, allowing Athens to fully exploit one of the largest hinterlands of any city-state in mainland Greece. The average city-state controlled between 50 and 100 sq. km (20–40 sq. miles) of land. The size of Attica is 2,650 sq. km (1025 sq. miles). This makes the state of Athens four times the size of its nearest neighbour, Megara, and twice the size of Athens' commercial rival, Corinth. Only Sparta, which controlled a region of 8,400 sq. km (3,250 sq. miles), exceeded Athens in size.

Athens was well positioned to provide alternative leadership to Sparta in the aftermath of the Persian war. It had not taken long for dissatisfaction with Spartan leadership to arise among the allied cities. In particular, they were dissatisfied with the Spartan reluctance to press their advantage over Persia and pursue an aggressive campaign of revenge. This, coupled with the perceived autocratic tendencies of the Spartan king, Pausanias, led the allies to approach Athens to lead them against Persia. Sparta recalled their king from the Hellespont where he was leading Greek operations against the Persians, and tried to send a replacement to take over the command, but they were too late. Events had moved on, and Athens was now the leader (Greek *hegemon*) of a new alliance designed to punish Persia, the Delian League.

It was the Delian League that would form the basis of the Athenian empire. The League offers a model of empire that stands in contrast to a number of traditional notions about empire. There were no governors of provinces. Athens allowed the majority of city-states under

## KEY DATES

| | |
|---|---|
| 480 BC | Persians defeat Athenians at Thermopylae, but are themselves routed in a naval battle at Salamis |
| 479 BC | Greeks end Persian invasion with land victories at Plataea and Mycale |
| 478 BC | Formation of Delian League led by Athens |
| 461–446 BC | Sparta revolts against Athenian domination in the first Peloponnesian war |
| 447–433 BC | Major building work on the Acropolis, including Parthenon |
| 440 BC | Athenians besiege Samos after it attempts to secede from Delian League |
| 431–404 BC | Persia and Sparta confront Athens in the second Peloponnesian war |
| 416 BC | Capture of island of Melos |
| 415–413 BC | Athenian expedition to Sicily |
| 378 BC | Foundation of the Second Athenian League |
| 371 BC | Defeat of Sparta by Thebes at the battle of Leuctra |
| 338 BC | Philip II of Macedon defeats Athens at Chaeronea, initiating Macedonian hegemony |
| 336 BC | Assassination of Philip and accession of Alexander the Great |

its rule in the League to remain autonomous in the conduct of their internal affairs. It instituted no universal system of laws. Nor did it ever extend its citizenship to anybody, except to a few honoured foreigners. Instead, the Athenian empire was one based on the recognition of the pre-eminence of Athens, and that certain privileges went with this status. These privileges included the right to demand and assess tribute to pay for the upkeep of the fleet, the right to arbitrate in disputes between members of the League, and the right to determine what lay in the League's best interest. Theoretically, members of the League also had a say in its administration. However, such niceties were not observed for long. It is telling that even today it is not possible to reconstruct the constitutional arrangements of the original League, so little historical impact did these arrangements have.

Once a city was admitted to the League, it was difficult to leave. Athens was ruthless in pursuing allies who abdicated their responsibilities. Under the pretext of maintaining the League, allied cities that revolted were crushed and new, more loyal regimes were instituted. At its height, Athens considered itself to be leader of over 400 city-states, although only 190 seem to have been regularly paying tribute.

It is striking just how quickly Athens turned the actions of the Delian League to its own advantage. For example, immediately after taking leadership of the League and removing the Persian garrison from Thrace, the Athenian fleet attacked the Greek island of Scyros. The reason for this attack was supposedly to make the seas safer by destroying a nest of pirates. Such an action was defensible on a broad interpretation of the remit of the Delian League. Less defensible was the establishment of an Athenian colony on this strategic island, one that Athens had been eyeing for some time. The next Greek victim of the League was the state of Carystos on the island of Euboeia. Its crime had been to assist the Persians (admittedly under considerable duress) in 490 BC. It had remained neutral during Xerxes' invasions. For such fence-sitting, Carystos paid a high price. The city was overrun, enrolled into the League and an annual cash subscription was levied. The unpleasantness of this incident is only magnified by the decision of a number of Athenian parents to name their children Carystonikos ('Victory over Carystos') at this time. Exulting in the defeat of fellow Greeks takes off some of the shine of this supposed defender of Greek freedom.

It did not take long before a number of states decided to attempt to withdraw from the League. The first was Naxos in 470 BC. For such temerity, the city was besieged. When Naxos eventually capitulated, it was deprived of its fleet, re-enrolled in the League, and a cash contribution levied upon it. The capture of Naxos was regarded by critics of the empire as the first truly illegal act undertaken by Athens. Yet an even worse breach was to follow quickly upon it, namely the Athenian treatment of the island of Thasos. The cause of the dispute between Thasos and Athens was the Athenian intention to found a colony on the gold-rich coast off the island. This region had long been under the control of Thasos and was a considerable source of the island's wealth. Faced with this threat, Thasos seceded from the League. The Athenians immediately sent a fleet to quell the rebellion. After three years of fighting they were eventually successful, and Thasos was once again enrolled into the League. In addition, Thasos was required to dismantle its walls, pay a cash indemnity to the League, and hand over control of the mineral coastline to Athens. This pattern of Athenian self-interest driving League activities was to continue for the next half century. It is no wonder that Athens eventually stopped referring to the League in inscriptions as 'Athens and her allies' and started calling it 'the cities which Athens rules'.

## The machinery of empire

The principal obligation required of members of the Delian League was to support the alliance through maintaining the fleet. This support could come through either the provision of money to Athens to buy ships and crew them or the provision of actual ships and crews to serve under Athenian control. The majority of states chose the former option, handing over an amount of 'tribute' each year, and reducing the size of their navies accordingly.

That so many states effectively paid for their own enslavement and diminished their capacity for resistance reflects two factors. The first is the high cost and effort required to maintain a fleet. Even Athens, which enjoyed a number of economic advantages owing to its size, probably had little left over from the allied contributions after it had paid its fleet costs. Paying cash gave all the benefits of having a fleet (defence against Persia, removal of pirates) without the administrative difficulties.

The second factor is general acceptance of Athenian domination of the sea. It is extraordinary to see how quickly Athenian hegemony was accepted throughout the Aegean. Whatever the situation at the formation of the Delian League, it soon became apparent to the various states that nothing was going to happen in the Aegean without the consent of the Athenians. There was little point in maintaining a fleet because the sense of independence it provided was illusory. Some states such as the large island states on Chios, Lesbos and Samos chose to buy into the illusion, enjoying the symbolism that supplying ships as opposed to money gave them. However, despite the symbolism, they enjoyed no greater autonomy than any of the money-paying states. When Samos and Lesbos rose in revolt, they were crushed with the same effectiveness.

The provision of tribute was not just about economic resources and the maintenance of military might. Tribute also served an ideological function. The hegemony of Athens was signalled from the very formation of the Delian League when it was granted the right to appoint its treasurers, a message reinforced when Athens moved the treasury from Delos to Athens. The symbolism of the act was not lost on anybody. Traditionally historians have regarded the act as the final sign of the complete destruction of the ideals of the Delian League. Athens tied a number of aspects relating to the tribute into its own civic calendar. They timed the reassessment of tribute to coincide with the Great Panathenaia, a festival held every four years that celebrated the birthday of Athena. Allied ambassadors were required to attend and bring offerings to the festival. Immediately afterwards they were told what their annual contribution towards the upkeep of the empire would be. Even more pointedly, tribute when it was collected was brought to Athens in time for the Great Dionysia, the annual dramatic festival in honour of Dionysus. Indeed, the display of tribute was one of the preliminaries to the dramatic festival. The money was piled up onto the stage for the contemplation and enjoyment of the satisfied Athenian audience.

In addition to its fleet, Athens employed a large number of officials to maintain order throughout its empire. According to one source, at its height in the mid-5th century BC Athens had over 700 officials devoted to the running of the empire. A considerable number of these were stationed in allied city-states. These officials served a variety of functions. They were involved in the transfer of tribute to Athens, liaising with local officials over the handling and collection of the money. They oversaw the carrying out of Athenian decrees. They reported to Athens on affairs within the local city, and acted as a contact point for Athenian embassies. In cases where a city had previously risen in revolt against Athens, there would also be a garrison of Athenian soldiers stationed there, responsible for keeping order and ensuring that the city remained loyal. Likewise numerous embassies and heralds were dispatched as the need arose to convey imperial policy to outlying city-states. Yet service as an official stationed in the allied cities does not seem to have been particularly popular among Athenian citizens. For this reason, those unlucky enough to have been allotted these postings were often tempted to try to excuse themselves or bribe another to take their place. Eventually Athens had to pass a law forbidding such practices.

The Athenians also enrolled a number of prominent locals into the service of their empire. These locals were awarded the title of 'proxenos'. These proxenoi were concerned with looking after the interests of Athenian visitors to a state. They provided hospitality, introductions to relevant individuals and institutions, and even in some cases financial support. In return, they were granted special privileges in Athens and legal protection against reprisals from their fellow citizens. Admittedly, this protection almost always came too late in times of revolt. Nevertheless, loyal *proxenoi* could rely on Athens to avenge their deaths.

## Creating culture

There were few aspects of Athenian public life that were not affected in some way by the empire. It undertook a building programme that befitted its new status as an imperial capital. The empire made Athenians think differently about their history, and it impacted on the religious practices of the citizens and allies. The story of empire infused history and myth and this amalgam seeped onto the Athenian stage, into the visual arts, and ultimately into the minds of the citizens. For example, two of the most distinctive features in the classical period – its Athenocentrism and its focus on the barbarian – are both ideas developed in the service of the empire. Both these features acted to create a myth about Athens as the pre-eminent Greek state, one blessed by the gods whose rule was not only destined, but necessary.

It was not unusual for Greek city-states to promote their own locale heavily, so in that respect Athens' self-publicity was not peculiar. However, it is difficult to find a city that matches the Athenian effort in burnishing the individuality and superiority of its institutions. The attempts are almost pathological, and suggest that Athens was desperately trying to cover up its own insecurities as *hegemon*. Athenian ideology attempted to rewrite the historical accident that led to Athenian leadership of the Delian League into a law of nature, and the full panoply of the arts was devoted to this endeavour.

There are numerous instances of this Athenian sense of superiority at work. For example, the special place that Athens enjoyed in the heart of the goddess Athena was a theme constantly reinforced through ritual, vase-painting, and most notably the rebuilding work on the Acropolis. However, it was not just Athena who was depicted showing special favour to the Athenians. One of the claims that Athens liked to make was that Attica was the birthplace of agriculture. In the town of Eleusis, the goddess Demeter first taught the art of agriculture to prince Triptolemus, who then sped off in a winged chariot to teach the art to the rest of the world. This story, which makes Athens the cradle of civilization, was told in drama, art and ritual. Allies, for example, were required to send offerings of 'first fruits' of corn and barley to Eleusis in remembrance of this act of kindness. Although all these stories had existed long before the empire emerged, it was the empire that created a new and intense market for them, allowing them to be promulgated in ways and to an extent that had been previously unimaginable.

Similarly, tremendous focus was placed on the role of Athens as leader in the fight against the Persians. After all, this was the claim on which Athenian superiority rested. In Athenian hands, the Persian wars became a second Trojan war. Marathon was reworked as the most perfect of battles. Numerous monuments were erected around the city and throughout Greece to remind people of the Athenian role in the wars. It is no accident that one of the few dramatic tragedies that features an historical event takes as its subject the Athenian victory at Salamis. As a consequence of such ideas, the Persians came to be regarded as a breed apart, a group whose very nature was deficient. Classical art picked out every ethnic difference whether it was Thracian tattoos, the baldness of the circumcized Egyptians, or the soft effeminate dress of the Persians. Empire invented the barbarian, an ironic circumstance given the 'barbaric' flavour of so many of its own institutions (such as tribute).

All this activity attracted the attention of other Greeks. Artisans, poets and dramatists flowed into the Athenian harbour as well as grain and timber. The increasingly wealthy Athenian elite developed a taste for novelty as a way of separating themselves from their fellow citizens. Talented foreigners were able to find many outlets for their skills in

Athens, whether it was as teachers, musicians, poets, dramatists or even just semi-professional conversational partners.

Of course, one makes a mistake if one imagines that all this intellectual endeavour was just about supporting imperial ideology. Empire provided a spur to cultural development through the production of resistance as well as compliance. Art is different from propaganda, and one can easily see, especially in the art forms such as drama, a desire to question the excesses of Athenian imperial rule. Comedy was only too wise to the balance sheet of empire, and was happy to point out its undesirable consequences and its grotesquery. Likewise tragedy, although conventionally setting its plays in the mythical past, often took violence and the abuse of power as its themes, concepts all too pertinent to the running of the empire. It is hard to imagine that many Athenians who witnessed the fall of Troy and the enslavement of the court of Priam in Euripides' *Trojan Women* weren't prompted to think of the massacre and enslavement of the island of Melos only a few months before, especially as a number of members of the audience would have had a reminder of this brutal act in the form of new Melian slaves in their households. Yet despite whatever questions these performances evoked, their effect is debatable. The comic Aristophanes who devoted numerous plays to the topic of peace never seems to have convinced his audience to abandon war.

## Opposition to Athenian rule

One of the important functions of empires is the control and distribution of resources. As a consequence, every empire has both its beneficiaries and those who lose out. Many took advantage of the opportunities offered by the Athenian empire. The urban poor found themselves employment in the Athenian navy. The wealth of Athens attracted merchants and craftspeople from all over the Greek world. Commodity exporters such as the wine-producers of Chios also did extremely well. In the marketplace of Athens it was possible to find Egyptian perfume sellers, Libyan grain merchants, Phoenician textile workers, and Thracian princes keen on enjoying some sightseeing. Wealthy Athenian citizens were not slow to see the potential under the empire for extending their landholding interests, and a number of citizens seem to have owned large foreign estates. Yet, all of these benefits came at a cost. Merchants were required to pay landing-taxes to help support Athenian religious cults. Foreigners who wished to live in Athens had to pay fees to the state. Athens could be rapacious in its demand for resources. We have already seen the consequences for Thasos that arose from Athenian desire to control its mines. Similarly, Athens endeavoured to secure for itself the best in timber and grain, even when those resources were much needed by its allies.

Allies did not always enjoy life under Athenian rule. Athenian officials stationed within cities could be a source of tension. Not bound by local laws, there was much potential for corruption and illegality. Athenian officials were infamous for their drunken debauchery and seduction of the wives of locals. Regimes that enjoyed the support of Athens used that support in the persecution of their opponents. If local elites showed disloyalty, Athens would often impose democratic regimes onto the states. Internal recriminations, bloodletting and exile were almost always the immediate consequences of these actions.

This occasional, but dramatic interference in their internal politics was one of the main grievances of the allies. Another was the confisca-tion of land and the imposition of colonies that usually occurred after rebellion. The most famous case of such behaviour took place following the revolt of Mytilene in 428 BC. Mytilene was an important ally of the Athenians, and Athens took her betrayal to heart. The historian Thucydides presents us with an account of the passions roused fol-lowing the revolt and subsequent capture of the island by Athenian forces. For him, the handling of the Mytilene affair exposed both the impetuousness of the Athenian people and their ruthless calculation in ruling their empire. In a meeting of the Athenian Assembly, the desire for revenge was strong and the Assembly voted to put to death all adult male citizens and to enslave all the women and children.

Immediately a ship was dispatched taking these orders to the Athenian commander on Lesbos. However, the very next day, the Assembly had a change of heart, and it was decided that only the ringleaders of the revolt should be executed. Orders countermanding the previous ones were sent. Thucydides recounts how these two triremes raced across the Aegean, one bringing a death sentence, the other a reprieve. The crew of the second trireme rowed without taking a break for meals or sleep and arrived at Mytilene just as the Athenian commander was about to carry out the massacre. The Mytileneans were spared, but Athenian 'leniency' was still harsh. The Mytilene fleet was commandeered into the Athenian navy, the city's walls were pulled down, over 1,000 men involved in the revolt were executed, and most of the island of Lesbos confiscated.

Yet, it was not just allies who were opposed to the empire. Some Athenians were not endeared to it either. As Athens developed its own foreign policy connections, it was venturing into an area that had previously been the sole preserve of elite aristocratic families. Many were happy to be co-opted, trading upon their family connections to secure positions on embassies or serve as generals to regions to which they had ancestral ties. However, a number resented this new democratic order.

This internal opposition to the empire took a number of forms. Most of it was just talk, yet sometimes talk translated into action. The most prominent act of urban terrorism in Athenian history seems to have been carried out by this opposition. One morning in 415 BC, Athens awoke to find that the much-beloved statues of the god Hermes had been mutilated. These distinctive statues took the form of a head of the god placed on a square pillar decorated with a set of male genitalia. They were dotted throughout the cityscape of Athens, clustering at crossroads and near people's houses. The mutilation was linked to the forthcoming expedition to Sicily, an attempt to establish Athenian dominion in the West. As Hermes was the god of travel, many saw the mutilation of the statues of Hermes as a political protest against

Athenian military expansion. Such was the climate of fear and distress caused by this act of sacrilege that the Athenians resorted to informers and torture to locate the culprits. A number of prominent Athenians were arrested, executed and their property confiscated.

Members of allied city-states who were opposed to Athenian rule were also known to resort to violence and Athenian citizens found themselves subject to occasional attack as they ventured abroad. In order to counteract these acts of brutality, a heavy fine was exacted on any city that allowed an Athenian to be murdered on its soil. Of course, such attacks are not surprising in cities where revolt had been crushed and new regimes installed. It is telling, however, that we find references to such attacks in even supposedly loyal communities such as those on the island of Chios. More significant than random, sporadic acts of violence was widespread revolt. None of Athens' major allies were immune to the lure of revolt. Often they revolted more than once.

## War with Sparta

The war with Sparta and her allies, conventionally called the Peloponnesian war, represents the most significant historical event in the history of the Athenian empire. This war, lasting for over 27 years, divided the Greek world, and eventually would lead to the downfall of the Athenian empire.

To many, it seemed that Athens established its empire through stealing the hegemony of the Greeks from Sparta after the end of the Persian wars. Athens may have claimed that leadership of the Greeks was not the exclusive domain of the Spartans and that it was given freely to Athens by her allies, but it is unlikely that these arguments ever held any sway outside the borders of Attica. Certainly, the Spartans were not pleased with Athenian imperial expansion. Their initial reluctance to oppose the Athenian usurpation of control owed more to their internal politics and an aversion to foreign campaigns than it did to a desire to see Athens in control of the Aegean. The Persian wars had gone on long enough, and the Spartans disliked the thought of continuing the fight against Persia. Spartan elites resented the tremendous power that Spartan kings wielded while abroad on campaign, and so wished to recall the leaders home. Moreover, Spartans were wary of leaving their lands too long lest it encourage rebellion among their helot serfs. Sparta was content with the leadership of the Peloponnesian League, an alliance of states bound together by pacts of mutual defence. Where Sparta led, these states were obliged to follow. Yet, if Sparta expected gratitude for the ease with which Athens obtained the leadership of the rest of the Greeks, they were sadly mistaken. Throughout the first half of the 5th century BC, we see Athens continually aggravating Sparta and her allies, in particular the states of Corinth and Thebes.

Corinth was the other major power in the Peloponnese, and in many ways it felt the brunt of Athenian expansion far more than Sparta. Athens made alliances with rivals of Corinth. It threatened to upset the balance of power in the region by expanding its influence westwards. Between 461 and 446 BC, we see almost constant acts of hostility, both diplomatic and military, between Corinth and Athens.

Athens expanded northwards as well as west. It seems that Athens seriously considered the idea of establishing a land empire to match her naval one. For example in 457 BC, Athens captured a number of Boiotian towns and enrolled them as tribute-paying members into its empire. Although these towns were subsequently liberated, this action clearly indicated Athens' intentions in the area. It also ensured that it incurred the enmity of Thebes which regarded Boiotia as its domain.

As we can see, this period of 47 years after the formation of the Delian League is characterized by two features, namely the continued imperial expansion and 'bedding-down' of the Athenian empire, and a series of scrappy disputes between Athens and members of the Peloponnesian League and its allies. These disputes determined nothing, except to create a climate of hatred.

In such a situation, we may be forgiven for thinking that large-scale war between Athens and Sparta was inevitable. Certainly, the historian Thucydides, who chronicled the eventual conflict, thought so. 'The truest cause of the war was the growth of Athens' power and the fear this caused in Sparta.' Nevertheless, there is every reason to believe that when war did break out neither side imagined that it would extend much beyond five years, nor that it would extend to regions as far away as Sicily and Thrace.

The first phase of the war is generally called the 'Archidamian' war after the Spartan king, Archidamus, who led the Spartan army to invade Attica on three separate occasions (431, 430 and 428 BC). This phase is typified by these annual invasions of Attica and the steadfast refusal of Athens to fight Sparta in open combat. This policy, attributed to the Athenian statesman, Pericles, was based on the idea that Athens could function effectively as an island behind its walls, relying on her port and command of the sea to provide her with the necessary supplies. Such a stalemate was unsustainable. Sparta was not used to such prolonged and indifferent warfare and, even with all its imperial wealth, Athens did not have the resources to maintain such a policy forever. Moreover, life on 'Athens island' was far from idyllic. The population of Attica was cramped into too small a space. The situation was not only uncomfortable, it was unhealthy. An outbreak of plague swept through the city, with devastating effects. The population was decimated and the city lost many prominent individuals, most notably Pericles, the architect of the Athenian defence strategy.

Almost simultaneously, there was a change of policy by both sides. Sparta decided to strike at Athens' imperial resources directly, sending an expeditionary force to northern Greece to stir up trouble, and to impede the transport of grain to Athens so that hunger might force the city population out from its walls. Athens, for her part, decided to adopt a strategy of harrying the Peloponnesian forces through a series of piratical raids and the establishment of fortresses on the coastline. Both strategies met with a great deal of success. The Spartans in Thrace, led by the skilled tactician, Brasidas, liberated a number of cities from Athenian rule, and caused tremendous problems for Athenian control of the area. Meanwhile, in the Peloponnese, the Athenian commander Cleon managed, as much through luck as tactics, to capture a significant section of the Spartan army on the island of Sphacteria near Pylos. Curiously, in an attempt to break the previous stalemate, both sides had entangled themselves in another one of even greater complexity.

This lack of clear resolution meant that in 421 BC Sparta and Athens entered into a peace treaty to end the conflict between them. This so-called 'Peace of Nicias', named after the Athenian politician who had been instrumental in its negotiation, proved not to offer a long-term viable settlement of affairs in Greece. For a start, neither Corinth, Thebes nor Megara would agree to be bound by its terms. More importantly, it did nothing to introduce any structural mechanism to curb Athenian imperial ambitions.

Within a few years of the establishment of the treaty, we see Athenian expansion again causing problems with Sparta. In 419 BC, Athens entered into an alliance with Sparta's age-old enemy, Argos. In 416 BC, Athens attempted to bully the island of Melos, an island settled by the Dorians and technically neutral, into its empire. When Melos refused, Athens besieged the city and in conquering it inflicted a terrible price on the Melians for their refusal to acquiesce to Athenian demands. In 415 BC, Athens embarked on a disastrous and overly ambitious expedition to seize control of Sicily. This expansion westwards was troubling to Sparta. If Athens had been successful in Sicily, Sparta would have found itself bracketed by Athenian controlled regions to the west and east and, with the wealth of the western Greeks at its disposal, Athens would have proved an almost unstoppable opponent. Sparta successfully aided the Sicilian opposition to Athens and the war continued.

The most significant factor in this second stage of the war is the courting of Persia by Athens and Sparta. Both sides realized that it was only the intervention of a major power like Persia that could settle the deadlock. Persia could provide Sparta with a fleet so that Athenian naval supremacy could finally be challenged. Persian resources could ensure that Athens need never worry about Spartan siege tactics or efforts to disrupt Athenian food supply. There had been attempts to court Persia from the very beginning of the war. However, in this phase they took on a new intensity and urgency. Sadly for Athens, Persia decided to come down on the side of Sparta. At that point Athens' fate was sealed.

Persia provided funds to equip a fleet under the command of the Spartan naval commander, Lysander. The fact that Sparta, a traditionally land-based military power, was experimenting with the sea shows the extent to which the conflict promoted ingenuity and change. Indeed, one of the features of the Peloponnesian war is the way in which it provided opportunities for ambitious figures such as Brasidas and Lysander, people who might otherwise have been overlooked in the Spartan system.

Of course, the Athenians didn't know that they were living on borrowed time and consequently put up a spirited defence. Indeed, it was infuriating for the Persians how long it took for the Spartans finally to overwhelm them. At Arginusae, near Lesbos, the Athenian fleet defeated the Spartans, and another fleet had to be constructed with Persian money. Yet the Spartan opportunity eventually came at the battle of Aegospotami in 404 BC, when they managed to catch the Athenian fleet unawares while it was still beached. Only nine Athenian ships managed to escape the massacre. It was this defeat that effectively put an end to the Athenian empire. Athens was forced to enter a humiliating treaty negotiated by Lysander in which its walls were torn down and a brutal pro-Spartan military junta was installed to govern the city, the so-called 'Thirty'.

## The second Athenian confederacy

Power abhors a vacuum. Alternatively, imperialism is addictive. Whatever the explanation, the period following the defeat of Athens is not one of the peaceful co-existence of mutually autonomous states as Spartan rhetoric during the war promised. Instead, we see three powers, Sparta, Thebes and Athens, all jostling to dominate the Greek world. It was a time of shifting alliances, dramatic reversals of fortune, and complex diplomatic intrigue.

The imperialism of Sparta is surprising. Prior to the outbreak of the war, Spartan foreign policy had been distinguished by a reluctance to venture far from their traditional power base in the Peloponnese. Now the war had expanded their world view, and encouraged a new ambition.

This newly found ambition saw the Spartans turning on their former ally, the Persian king Artaxerxes. They backed a pretender to the throne, and when this failed they undertook to wage a war to free the Ionian cities now under Persian rule. This swaggering, imperialist Sparta was bad at making friends. In addition to incurring the enmity of Persia, Sparta now lost the support of her former allies, Corinth and Thebes.

The betrayal by Sparta persuaded Persia to start supporting Athens as a bulwark against Spartan aggression. They gave funds to the remnants of the Athenian fleet, and this fleet under the command of Conon, one of the survivors of the battle of Aegospotami, was successful in reducing the power of the Spartan navy.

In Athens, the oligarchic regime of the Thirty had only lasted for a couple of years. After losing the backing of its Spartan supporters, the regime had been removed and democracy restored. Athens seemed to be recovering from defeat. Indeed, it was recovering a little too quickly for Persia's comfort. The Athenian navy sailed the Aegean demanding funds and supplies from islanders and communities on the coast of Asia Minor. The Athenians encouraged rebellion in the Persian empire by inciting the Persian client king, Evagoras of Cyprus, to rebel.

This new-found enthusiasm of the Athenians needed to be checked. And so the former enemies, Persia and Sparta, joined forces to curb Athenian plans for expansion. In 387 BC, the Spartans captured the Hellespont and, faced with the possibility of starvation, the Athenians were forced to negotiate a settlement of their differences with Persia and Sparta, and in 386 BC a compromise was struck, the so-called 'King's Peace'. There was to be peace throughout the Greek world, but this would come at a price – there were to be no more Greek empires. Instead, all Greek states were to be autonomous.

In theory, this should have put an end to Athenian imperial ambitions. In practice, it seems only to have put them on hold temporarily and encouraged Athens to think of imaginative ways around this requirement. The Athenian solution initially was to construct a series of bilateral defensive treaty relations in which Athens and another state promised mutual support in the event of attack. Such actions were not excluded under the terms of the King's Peace. Out of these treaty relations blossomed the second Athenian Confederacy. Founded in 377 BC, this confederacy was designed to provide opposition to Spartan domination. The leader would be Athens, and the league was to be maintained through a series of 'contributions'.

The Athenian empire was back. Or was it? We possess the foundation document of this league, which makes for interesting reading. What is clear is that these allies knew the perils of entering into such an alliance with Athens. The document outlines what will constitute unacceptable behaviour by Athens. Autonomy is guaranteed. Tribute is explicitly banned. Athens is prohibited from establishing garrisons or governors. Athenian citizens are prohibited from foreign landholding. Any attempt to alter these conditions would result in the death of the proposer. Each member state of the confederacy was to have a vote in an assembly of allies, and this assembly had equal authority to the Athenian people. In a symbolic gesture, a copy of the charter was erected in Athens beside the statue of Zeus Eleutherios (literally the 'Zeus of Freedom'). The charter of the Second Athenian Confederacy is an attractive package, and it is easy to understand why so many city-states were keen to sign up to it. The final tally of members is put as high as 70, and it can't have been much less than 60.

By and large, Athens kept the promises made in this charter document. There were a number of pragmatic reasons to do so. Athens was not nearly as strong as it had been in the previous century. Constant pressure from Sparta, and later Thebes, meant that it couldn't afford widespread dissension among the allies. Yet this didn't stop Athens using its position as the lead city to bully other city-states outside the league, or extracting advantages when it could. On liberating Samos from Persian rule, for example, Athens quickly imposed a series of colonies on the island so that the Samians were effectively displaced. The community on Sestos had all its adult males slaughtered and the rest of the population sold into slavery. Secession remained a problem. Ceos tried to secede and was brought forcibly into line. Military emergencies could cause Athens to bend its rule and establish garrisons at strategic points for the greater good. The extent to which Athens should be regarded as an imperial oppressor in this period will vary according to which city-state one might have asked. One suspects that the answer from Sestos and Samos would have been very different from a state like Tenedos, which remained a loyal member of the confederacy right until the end. What is perhaps significant is that the matter is debatable in a way that it is not for the 5th century.

Ultimately, the downfall of the Athenian confederacy came about thanks to the influence of other powers rather than any act on the part of Athens. In 371 BC, Thebes defeated Sparta at the battle of Leuctra, a setback from which Sparta never recovered. This newly emergent Thebes was not prepared to allow Athens to be the dominant power in Greece. It seems to have actively incited states to revolt against Athens. Persia, meanwhile, adopted a similar tactic for states close to the Persian sphere of influence. In 357 BC, these actions came to fruition and a number of important states, most notably Ceos and Rhodes, attempted to secede. This attempt initiated the so-called 'Social War'. This war demonstrates the weakness of the Athenian position. After a two-year campaign season, Athens no longer had the resources to continue and any ally who wished to secede was permitted to do so.

The last power to enter the stage is Macedonia, the state which finally put an end to the Athenian confederacy. The rise of Philip of Macedon is a supreme exercise in the art of diplomacy and double-dealing. He played Thebes and Athens off against each other, all the while extending his influence southwards and eastwards. By the time he effectively controlled Thessaly, Thrace and the Chersonese, it was too late for his enemies. Thebes and Athens allied themselves to oppose him, but they were routed by his superior military forces at the battle of the Chaeronea in 338 BC. This marks the end of Athenian imperialism. Athens and her allies were reorganized into Philip's new league, the League of Corinth. After the battle of Chaeronea, Philip is reported to have walked among the dead. Seeing the bodies of his opponents piled high, he wept for the loss of such brave men. No one we know apart from Athens wept for the loss of the Athenian empire; a new imperial age was beginning.

# THE EMPIRE OF ALEXANDER AND HIS SUCCESSORS

## 338–60 BC

MICHAEL SOMMER AND THOMAS HARRISON

When Alexander the Great was born in Pella, the capital of the small kingdom of Macedonia, in 356 BC, it was the dawn of a new era. His father Philip II, the newly invested Macedonian ruler, was about to change permanently the political map of the Aegean world. Within a few years, he reached Thermopylae, the gate to Greece. Little more than a decade later, Macedonia was de facto the hegemonic power in Hellas: Philip forged alliances with some Greek city-states, isolated Athens and subdued the entire south of the Balkan peninsula. Nothing, however, announced the truly world-shaking changes that were imminent when Philip was murdered in 336 BC and Alexander came to power.

### From Philip to Alexander

No single ruler changed the ancient world to the same extent as Alexander the Great. In the 13 short years of his reign, the tiny kingdom of Macedonia, at the periphery of the vast Persian empire of the Achaemenids, became the greatest power the world had seen so far. A new era had begun which we call 'Hellenism'; Greek language, culture and customs took off throughout the Near East and Central Asia. When Alexander died in 323 BC, he had led his soldiers across the Hellespont and the Taurus mountains, through the deserts of Libya and the endless plains of Mesopotamia, across the Hindu Kush, into India and through the hostile Gedrosian desert in Iran. Thousands had died or been expelled from their homes, their cities plundered and their possessions confiscated. But after Alexander's death, his empire fell apart even faster than it had been built. One generation after the great conqueror, the Hellenistic world was divided into three major and a handful of minor kingdoms, all competing for the great prize: Alexander's legacy, universal power.

Alexander's conquests would have been impossible without the preparations laid down by his father Philip II (359–336 BC). It was he who had won for Macedonia leadership over Greece and the Balkans, and he left to his son not only a stable and enlarged empire, but also a mission. In the battle of Chaeronea in 338 BC Philip had defeated the city-states that had allied under the leadership of Athens. There had been strong antipathies between the Greeks – living mainly in city-states – and the Macedonians, who lived under a king. The Greeks believed the Macedonians in general to be barbarians, though they made an exception for the Macedonian royal line and allowed them to participate at Greek festivals. After his victory over the Greeks at Chaeronea, rather than subduing the Greek city-states and integrating them into his kingdom, Philip chose to unite them under the umbrella of the Corinthian League, at the same time ensuring that the League elected him as its leader and general for life.

One of the first decisions taken by the League was a call to arms against the Persian empire. The official aim of this campaign was to be revenge: some 150 years earlier, as we saw in the previous chapter, the Persians had destroyed many sites in Greece, among them the Acropolis of Athens, and looted many important works of art from Greece. The campaign against the hereditary enemy fulfilled the Greek elite's desire for revenge and thus formed a basis for a cooperation between the Greek cities, conquered by Philip, and the Macedonian kingdom. This also explained the king's second public declaration: it was his professed aim to 'free' the Greek cities in Asia Minor (the western coast of modern Turkey) from the Persian yoke – whatever 'freedom' might mean under Macedonian hegemony.

The Macedonian generals Parmenio and Attalus led a large army across the Hellespont, the narrow straits between Greece and Asia, in 336 BC. The timing of this venture was well chosen, as both the Persian king Artaxerxes III Ochus and his successor Artaxerxes IV had been murdered in 338 and 336 BC respectively. The dynasty of Iranian Achaemenids, which had ruled over an empire from the Hindu Kush to the southern border of Egypt, was thus ensnarled in internal strife. From this, in 336 BC, Darius III emerged as the new Persian king, aged around 45 at the time of his accession – and his main goal, of necessity, was the consolidation of his empire.

Shortly after the campaign for 'freedom' had started, Philip fell victim to a murderous assault. He was succeeded by the 20-year-old Alexander, the third Macedonian king to bear the name. Philip had not had an especially close relationship with this son, having married his second wife Kleopatra during the boy's childhood. The young man had grown up under the influence of his mother Olympias, a princess from Epirus, and the Greek philosopher Aristotle, who had stimulated Alexander's great interest in Greek culture. With Aristotle, he had read the Homeric epics, and he was to keep a copy of the *Iliad* under his pillow for the rest of his life. An identification with the Homeric heroes became a major driving force for the young Macedonian prince, who idealized himself to be the Achilles of his own generation.

Alexander principally owed the relatively smooth transition from Philip to himself to his father's generals. Once made king, the young man had many of his internal rivals and enemies murdered, thus establishing his power in Macedonia. He dealt successfully with unrest on Macedonia's northern and western borders that had been provoked by Philip's assassination and the subsequent succession crisis: Illyrian and Thracian tribes prepared for an invasion of Macedonia, but were defeated in a campaign during which Alexander crossed the Danube in the north. From a Hellenic point of view, the river formed the border of the *oikoumene*, as the Greeks termed the inhabited, civilized world. This was the first of a number of times that Alexander reached

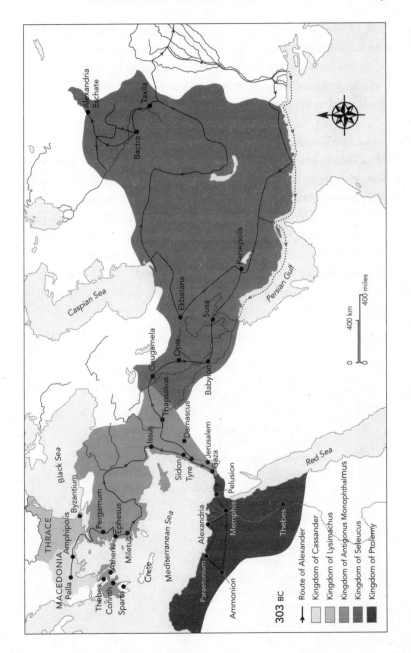

Alexandria
Eschate

Taxila

Bactra

Persepolis

Persian Gulf

Ekbatana

Susa

Caspian Sea

Gaugamela

Opis

Thapsakos

Babylon

Issus

Damascus

Red Sea

Sidon

Jerusalem

Tyre

Gaza

Pelusion

Black Sea

Byzantium

Pergamum

Ephesus

Miletus

Alexandria

Memphis

Thebes

THRACE

Amphipolis

Athens

Crete

Mediterranean Sea

MACEDONIA

Pella

Thebes

Corinth

Sparta

Paraetonium

Ammonion

**303 BC**

Route of Alexander
Kingdom of Cassander
Kingdom of Lysimachus
Kingdom of Antigonus Monophthalmus
Kingdom of Seleucus
Kingdom of Ptolemy

400 km

400 miles

0

0

and crossed a river that symbolically marked the end of the known world: similar turning points were to become the Oxus (Amu Darya) river in Central Asia and the Hyphasis (Beas) river in India. The act was, as we hear from ancient authors, motivated by Alexander's 'inner urge' – the same motive that underlay his campaigns against Persia.

When a rumour of Alexander's death in battle circulated, the important Greek city of Thebes left the Corinthian League and removed the Macedonian garrison. This prompted a sympathetic response from Athens, suggesting that the new order imposed on the Greek world by Philip was not one welcomed widely by the Greeks themselves. They wanted their freedom, rather than peace guaranteed by a foreign king. At the same time the Persian king was sending lavish gifts of money to politicians within Greece in an attempt to destabilize the Macedonian hegemony. When Alexander reacted by razing the city of Thebes to the ground in 335 BC, no other Greek city went to help it. Instead, the

## KEY DATES

| | |
|---|---|
| 338 BC | Victory for Philip of Macedon at Chaeronea |
| 336 BC | Death of Philip |
| 334 BC | Alexander invades Persian empire |
| 333 BC | Persian king Darius loses battle of Issus |
| 332 BC | Foundation of Alexandria |
| 331 BC | Huge victory for Alexander at battle of Gaugamela |
| 326 BC | Alexander invades northern India |
| 323 BC | Death of Alexander at Babylon |
| 301 BC | Victory of Seleucus and Lysimachus at Ipsos |
| 274–271 BC | First Syrian war between Ptolemies and Seleucids |
| 260–253 BC | Second Syrian war |
| 246–241 BC | Third Syrian war |
| 197 BC | Romans defeat Philip V of Macedon at Cynoscephalae |
| 189 BC | Romans defeat Antiochus III at Magnesia |
| 146 BC | Roman sack of Corinth |
| 31 BC | Battle of Actium |

members of the League congratulated Alexander on his victory and acquiesced in the destruction of the city. It was only to be rebuilt in 316 BC. Though the new king now reigned supreme and could start his war of aggression against Persia in the next year, the revolt reveals to what extent the rising empire depended on Alexander as a person.

## Conquering the Persian empire

In the spring of 334 BC, a large army consisting of 30,000 men on foot, 5,000 on horseback and an elite of 12,000 experienced Macedonians crossed the Hellespont. As we have noted, it was officially a war of revenge for the Persian destruction of Greek temples and cities 150 years before. However, there were few contingents from the Greek city-states in Alexander's expeditionary force. This suggests that the motive of revenge on behalf of the Greeks was unlikely to have been Alexander's main priority when he set out on his expedition. Why he initiated his campaigns and how far he could have conceived of his subsequent success are ultimately matters for speculation.

It seems likely that Alexander at first thought only of 'liberating' the long-established Greek cities of Asia Minor. Even Alexander would have realized that such an army, however experienced, would not have been able to pursue larger geopolitical aims. The Persian king in the distant centre of his empire, on the other hand, regarded the small army of Macedonians and Greeks as a threat only to the outlying provinces (or 'satrapies') of his empire; it was not a problem that he would need to be involved in, and so he delegated the task of dealing with Alexander's threat to his satraps (governors) and the Greek admiral Memnon of Rhodes. Alexander, relying – as in all his military victories – on the speed and manoeuvrability of his army, defeated the satraps in the first large battle of Alexander's campaign at the river Granicus, and opened up the route towards the border of Syria. The Greek cities were thus, whether they wanted it or not, 'set free', as was the large non-Greek territory which now found itself under Macedonian rule. Only when Alexander crossed the Taurus mountains did the Persian king oppose him in person with a huge army at the Gulf of Issus – where he was duly defeated by Alexander. The celebrated Alexander Mosaic from Pompeii probably depicts the decisive moment, when the Persian king, attacked by Alexander, turns around to leave the battlefield. Darius fled with only a few soldiers across the Euphrates, while his camp, and with it his family, were taken over by the Macedonian conqueror. At Damascus the most important of Alexander's generals, Parmenio, managed to get hold of Darius' war chest, thus solving the Macedonians' previous financial problems.

Instead of pursuing and fully defeating the Persian king across the Euphrates, however, Alexander decided to march southwards, along the Mediterranean coastline towards Egypt. The city of Tyre, on an island off the coast of present-day Lebanon, welcomed Alexander's envoys but refused the Macedonian king's request to perform a sacrifice in the local temple of Melqart, the supreme god of the Phoenician city. Alexander put the island city under siege, which it resisted for seven months. Eventually the city was conquered when Alexander's engineers built a dam to the island. By now, the Persian king had realized the gravity of the threat that the Macedonian posed to his empire and his kingship, and asked for a peace on conditions which were very favourable for Alexander. The historian Arrian, writing at the height of the Roman empire but using near-contemporary sources, describes how Parmenio advised Alexander to accept the Persian king's terms, claiming that if he were Alexander he would be glad to stop the war under those conditions. But his advice was royally snubbed. Alexander retorted that he would also be glad to stop the war if he was Parmenio, but as he was Alexander, he would not. He claimed that all of Darius' money and empire belonged to him, and that in short, he aspired to become the king of Persia himself.

This ambition was to become a major factor in the subsequent alienation of the Macedonian elite. For the time being, however, Alexander was protected by the overwhelming success of his campaigns, and, now that the Phoenician-Cypriot fleet of the Persian king no longer posed a threat, he pushed on, largely unopposed, towards Egypt. There he visited Memphis, the ancient capital, where he conducted Greek-style games and made an offering to the Egyptian god Apis, a deity worshipped in the form of a living bull, and where we get a first glimpse of Alexander's constant endeavour to reconcile Greek and Near Eastern traditions. Leaving Memphis, he sailed down the Nile's westernmost branch and founded, on the delta's coast, a city named after himself: Alexandria. In the temple of Amun-Ra in Siwa, an oasis in the middle of the Libyan desert, he was proclaimed the son of Zeus.

The oracle of Amun-Ra at Siwa had been well established for several centuries. Greeks who had settled in nearby Cyrene in the 7th century BC had spread the oracle's fame, linking it to their own supreme god, Zeus. Here in Siwa, Amun-Ra announced with a nod his acceptance of the future pharaoh, Alexander. What exactly happened when Alexander entered the sanctuary is not known. Callisthenes, one of Alexander's earliest biographers who accompanied the king on his campaigns, provides a description of the events, extant in a fragment, which is rather cryptic:

> 'Hence the oracle of Ammon, which was formerly held in great esteem, is now nearly deserted.... Alexander was ambitious of the glory of visiting the oracle, because he knew that Perseus and Heracles had before performed the journey thither.... The priest permitted the king alone to pass into the temple in his usual dress, whereas the others changed theirs; ...all heard the oracles on the outside of the temple, except Alexander, who was in the interior of the building; ...the answers were not given as at Delphi..., in words, but chiefly by nods and signs, as in Homer: "the son of Kronos nodded with his sable brows," the prophet imitating Zeus. This, however, the man told the king in express terms: that he was the son of Zeus.'

The episode at Siwa determined much of Alexander's future reign; henceforth, his divine descent formed part of the monarch's officially divulged image. Being now Zeus Ammon's son he was separated from his fellow Macedonian aristocrats by a barrier, at first barely visible, but still decisive. No longer was he a military ruler elected by the army and bound by Macedonian tradition: his rule had become rooted in a Near Eastern theocratic tradition that went back several millennia. But his being the son of a god had probably more to it than the 'official' reading reveals: for a man raised with Greek myths the events of Siwa were designed to move him into one sphere with the Homeric heroes. Like Achilles, he had a divine pedigree himself now, and one which was even better: while the hero who had defeated the Trojan Hector had the relatively obscure sea god Nereus as grandfather, he, Alexander, could call Zeus himself his father. The evidence suggests that Alexander genuinely believed in his heroic mission.

In 331 BC the Macedonian king, leader of the Corinthian League and Egyptian pharaoh, revived the campaign against the Persian king, Darius. Having crossed the Euphrates and Tigris rivers, Alexander fought against Darius at Gaugamela and defeated him; his soldiers subsequently proclaimed him to be 'King of Asia'. He entered the two royal residences at Babylon and Susa, where he took over the unbelievable treasures of the Persian king. Early in 330 BC he finally reached Persepolis, one of the most important residences of the king and the empire's ceremonial capital. Then, shortly after a brief period during which he tried to find an accommodation with the local nobility, he set fire to the royal palace. Why did Alexander do something so apparently irrational? Some ancient authors suggest that it was an accident, the result of a prostitute's late-night high jinx, others that it was an intentional political signal. The archaeological remains, however, reveal that the fire was clearly planned. One clue to the significance of the event is that immediately afterwards Alexander released the contingents in his army that had been drawn from the Corinthian League; this suggests that the destruction of Persepolis was presented as the fulfilment of the Greek's revenge for the Persian destruction of the Athenian Acropolis in 480 BC.

## The King of Asia

Even though the campaign of 'revenge' had now been concluded, Darius was still alive and unwilling to yield to Alexander's power. Alexander pursued Darius through the east of his empire, in the mountainous regions of the Hindu Kush. But after Darius was murdered by one of his own men, the satrap of Bactria and Sogdia, Bessus, Alexander took the opportunity to adopt a new ideological mantle – that of the avenger of his former enemy. It was he who was the legitimate heir to Darius, a fact that was reflected in his homage to the murdered king.

Alexander was now the king of Macedonia, the Egyptian pharaoh and Persian king. He secured his conquests by founding cities in his name and by building military colonies for the Greco-Macedonian soldiers. As successor to the Persian kings he was also concerned to make his peace with the traditional elite of the Persian empire, and to integrate them into his imperial system. He adopted a ceremony whereby those who approached him had to fall to the ground like dogs, or *kynes*, which came to be known in Greek as proskynesis. This was a Persian court ceremony, and did not please his fellow Macedonian noblemen, who became increasingly uneasy about the direction his kingship was taking. It was also by an Iranian rite that he married Rhoxane, the daughter of a Sogdian chieftain from the mountains north of Afghanistan. The heir that was to be expected from this marriage could embrace both the West and the East in his rule.

The Persian kings' claim of absolute power, however, was incompatible with the traditional military monarchy. By following in the kings' footsteps, Alexander alienated himself from the people of his inner circle. He ignored them, and appointed increasingly more Persians to the highest offices, thus stirring envy among the Macedonians whose positions had previously been uncontested. It became obvious that the war – which had started as a revenge campaign against the Persians – was now being led by someone who was more and more influenced by Persian traditions and manners. The Macedonians who openly criticized Alexander, however, did not live for long; he either killed them himself or had them murdered. In 327 BC, seven young noblemen planned a plot against Alexander. One of them, Hermolaus, confessed when charged with treason and claimed before the Macedonians 'that he had conspired against the king's life, because it was no longer possible for a free man to bear his insolent tyranny'. The son of the Macedonian general, Parmenio, was duly executed as well. Alexander's new empire was Macedonian no more.

Aged 25, the king of what had been a petty kingdom at the periphery of the Persian empire had already changed the world. Yet the conquest of the Persian realm was not enough for him – he had, as the sources tell us, an 'inner urge' to pursue his conquests to the limits of the known world. He pushed his campaign eastwards, and no power, or so it seemed, was able to stop him. He believed that he was about to surpass Achilles and Hercules. In 327 BC, he crossed the Khyber Pass into India, following the god Dionysus' footsteps, whose expedition to India held a prominent place in Greek mythology. The son of Zeus-Ammon crossed the Indus river – as with his crossing of the Danube, crossing an apparently uncrossable border – and defeated King Porus in northwestern India in the last large-scale battle of the campaign, before he finally reached the river Hyphasis (Beas), today situated in the border regions of Pakistan and India.

Alexander still hoped to reach the eastern ocean, which at the time was believed to be the end of the world. But scouts reported that to the east of the river there were only endless fertile plains, and beyond them yet more mountains to cross. The soldiers' patience was wearing thin and mutiny was in the air:

> 'Conferences were held throughout the camp, in which those
> who were the most moderate bewailed their lot, while others

*resolutely declared that they would not follow Alexander any farther, even if he should lead the way'.*

In Arrian's narrative of the events, Alexander makes a final, desperate attempt to bring them back in line. After listing the lands they had conquered together, he goes on:

*'If in addition to these, the river Indus flows through our territory, as do also the Hydaspes, the Acesines, and the Hydraotes, why do you shrink from adding the Hyphasis also, and the nations beyond this river, to your empire of Macedonia? Do you fear that your advance will be stopped in future by any other barbarians?'*

His pleas were in vain; the soldiers insisted on returning to Babylon. Alexander gave in to the pressure and declared the Hyphasis (as a decade earlier he had declared the Danube), the border of the *oikoumene*. What lay beyond was no longer worth conquest. On their way back to Babylon, the bulk of the army had to cross the Gedrosian desert, a sunburnt, waterless hell in southern Iran, where more soldiers died than in any of his battles. On Alexander's arrival at Susa in 324 BC, a mass marriage was arranged in order to consolidate the fusion of the Greco-Macedonian and the Persian elites: the king himself married two Persian princesses, and 80 of his most important courtiers found themselves forced to marry Persian women, as did 10,000 of Alexander's soldiers. The event contributed to further alienation of the traditional Greek and Macedonian circles. An edict ruling that the Greek cities had to re-accept those individuals who had been exiled from their communities led to yet more unrest; the edict was a clear breach of the traditional autonomy of the Greek city, and made it obvious that Alexander was only willing to respect the 'freedom of the Greeks' as long as it served his interests. Many Macedonians also opposed the king's apparent request to be venerated as a god.

When Alexander replaced the retired Macedonian veterans at Opis with Persians, his old soldiers mutinied. This was partly due to the fact that they would now have to fight alongside their former enemies, but mainly in objection to teaching the Macedonian art of fighting to the Persians. This implied a loss of their military supremacy, which had been one of the foundations of their privileged status that set them apart from other subjects in Alexander's empire. The king hoped to end the quarrel quietly, as Arrian reports:

> 'Alexander gave a public banquet, seated all the Macedonians round him, and next to them Persians and he himself and those around him drank from the same bowl and poured the same libations, with the Greek soothsayers and [Persian] Magi initiating the ceremony. Alexander prayed for various blessings and especially that the Macedonians and Persians should enjoy harmony as partners in the government.'

## Alexander's empire

Alexander's empire, with its capital in Babylon, embraced three entirely different components: Macedonian-style kingship, Near Eastern-style empire, and the Greek league (in legal terms, at least) of independent cities. For his Macedonian soldiers, Alexander was legally nothing but a first among equals. For the subjects in the former Persian empire, however, he was a king of nearly unlimited power, while for the Greeks he was a reluctantly elected leader. In the vast space of the former Persian empire, the king left the old territorial units unchanged, but gave the offices of the satraps to Macedonian officers, whereas subordinate officials were kept in place. After the victory over Darius at Gaugamela in October 331 BC he changed this policy and appointed members of the local elites to the highest offices, including that of governor.

It is obvious that Alexander envisaged an empire in which the ethnic origin and cultural affiliation of the ruling class mattered little, if at all. The theocratic approach to monarchy, which he had encountered at Siwa, and the autocratic style of government he adopted from the Persians, seemed to provide the appropriate tools for the integration of western and Near Eastern elements into the imperial layout. But the growing resentment among his own Macedonian soldiery, obvious at all levels, and Alexander's increasingly harsh reaction to it, make it doubtful whether the universal monarchy Alexander aimed for would have ever worked. Macedonian and Near Eastern concepts of leadership were by no means complementary, but mutually exclusive, and the readiness of the Greco-Macedonians to accept the quasi-divine escapism of their king had been dwindling long before the Macedonian phalanx mutinied at Opis. When Alexander died a premature death at Babylon, on 10 June 323 BC, the centrifugal forces got the upper hand. Asked on his deathbed who among his generals should succeed him, he reportedly answered: 'the strongest'. The empire was to fall apart.

## The contest for Alexander's legacy

Since Alexander's power had rested on his role as king of Macedonia, the assembly of the Macedonian soldiers regarded themselves as authorized to elect the next king. Two males were qualified through their descent: Alexander's half-brother Philip Arrhidaeus, who was reportedly mentally ill, and the as-yet unborn child of Rhoxane, to be named Alexander (IV) after his father. Neither they nor Alexander's mother Olympias and Alexander's wife Rhoxane were to live for long. The generals took matters into their own hands: they divided the empire along the borders of the satrapies, but at the same time all paid lip service to the idea of a united empire, referring to themselves only as satraps. Lysimachus received Thrace, Antigonus a large part of Asia Minor, Eumenes of Caria got Paphlagonia and Cappadocia, and Ptolemy the prize of Egypt. Antipater was to be strategos, or general of Europe, which consisted mainly of Greece and Macedonia, while the unofficial ruler in charge of the overall empire was Alexander's former cavalry leader Perdiccas, who had also been responsible for distributing the satrapies. He assumed the administration of Asia for himself. The original provincial satraps, whom Alexander had held in high esteem, lost their importance, and the idea of universal monarchy was abandoned – as became apparent when most of the marriages formed at Susa were dissolved.

The satraps' intermediate position between monarchy and theoretical subordination under a central king led to problems in representation which are apparent from the 'Satrap Stela', a memorial set up by Egyptians priests. The leader of Egypt, Ptolemy, had given land to the Egyptian temple of the town Buto and this land-donation was recorded in the hieroglyphs on the memorial. On its upper section it depicts an Egyptian pharaoh sacrificing to the gods of Buto, a symbol of the land-donation to the temple. The cartouches of the king – that is, the rings into which the name of the pharaoh is usually spelled out – are empty, but we learn from the text that the king depicted is Pharaoh Alexander IV, and that Ptolemy himself is only his satrap. However, the whole text is then an encomium of the achievements of the satrap who fulfils a pharaoh's role: it is he who gives land to the priests of Buto, following the model of an Egyptian king called Chababash. By taking on the duties of a pharaoh, Ptolemy gave direction to the internal strategy of the dynasty of the 'Ptolemies' which followed him. For their Egyptian subjects, the Ptolemies represented themselves as pharaohs, for the Greeks and Macedonians, as Hellenistic kings. Modern scholars refer to this as the 'double face' of Ptolemaic rule.

Eventually, in the summer of 306 BC, Antigonus held an assembly of his army, which acclaimed him as king. As the insignia of his newly acquired kingship, he assumed the diadem. Not much later Seleucus, Lysimachus and Cassander, the ruler of Greece and Macedonia, followed: the 'year of the kings' (306/305 BC) gave the final blow to the fiction of a continuation of Alexander's empire. Two years later, Alexander IV was executed.

In only one generation, through a messy pattern of wars between the former generals of Alexander, the *diadochi*, or successors, gradually established and reinforced their control over their separate kingdoms. The largest part of Alexander's empire was taken by the former general Seleucus; his domain, which was to become the Seleucid empire, took up much of the former Persian empire, stretching from inland Asia Minor to the verge of India. Ptolemy had stood his ground in Egypt, and Antigonus' power base had shifted from Asia Minor to Macedonia. Alexander's empire was in ruins, but Macedonian dynasties remained in power in an area that stretched from the Ionian Sea to the Indus. Structurally, the emerging territorial kingdoms (Ptolemaic Egypt with parts of the Aegean; the Seleucid Near East; and Antigonid Macedonia) and the smaller units (Attalid Pergamum; the island of Rhodes; and a handful of petty kingdoms in Asia Minor) could hardly have been more diverse. In the west, the Greek city-states, the *poleis*, remained the dominant form of political organization. Their political scope began to increase again with the partition of Alexander's empire and the establishment of the relatively weak Antigonid dynasty in Macedonia.

The case of Rhodes demonstrates that even relatively small political entities could maintain their independence against far larger and more powerful territorial states. Rhodes had been a commercial hub in the eastern Mediterranean throughout the 4th century BC. Crucial for Rhodes' wealth was the grain route between Egypt and Athens, in which Rhodians acted as intermediate traders. In the year of the kings, 306/305 BC, Demetrius, the son of Antigonus, tried to put an end to Rhodian independence. The Macedonian, who had earned himself the surname Poliorketes (the 'besieger'), put in a great deal of effort and technological sophistication in the attempt to overcome Rhodes, but in vain; their victory yielded the Rhodians the respect of the entire Hellenistic world. Those who visited the island were welcomed by the Colossus of Rhodes, a huge statue, some 30 m (100 ft) tall, of the sun-god Helios, patron of Rhodes. The statue, erected by the sculptor Chares of Lindus, was finished in 280 BC: soon, it was counted among the Seven Wonders of the World. The statue stood for only 53 years, when it was largely destroyed by an enormous earthquake that hit the island and devastated its towns. However, the Colossus was a symbol for the Rhodians' quest for freedom, for their sea power and the wealth accumulated through trade: 'Not only above the sea they built him, but also atop the land, as a glorious light of unenslaved freedom. For theirs who grew from Heracles' lineage, is the sovereignty over sea and land.' Thus an epigram from the Anthologia Palatina, a collection of Greek poetry, praises the Colossus and its freedom-loving builders.

In the formerly Persian east, the word 'freedom' had a different tone. Here, the new rulers reinforced their entitlement to the land with the claim that the old Persian territory was 'spear won'. That meant in practice that indigenous landowners could be deprived of their property and replaced by Greek and Macedonian immigrants. Alexandria in Egypt became the model for a surge of new colonial cities founded by Alexander and his successors, mainly in Syria and Mesopotamia, but also in areas as distant as Central Asia. The influx of Greco-Macedonian settlers to Asia remained steady throughout the 3rd century BC. The concept of 'spear won' territory that turned parts of the Near East into urban landscapes dominated by Greek-style *poleis* had its intellectual forerunners in philosophers such as Aristotle and orators such as Isocrates, who had claimed that the inhabitants of the Persian empire were natural-born slaves and their land was a legitimate prize for Greek conquerors – an idea turned into practice by Alexander's victories.

On the other hand, the foreign-born dynasts had to come to an understanding with the local elites on whom they needed to rely. In Egypt, the indigenous temple priesthoods benefited from Macedonian rule by becoming economically more independent and were able to commission large sanctuaries such as Edfu. But life under Macedonian rule also changed the cultural patterns of the Near Eastern societies. Some, like the Phoenician coastal cities in present-day Lebanon, had been in touch with the Hellenic world for centuries. But many inhabitants of inland Syria and Mesopotamia came into contact with Greek culture and Greek lifestyle only after Alexander's conquests. Many members of local elites began to emulate the invaders in some ways, while remaining distinct in others. A good example of the impact the political changes had on a local elite is the Jewish family of the Tobiads in present-day Jordan. Ever since the Jews had returned from the Babylonian exile in 538 BC, members of this family had served as regional administrators on behalf of the Persian king – a position they retained under the Ptolemies. Ancient papyri reveal the close relationship between Tobias and the king. When the Seleucids conquered Syria in the Fifth Syrian War, the Tobiads continued to play an important role. At Irak-el-Amir, Hyrcanus, Tobias' grandson, had a large palace built for himself, modelled on a Greek temple and imitating the now lost palaces of the Ptolemies in Alexandria and of the Seleucids in Antioch. The building illustrates how local elites gradually 'hellenized' themselves.

While the locals became more Greek, the Macedonian dynasties became increasingly local, thus culturally drifting further apart. What united them, however, was the importance kingship, dynasty and the ruler's personal charisma had for the coherence of the Hellenistic societies. Over and over again, Hellenistic kings had to prove their ability to convey to their subjects security, wealth and good luck. They had to be generous, fortunate and, above all, victorious in battle. The model was, not surprisingly, Alexander himself, who had possessed these qualities in abundance. Accordingly, Hellenistic monarchs boasted honorific names such as 'saviour' (*soter*), 'benefactor' (*euergetes*) or 'victor' (*nikator*) – even though, in most cases, the reality was more prosaic. Hellenistic kings had their subjects indulge in lavish jollifications. The processions put on stage by the Ptolemaic rulers in their capital, Alexandria, were famous. In the 270s BC, Ptolemy II honoured his deceased father with a procession that dwarfed anything the Greek world had seen so far. Carts with larger-than-life statues of Alexander and Ptolemy I were accompanied by a personification of *arête*, the rulers' virtue – statues of deities and a statue with a golden wreath, symbolizing the city of Corinth. All this was followed by carts 'with richly dressed women, representing the cities which once had been subject to the Persians, in Ionia and elsewhere in Asia and on the islands. They all wore golden wreaths.' The spectators were duly impressed, but the treasury was afflicted with exorbitant expenses.

Another side effect of the Hellenistic rulers' pursuit of glory was their constant urge for war. Generations of Seleucid rulers felt the need to imitate Alexander by waging a major campaign (*anabasis*) to enforce their claim on the eastern satrapies. In spite of such efforts, these provinces continued to drift away from the centre. Still more devastating was the ongoing climate of tension between – and within – the Hellenistic powers; the Seleucids and the Ptolemies went to war over Syria as many as six times and the petty kingdoms of Asia Minor fought a constant war of attrition against the Seleucid empire. The Antigonid kings of Macedonia had a hard time holding the city-states of the Greek mainland at bay. Dynastic strife loomed as soon as a king seemed to betray his subjects' trust. In spite of the immense wealth, especially in the Ptolemaic and Seleucid kingdoms, these states were profoundly unstable, prone to overstretching their resources and to exhausting themselves in never-ending wars.

## A clash of civilizations?

Where people are moving, ideas also get in motion. As a matter of course, Greek concepts, ways of life and technologies spread with the Greco-Macedonian conquerors as they advanced through Asia and settled in new homes in Syria, Mesopotamia and Egypt. Our understanding of Hellenism in the east would be flawed, however, if we imagined cultures coming in contact with each other as a one-way process. Learning from each other and adopting ideas worked in both directions, as the example of Alexander at Siwa makes clear. What the Greeks did bring to the Near East, was their model of the self-governing, autonomous city, the *polis*, populated not by subjects, but by citizens. Greco-Macedonian settlers, among them many discharged soldiers, founded new, or took over existing, cities even in areas as remote as

Bactria, in present-day Afghanistan. Though they were in the minority throughout, the Greco-Macedonians usually formed the dominant element of the population where they settled. On the other hand, the east had its own urban tradition, stretching back at least 3,000 years. Most of the indigenous cities in the former Persian empire continued to exist, virtually unchanged. But Greek personal names – adopted by local people – and some Greek political institutions even found their ways to cities like Babylon and Uruk, in the heart of Mesopotamia, where few, if any, Greeks ever settled.

Nowhere were the pitfalls of culture contact more tangible than in Jerusalem, once the city of Solomon's Temple and still the religious centre of Judaism when the Seleucids conquered Palestine from the Ptolemies in the Fifth Syrian War at the very beginning of the 2nd century BC. A substantial faction of the city's priestly elite, led by the high priest Jason, was profoundly 'hellenized' by the 170s BC and attempted to turn Jerusalem into a Greek *polis*. The Hebrew Bible's Book of Maccabees reports:

> 'And some of the people determined to do this, and went to the king [Antiochus IV]: and he gave them license to do after the ordinances of the heathens. And they built a place of exercise [a gymnasium] in Jerusalem, according to the laws of the nations.'

Gymnasia, like theatres and stadiums, were emblematic for a city's 'Greekness'. In addition, they 'removed their marks of circumcision and repudiated the holy covenant'. Menelaos, who succeeded Jason through bribery, struck a deal with Antiochus and repeatedly allowed the Seleucid king – who was financially in dire straits – to loot the temple treasury. Menelaos was then ousted by his own predecessor, Jason, an action Antiochus could hardly tolerate. He duly issued a decree banning Jewish religious practice (167 BC), and thus provoked the Maccabean Revolt, named after the priestly family that sparked the uprising. The revolt virtually ended Seleucid rule in Judaea. What at first sight appears to be a cultural war between Greco-Macedonian rulers and Jewish subjects, at a closer look emerges as an inner-Jewish conflict in which Antiochus became involved. The 'hellenization' of the city of Jerusalem was a project that some of the Jewish elite could benefit from substantially. People like Jason and Menelaos hoped to steel their social hegemony by turning Jerusalem into a *polis*. Abandoning Jewish religious traditions was essential for their scheme, and Antiochus was their natural ally. But the plan got out of hand and the Maccabees took over as a de facto sovereign dynasty of priests.

The greatest of all Greek cities in the Hellenistic east was Alexandria. Alexander the Great had founded his own city, on the westernmost branch of the Nile, during his campaign in Egypt. Its foundation led to a fundamental shift of the geopolitical 'axis' of Egypt towards the Mediterranean coast. The design of the city was probably the work of Deinocrates, who followed a rectangular (called 'Hippodamian', after the architect Hippodamus of Miletus) layout of the roads, not very different from modern Manhattan. A dam, called 'Heptastadium', connected the city to the island of Pharos, where Sostratus of Cnidus built a giant lighthouse, called simply 'Pharos'. It was later considered to be one of the Seven Wonders of the World. It was Ptolemy I, who – according to the 'Satrap Stela' mentioned previously – had moved the royal residence from Memphis to Alexandria in 311 BC. Soon the new foundation became the most populous city of the ancient world, and the largest port of trade. Alexandria with its library that embraced the wisdom of the entire classical world, and the museion, an institution devoted to scholarship and the arts, became a cultural centre of prime importance, excelling in literature, philosophy and the sciences.

When Ptolemy I got hold of the satrapy of Egypt, he had Alexander's corpse transferred from Babylon to Saqqara, the necropolis of Memphis. His son, Ptolemy II, transported it to Alexandria, buried it in a tomb, called sema, and established the cult of Alexander-Ktistes. The cult of a *heros ktistes* ('founder hero') was a feature Alexandria shared with most Greek cities, especially the 'colonial' foundations on the Black Sea littoral and in the Mediterranean West. But Alexander was more than that: Ptolemy made him the founder god of his empire, with his own priest who featured second (after the king) in the ceremonial hierarchy of Ptolemaic Egypt. Coins issued under his rule portrayed Alexander with the attributes of Dionysus, Amun and Zeus. After Ptolemy Soter's death, Ptolemy II Philadelphus deified his father as Theos Soter ('God Saviour'), to whom the festivals called the Ptolemaia were dedicated. The dynastic cult allowed the Ptolemies to share in Alexander's charisma as the victorious king. Under Ptolemy II, the living royal couple was included in the ruler cult, a practice adopted also by later generations of kings.

Alexandria was thus closely linked to the dynasty, its cult and the royal institutions. But like any Greek *polis*, Alexandria had its own city law and autonomous institutions: officials, council, people's assembly. But Alexandria was not entirely Greek: Greeks and Macedonians were just one minority in the most multicultural city of the Hellenistic world, with other ethnic groups forming substantial minorities, too, notably the Jews. The vast majority of the kingdom's population, and probably even that of Alexandria, were native Egyptians. Egyptians, Jews and Greco-Macedonians formed three distinct civic bodies within the city, each keen on maintaining their cultural traditions. Only Macedonians and Greeks enjoyed full citizenship.

The divide was not hermetic, though: Egyptians could rise in the ranks of Ptolemaic society by joining the army, or by learning Greek and taking on administrative responsibilities. There was intermarriage between the ethnic groups, and religious syncretism – the contamination of one faith with elements of another – was ubiquitous. Egyptians were quick to integrate the Macedonian dynasty into their own cultural and political framework. The earliest version of the so-called Alexander Romance, a compilation of popular fiction entwined around Alexander's life, has it that Alexander was the son of Nectanebo II, the last Egyptian pharaoh ousted by the Persians when they re-conquered

Egypt in 342 BC. When Alexander conquered Egypt, it was the fulfilment of an oracle which once had announced that one day a rejuvenated Nectanebo would take possession of his ancestral throne. The story undoubtedly had its origins in a hellenized indigenous environment in Egypt, and was designed to reconcile the Ptolemaic dynasty with old local traditions. Egyptian inhabitants of Alexandria appropriated the founder hero of their city and the entire kingdom for themselves, thus laying the grounds for the locals to identify themselves with the Macedonian conquerors.

Recent fieldwork has brought to light much of Hellenistic Alexandria, which until a few years ago had been deemed to be lost forever. Large parts of the ancient city, especially the palace quarter next to the harbour, had sunk beneath sea level, probably due to a series of earthquakes. In 1996, a team of French underwater archaeologists embarked on a mission to map the royal quarter. A large building with a colonnaded esplanade, which stood on the island of Antirrhodos, was identified as the Ptolemies' Royal Palace. Statues and other artifacts found in the harbour reveal that the Macedonian rulers embellished their dwellings in an Egyptianizing style, which tied in with the ancient traditions of the kingdom of the pharaohs. All this suggests that Ptolemy and his successors felt truly at home on the Nile, just as they were perceived by many of the local people as legitimate heirs of the pharaohs.

## The end of Hellenism

In 31 BC, in the naval battle at Actium, Octavian's admiral Marcus Agrippa won a decisive victory over his rival Mark Antony and Cleopatra, the queen of Egypt. Eleven months later, Mark Antony and Cleopatra were dead, Ptolemaic Egypt, the last of the Hellenistic empires, conquered by Octavian's legions. Was this the end of Hellenism? The answer is: yes and no. Yes, because Rome had proved stronger than any of the monarchies that had succeeded Alexander's empire. Their intrinsic political instability, conditioned by the charismatic character of monarchic rule and the fragile balance of power between them, had made them an easy prey for the expanding Roman Republic, in spite of the immense resources their rulers commanded. Political Hellenism was dead in 30 BC, the year when Egypt became a Roman province, but it had been in agony since the middle of the 2nd century BC when Hellenistic monarchs became increasingly dependent on Rome.

Yet Hellenism as a cultural system, a lifestyle and a symbolic framework for art, architecture and town planning, as well as for literature, philosophy and religion, survived. *Graecia capta ferum victorem cepit* – 'conquered Greece defeated the savage victor' – thus versified Horace, the Roman poet writing under Augustus, the victor of Actium. Hellenism lived on in the uncounted cities that dotted the Roman empire, from the river Clyde to the Euphrates in Mesopotamia; it lived on in the self-representation of the Roman emperors, through buildings, inscriptions and coins; it also lived on in Christianity that, in Late Antiquity, absorbed many of the intellectual achievements of the classical world. Alexander's political legacy may have had inept heirs, but the cultural heritage of Hellenism shaped a world stretching from the Atlantic to the Indus far beyond Antiquity.

# THE PARTHIAN AND EARLY SASANIAN EMPIRES

## c. 247 BC–AD 300

TED KAIZER

Forget about Gauls and Africans, Britons and Germans as Rome's most mighty enemy: from their first encounter in 92 BC – when a tête-à-tête between the Roman general Sulla and the Parthian envoy Orobazus took place – Parthia and its King of Kings swiftly came to be represented by Latin and Greek authors as the principal foe. Over the next 300 years, the two superpowers of the ancient world would regularly clash, especially over the mountainous region north of Syria known as Armenia, a famous breeding land for horses, and hence a potentially advantageous protectorate for both Parthians and Romans. Unfortunately, there are virtually no indigenous Parthian texts available to us, and we are therefore to a hazardous degree dependent upon classical sources, so that we have to study the Parthian empire above all through the eyes of its adversaries.

Ultimately replacing the residue of the once mighty Seleucids in Mesopotamia, the Parthians had their actual origins elsewhere. As the tribe of the Parni, part of a much larger nomadic confederation known as the Daha, they moved from the steppe area east of the Caspian Sea into the lands known as Parthava, in northeastern Iran, which had been known under that name as a satrapy of the Achaemenid empire since at least the later part of the 6th century BC. The original invasion of 'Parthia' by the Parni was traditionally set in 247 BC, under the chieftain Arsaces, after whom the Arsacid era and the Arsacid dynasty were later named, although this date is now heavily disputed. The campaigns by the 2nd-century BC kings, especially Mithridates I (171–138 BC), helped to install Arsacid rule over manifold territories which had their own cultural traditions and their own ruling families, and at its zenith the Parthian realm stretched from the Euphrates to the Indus. In less than a century and a half, the Arsacids had been truly transformed from nomads overrunning large parts of eastern Iran into world rulers, and in 113 BC Mithridates II took over the ancient Persian title 'King of Kings', proudly reflecting his domination over a patchwork of minor kings. However, the very presence of these vassal states, and the occasional efforts by their rulers to gain a larger degree of independence, made the Parthian empire vulnerable, especially in times of dynastic conflict, to which the house of the Arsacids seemed particularly prone.

A good example of the fluctuations in relations between the central Arsacid residence at Ctesiphon, situated on the Tigris in southern Mesopotamia, and the peripheral kingdoms elsewhere within the Parthian world is Hatra, a stronghold in the north-Mesopotamian Jazirah steppe. Hatra gained some notoriety for imposing losses on the Roman emperors Trajan and Septimius Severus, who both failed to take the city on different occasions. The material remains of Hatra's sophisticated culture only appear in our evidence in the late 1st century AD, when the city was ruled by a series of indigenous 'lords'. But in the second half of the 2nd century AD, this system of lordship was replaced by the installation of a royal house, and Hatra's rulers were henceforth known as 'King', or more specifically 'King of Arabia' and 'King over the Arabs', whatever that may have meant. This important change clearly implies that the Parthian overlords permitted the creation of a notionally new kingdom within the boundaries of their empire, or perhaps they were simply forced to accept it.

Our search for Parthian institutions and for typically 'Parthian' elements in their society is often frustrated by the lack of sufficient evidence. This is well illustrated by the example of Dura-Europos, a small town on the Euphrates known among scholars as 'the Pompeii of the Syrian desert', thanks to its exquisite and important archaeological discoveries. Here there is very little that demonstrates Parthian occupation during the years under their control. The evidence for Parthian writing at Dura is scant, while its architecture harks back to early Near Eastern styles.

The documentary evidence from Dura clearly shows that the Parthians did not make major changes to previous administrative and societal structures. They did have their own language (Pahlavi), but Aramaic, the official language of the Achaemenid Persian chancellery, and Greek, the lingua franca of the Hellenistic world and later of the Roman East, remained more popular among the population of their empire. The impression gained is one of increasing decentralization and of opportunism on the part of the Parthian overlords. Their empire flourished through trade, and both Parthian and local merchants acted as intermediaries between the Roman world and the Far East. From China and India they carried a rich assortment of colourful textiles and fragrant spices to the vassal kingdom of Characene on the Persian Gulf, from where they travelled up the Euphrates, and then made the dangerous desert crossing to Palmyra in the middle of the Syrian steppe – still an independent city in the 1st century AD according to Pliny's description: 'as it were isolated by Nature from the world, having a destiny of its own between the two mighty empires of Rome and Parthia, and at the first moment of a quarrel between them always attracting the attention of both sides'. In the 1st century AD, Isidore of Charax produced, typically in Greek, a list of fortresses and strongholds situated in the Parthian realm, including Dura-Europos. Although his *Parthian Stations* has sometimes been viewed as an itinerary following the Parthian trade route, it is in fact a description of the ancient royal road which was maintained in the first place for administrative and military purposes.

To what extent the Parthians understood their realm as an 'empire' in the way the Romans did theirs remains unclear. Whereas Rome ultimately wanted to occupy as much territory as was feasible, the Parthians seem to have viewed their domain more in terms of a collection of peoples answerable to the King of Kings, regardless of their

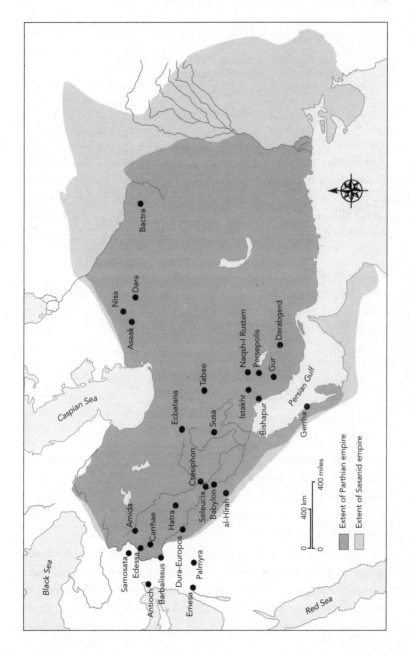

Bactra

Dara

Nisa

Asaak

Naqsh-I Rustam

Persepolis

Gur Darabgerd

Tabae

Ecbatana

Istakhr

Susa

Bishapur

Persian Gulf

Caspian Sea

Gerrha

Ctesiphon

Seleucia

Babylon

al-Hirah

Amida

Carrhae

Hatra

Samosata

Edessa

Barbalissus

Dura-Europos

Palmyra

Antioch

Emesa

Black Sea

Red Sea

400 miles

400 km

Extent of Parthian empire

Extent of Sasanid empire

## KEY DATES

| | |
|---|---|
| c. 247 BC | Traditional date of invasion of Parthia by the Parni and start of Arsacid era |
| 171–138 BC | Great expansion of Parthian empire under Mithridates I |
| 69 BC | First-ever crossing of Euphrates by Roman troops when Licinius Lucullus invades Parthian territory |
| 53 BC | Roman general Crassus defeated at Carrhae-Harran |
| 36 BC | Mark Antony's campaigns against the Parthians end in failure |
| AD 114–117 | Trajan campaigns against Parthia |
| 162–166 | Parthian war of Lucius Verus |
| 198 | Septimius Severus captures Parthian capital Ctesiphon |
| 224 | Artabanus IV, last Parthian king, defeated; beginning of Sasanian rule |
| c. 240–244 | First campaign of Shapur against the Romans; fall of Hatra |
| 244 | Gordian III killed in battle against Sasanians |
| 252–253 | Second campaign of Shapur who invades Syria and captures Antioch |
| c. 259/60 | Odaenathus of Palmyra defeats Sasanians near Orontes |
| 260 | Shapur I defeats and captures Valerian (Shapur's third campaign) |

level of independence. Some scholars have argued that Parthia was, in essence, similar to the Hellenistic kingdoms, while others prefer to follow the attitude of the Roman poet Horace, whose phrase 'Phraates has been restored to the throne of Cyrus' explicitly presents the Arsacids as rightful heirs to the Achaemenid Persians. In the end, perhaps the most lasting – and in any case the most visible – Parthian legacy was the peculiar dress code, which stood in sharp contrast to Rome's toga and tunic. The typically Parthian costume that became the mode over most of the Levant consisted of the famous baggy trousers that are often depicted on sculptures and frescoes, and local notables at cities such as Palmyra could appear on one and the same monument both in western and in eastern dress.

## Early Parthian conflicts with Rome

The story of Rome vs Parthia gets under way in 92 BC, when the Roman general Sulla met with the Parthian envoy Orobazus in the presence of the Cappadocian nobleman Ariobarzanes, for whom the Roman commander acted as a patron. Three chairs were prepared, and Sulla is said to have given audience while seated in the middle, between the two other men. For this apparent act of complacency on the part of Orobazus, who had openly acknowledged Roman superiority, he was put to death on his return by the King of Kings. When Sulla's former lieutenant Licinius Lucullus invaded some of the lands across the Euphrates in 69 BC, in the context of the Third Mithridatic war that Rome fought against the powerful monarch Mithridates VI of Pontus and his son-in-law Tigranes II of Armenia (who had himself annexed Parthian territories), this event – the first time ever Roman troops had crossed the river – was hailed by some as 'the greatest victory the sun had ever seen', as Plutarch records it later.

Only 16 years later, in 53 BC, did the unthinkable happen: no less than seven Roman legions were routed at the ancient city of Carrhae, also known as Harran and famous for its temple of the Moon, by Parthian opposition. The Roman commander Marcus Crassus – famous both for his secret alliance with Julius Caesar and Pompey the Great and for his corruptly acquired fortune – got caught in a trap and lost his life at the battle. Some 20,000 of his soldiers are said to have died with him, another 10,000 were deported by the Parthians, and the imperial army shamefully lost its eagles. Crassus' biographer, Plutarch, gives a vivid account of the horrendous end to the great man's life. He describes how the Parthian commander Sillaces arrived at the royal court with the decapitated head of Crassus, at the very moment that Euripides' *Bacchae*, which was being performed in the presence of the king, had reached the point where the head of Pentheus, king of Thebes, is supposed to be shown by his frenzied mother Agave. Plutarch poignantly states how Crassus' expedition therefore closed 'just like a tragedy':

> 'While the actor was receiving his applause, Sillaces stood at
> the door of the banqueting hall, and after a low obeisance cast
> the head of Crassus into the centre of the company.'

The final act of Crassus' life thus also illustrates how the Parthian court proved to be populated by connoisseurs of Greek tragedy, which is a far cry from the stereotypical image of the 'barbarian' generally encountered in classical sources.

The recovery of the lost standards of Crassus' army became a major issue for the Romans. Whereas in 36 BC the triumvir Mark Antony was unsuccessful in retrieving the eagles, Augustus could proclaim in the *Res Gestae*, his posthumously published list of achievements:

> 'I compelled the Parthians to restore to me the spoils and
> standards of three Roman armies and to ask as suppliants
> for the friendship of the Roman people.'

This came about while Augustus was in the East from 22 to 19 BC. He settled the Armenian situation by installing as king a member of the indigenous royal house who had once been a resident at the Roman court and who could therefore be expected to be loyal. Augustus' stepson, the later emperor Tiberius, delivered the candidate to the empty throne in person, and in 20 BC a diplomatic agreement was reached with the Parthian king Phraates IV, who accepted the Armenian solution in exchange for Rome's promise not to interfere in Parthia itself. He also handed back the eagles lost by Crassus at Carrhae. Despite its diplomatic solution, the return of the standards was presented in Rome as a military victory, and the event became one of the cornerstones on which the ideology of the new principate was founded. The poet Horace wrote in the *Secular Hymn*, commissioned by Augustus specially for the 'Games of the Century', celebrating Rome's entering a new age in 17 BC:

> '*Now Parthia fears the fist of Rome, the fasces potent on*
> *land and sea!*'

State coinage referred to the recovered eagles by portraying kneeling Parthians, a triumphal arch was built on the Forum to celebrate the occasion (it is now lost, but we know it from imagery on coins), and on Augustus' return from the East in 19 BC the Senate consecrated an altar of Fortuna Redux, the good fortune bringing soldiers home, in his honour. Perhaps most famously, the return of the standards is shown on the cuirass which Augustus wears on a statue from Livia's villa at Prima Porta. A bearded Parthian hands over the eagle to a Roman soldier (or perhaps Tiberius) while the gods look on in approval: the sun-god in a *quadriga*, Caelus holding the firmament, the personifications of Dawn and Dew, the divine twins Apollo (Augustus' main deity) and Diana, and the earth goddess Tellus with a horn of abundance as symbol of prosperity.

When the rivalries began to resurface in Armenia some 20 years later, Augustus sent his grandson (and adopted son) Gaius Caesar to the East, where the young crown prince met with the Parthian king Phraataces, the bastard son of Phraates IV, on an island in the Euphrates. We have an eyewitness account by Velleius Paterculus, who wrote in his *History of Rome*:

> '*As for the meeting, first the Parthian dined with Gaius upon*
> *the Roman bank, and later Gaius supped with the king on the*
> *soil of the enemy.*'

The Euphrates had once again acted as the symbolic frontier between the two empires. Yet notwithstanding the mutual respect, as described by Velleius, the image projected at Rome was again different, and the cuirass worn by Gaius on a posthumously erected statue (he died in Lycia in AD 4) is decorated with the heads of the bearded 'barbarians'.

### Later Parthian conflicts with Rome

The fear of the Arsacids remained present in the Roman psyche, even though, in reality, after the 40s BC the military power of the Parthians was in fact hardly sufficient to allow offensive action into the now Roman-dominated lands of Syria and Anatolia. The great Roman historian Tacitus records how the Parthian king Artabanus II, 'despising [the emperor] Tiberius' old age as defenceless', threatened the Romans by 'bragging of the old boundaries of the Persians and Macedonians and that he would invade the lands once possessed by Cyrus and later by Alexander'. Cassius Dio describes how the Parthians had always been considered a match for Rome and discusses the Parthian equipment and aims and methods of warfare:

> 'The Parthians make no use of a shield, but their forces consist
> of mounted archers and pikesmen, mostly in full armour.
> Their infantry is small, made up of the weaker men; but even
> these are all archers. They practise from boyhood, and the
> climate and the land combine to aid both horsemanship
> and archery.'

The Romans not only learned from the surprise movements of the Parthian riders, but they also managed to take over many of their opponents' tricks by actually incorporating native troops as auxiliary units in the imperial army. Such units, filled with indigenous soldiers who continued to fight with their own weapons, were often employed far from their homeland. A 'cavalry unit of Parthians and Arabians' (*ala Parthorum et Arabum*) is known for example from the tombstone of an officer from the 1st century AD that was found in Mainz in Germany.

In the 2nd century AD Roman emperors still sought fame through war against the Parthians. Trajan created a series of new Roman provinces across the Euphrates (all of which were abandoned immediately after his death) and state coinage shows how the Parthian king receives his diadem directly from Trajan, with a legend saying *REX PARTHIS DATUS*, 'a king is given to the Parthians'. From AD 162 to 166, Marcus Aurelius' co-emperor Lucius Verus took nominal command of a military campaign in the East, although he is said to have left the actual fighting to his generals while he himself enjoyed a luxurious lifestyle in the cities of Roman Syria instead. Wars between West and East seem to have resulted – like in more modern times – in an avalanche of historical publications attempting to satisfy a more general audience. In a wonderful piece called *How to Write History*, the famous satirist Lucian, himself of Samosata (formerly the royal capital of Commagene), criticized the way in which incapable writers hurriedly brought out books about Verus' Parthian war that were full of inaccuracies:

> '*Every single person is writing history; nay more, they are all Thucydideses, Herodotuses and Xenophons to us. Yet most of them think they don't even need advice for the job any more than they need a set of rules for walking or seeing or eating.*'

In any case Ctesiphon was conquered in AD 198 by Septimius Severus, who created (like Trajan, but this time lasting) the province of Mesopotamia and took the victorious title Parthicus Maximus.

## The rise of the Sasanians

The 2nd-century Roman campaigns weakened the Parthian power, which was further subject to infighting. But if the combination of war with Rome and dynastic conflicts was insufficient to bring the Parthian empire to its knees, ultimately it proved to be too vulnerable to rebellions and struggles for independence by vassal states. Some 475 years of Arsacid rule came to an end in AD 224, when a regional governor called Ardashir (or Artaxerxes, as classical sources name him) revolted against his Parthian overlords, defeated Artabanus IV, and in the process established the neo-Persian empire of the Sasanians. Named after Ardashir's ancestor Sasan, they would soon make Rome long for the days of the rivalry with their Parthian sparring partners. The Sasanians were far more aggressive and powerful than their predecessors on Rome's eastern borders, which is said to have caused the young emperor Severus Alexander to send letters to the Sasanian ruler to 'halt the invasion and check his expectations'. In the words of the 3rd-century historian Herodian, himself from the Near East:

> 'In these letters he told Artaxerxes that he must remain within his own borders and not initiate any action; let him not, deluded by vain hopes, stir up a great war, but rather let each of them be content with what already was his. By writing letters of this kind, Alexander thought that he would persuade the barbarian to remain quiet or frighten him to the same course.'

The emperor's prose did not, however, have the desired effect.

Ardashir's son Shapur followed in his father's aggressive footsteps and benefited from the 3rd-century crisis in the Roman imperial system, where a series of so-called soldier-emperors reached the purple in rapid succession. In 244 the teenage emperor Gordian III died of his wounds following his army's defeat near Ctesiphon, and was succeeded by his praetorian prefect Philip, who was born in the Syrian Hauran region and has become known to posterity as 'Philip the Arab', and who was forced into a peace treaty with Shapur. In a second campaign, in 252, the armies of the King of Kings overran large parts of Syria, including the major city of Antioch, and in 260 the emperor Valerian was taken captive by the Sasanians. He eventually died in a Persian prison, having spent the remainder of his life as a footstool to Shapur. For the Christian apologist Lactantius the King of Kings clearly acted as an instrument of God's punishment of the impious emperor, and he describes in detail the humiliation Valerian had to undergo in a pamphlet called *On the Death of the Persecutors*:

> 'He squandered the remainder of his days in the abject form of slavery: for whenever Shapur... chose to get into the carriage or to mount on horseback, he commanded the Roman to stoop and present his back; then, placing his foot on the shoulders of Valerian, he said, with a smile of reproach, "This is true, and not what the Romans depicted on their tablets and walls".'

We have the unique and invaluable reaction of Shapur himself in a trilingual inscription, written in Arsacid Pahlavi, in the Middle Persian of the Sasanians and in Greek. It is inscribed at Naqsh-I Rustam, north of Persepolis, where the Achaemenid kings had found their final resting-place, and is commonly labelled by scholars, in a witty reference to the famous *Res Gestae* of Augustus, as the 'Achievements of the Divine Shapur'. After introducing himself, Shapur gives the neo-Persian perspective on the consecutive wars:

> 'When at first we had become established in the empire, Gordian Caesar raised in all of the Roman empire a force from the Goth and German realms and marched on Babylonia against the empire of Iran and against us. On the border of Babylonia at Misikhe, a great frontal battle occurred. Gordian Caesar was killed and the Roman force was destroyed. And the Romans made Philip Caesar. Then Philip Caesar came to us for terms, and to ransom their lives, gave us five hundred thousand dinars, and became tributary to us.'

Shapur's second campaign is said to have been a reaction to further Roman falsehood:

> 'And Caesar lied again and did wrong to Armenia. Then we
> attacked the Roman empire and annihilated at Barbalissos
> a Roman force of 60,000 and Syria and the environs of Syria
> we burned, ruined and pillaged all.'

His third campaign, in which Valerian was captured, is also described.

As if this priceless document is not enough, we also have two exquisite visual representations of the events, which merge Shapur's three campaigns into one. A rock-cut relief at the same site of Naqsh-I Rustam shows the victorious King of Kings with two figures who have commonly been interpreted as Philip the Arab and Valerian, the one kneeling while the other is grasped by Shapur. A similar relief, at Bishapur, shows the King of Kings, again on horseback, with no fewer than three Roman emperors: Gordian III is trampled under Shapur's horse, Philip the Arab is depicted as a suppliant, and Valerian stands captured.

The fact that both the relief and the inscription at Naqsh-I Rustam were cut in the rocks at the same place where the tombs of the Achaemenid kings were located is a good indicator of the length to which the Sasanians went to present themselves as the legitimate heirs to the 'old' Persians. Nevertheless, the claims by some Roman historians – namely that the Sasanians from the outset intended to take possession of all the lands once occupied by the Achaemenids – must be taken with a pinch of salt. The degree to which the Sasanians owed part of their legacy to that of the Arsacids is debatable, but their policy seems certainly to have been more aggressive and their attitude to religious freedom less tolerant.

The most famous religious victim was the prophet Mani, the founder of a gnostic world religion known as Manichaeism, which combined a dualistic system according to which the powers of Light had to fight the powers of Darkness with elements directly taken over from Buddhism, Zoroastrianism and Christianity. Born in the final years of Arsacid rule, Mani travelled to India once Ardashir had established himself as the first Sasanian King of Kings, possibly because Ardashir refused to provide proper patronage. On his return to the Sasanian empire, Mani found a protector in Shapur. A 10th-century Arab author describes their first meeting as follows:

> 'The Manichaeans said that when Mani came into his presence, there were on his shoulders two lights resembling lamps. And when Shapur saw him he was impressed and Mani grew in his estimation.'

Shapur may well have viewed Mani's preaching – which incorporated elements from different cultural backgrounds – as a way to glue together, in a religious mould, his empire. His successor Hormizd, who only reigned for one year, also supported the prophet, but Vahram I, who became King of Kings in AD 273, showed a very different attitude towards Mani. Influenced by the Magians – the Zoroastrian priests whose lifestyle was directly opposed to much of what Mani taught (above all asceticism, including a condemnation of the great Persian pastime of hunting) – Vahram disliked him from the start. Mani was imprisoned and eventually executed.

The more aggressive Sasanian political and military approach is clear from Shapur's various incursions into Roman provincial territory. The fear that his soldiers could instill in their opponents is reflected by the novelist Heliodorus of Emesa (present-day Homs in Syria), who records, in the ninth book of his *Ethiopian Story*, the shock experienced by the Roman soldiers when they first laid eyes on the eastern enemy. The historian Ammianus Marcellinus, who had experienced first hand the unsuccessful Persian campaign of the last pagan emperor, Julian 'the Apostate', was full of similar praise of the Sasanian army:

> 'Their military training and discipline, and their constant practice of manoeuvres and arms drill ... make them formidable even to large armies. They rely especially on their cavalry, in

> *which all their nobility and men of mark serve. Their infantry*
> *are protected like gladiators and obey orders like slaves.'*

## Palmyra against the Sasanians

Important developments within the Roman empire had taken place
after the capture of Valerian. His son Gallienus had made the Palmyrene
notable Odaenathus his official deputy in the East, with the new title
of Corrector Totius Orientis, in order to create stability in the region.
Palmyra had been fully integrated into the Roman provincial system
from the 1st century AD onwards. In 130 the emperor Hadrian visited
the oasis in person, and in the early 3rd century Palmyra had acquired
the prestigious status of a Roman colony. In the 250s Odaenathus
came to the fore as the leading citizen, who also made it big time as
a Roman senator and eventually consul. According to a late and not
necessarily reliable source – the 6th-century imperial diplomat Petrus
Patricius – Odaenathus was hoping to strike a deal with Shapur at the
time of the second Sasanian campaign (when, as far as the trilingual
inscription from Naqsh-I Rustam is concerned, Palmyra indeed seems
to have escaped being pillaged). In any case, together with his son
Herodian, Odaenathus won a famous victory over the Sasanians in
260. As is shown by an inscription on an arch at Palmyra, the son (and
we can therefore assume also the father) now took on the traditional
royal title of the major power in the East:

> 'This statue was set up for Septimius Herodian, King of Kings,
> crowned near the Orontes with the diadem of royalty for his
> victory over the Persians.'

In the late 4th century, Festus described Odaenathus, who had 'collected a band of Syrian country folk and put up a spirited resistance',
as Rome's avenger, who even managed to capture Ctesiphon.

Odaenathus and his son remained loyal to the Roman emperor,
but following their victory over Shapur, they considered themselves

the rightful heirs to the royal diadem of the Sasanians. A mosaic that was recently discovered at Palmyra seems to echo the episode. The Greek mythological hero Bellerophon, on his winged horse Pegasus, is shown (dressed in Parthian trousers) as killing the monstrous chimaera, while two eagles fly above him carrying a wreath, symbolizing victory. A second image, seemingly depicting an innocent hunting scene, has a horseman (dressed in the same way as 'Bellerophon') engaged in a fight with Persian tigers, again accompanied by an eagle with a wreath. Following the ingenious explanation of the archaeologist who discovered it, the mosaic – combining Greek mythology with local iconographic detail – is no less than an allegory for the victory of the Palmyrenes over the Persians, which earned Odaenathus and Herodian the title 'King of Kings'.

Following the untimely death of father and son under suspicious circumstances, Odaenathus' widow Zenobia ruled for their underage son Vaballathus and extended the Palmyrene kingdom over large parts of the Roman East. It was not to last for long, as the emperor Aurelian defeated Zenobia's troops and finally crushed Palmyra's power, bringing it back firmly in the bosom of the Roman empire. Rome's success rate on its eastern frontier would continue to ebb and flow, and the treaty with the Sasanians that followed the emperor Galerius' victory over them, in 298/9, resulted in Rome's greatest-ever extension of its territory across the Tigris. Nevertheless, the neo-Persian empire would finally come to an end only centuries later, following the Arab conquest of Mesopotamia and Persia.

# THE ROMAN EMPIRE

## 27 BC–AD 476

MICHAEL SOMMER

'Indeed, you best have proved that well-known saying, that the
earth is the mother of all and the universal country of all. Now
it is possible for both Greek and barbarian, with his possessions
or without them, to travel easily wherever he wishes, quite as
if he were going from one country of his to another…. And
what was said by Homer, "The earth was common to all", you
have made a reality, by surveying the whole inhabited world,
by bridging the rivers in various ways, by cutting carriage
roads through the mountains, by filling desert places with
post stations, and by civilizing everything with your way of life
and good order…. And now, indeed, there is no need to write
a description of the world, nor to enumerate the laws of each
people, but you have become universal geographers for all
men by opening up all the gates of the inhabited world and by
giving to all who wish it the power to be observers of everything
and by assigning universal laws for all men and by stopping
practices which formerly were pleasant to read about, but were
intolerable if one should actually consider them and by making
marriage legal between all peoples and by organizing the whole
inhabited world like a single household.'

'Like a single household' – Aelius Aristides, an orator and intellectual
in the 2nd century AD, could hardly have characterized the vast empire
that stretched from the Firth of Forth to the Nile, from the Atlantic to
the river Euphrates, more succinctly. In his speech 'On Rome' (*logos*

*eis Rhomen*), probably delivered to an audience in the city of Rome during the reign of the emperor Hadrian (117–138), Aristides, a Greek from the northwest of Asia Minor, compares and contrasts Rome to preceding empires, beginning with the Persians. The juxtaposition with Persia is a favourable one for the Romans as their empire is built on consensus rather than force, and turns subdued populations into shareholders of imperial rule. Unlike the Achaemenid Persian and Hellenistic empires, the Romans have much to offer their subjects. For Aristides, the Roman empire is synonymous with civilization.

This is certainly an idealistic perspective on Roman rule. After all it was the job of an orator to please his audience and to praise the empire of the city that hosts him. However, the image constructed by Aristides is not necessarily wrong. To be sure, Roman hegemony – like any empire in history – was established through force. But by the imperial period, Rome's elite was remarkably cosmopolitan, and the distinction between Romans and subjects had been diminished. People from the most distant parts of the empire had been admitted to the Senate. Trajan, the emperor under whom Aristides was born, was the first Roman ruler to be born outside Italy: his family, the Ulpii, came from the Roman colony of Italica in Spain. Still later, men whose mother tongues were Punic, Aramaic or Arabic could put on the imperial purple. These people were the living proof that the Romans had successfully 'romanized' their empire. But the repercussions of romanization were enormous: while the empire's non-Roman, non-Greek (hence 'barbarian') periphery became gradually more Roman, Rome itself became considerably more 'barbarian'.

In this sense, Rome indeed made the world 'common to all'. The empire created a universal framework of standards, values, role models, laws and means of communication that substantially reduced the distances between centre and periphery. The Romans gave local elites the chance to break the chains of parochial narrowness and rise to the higher echelons of imperial aristocracy. Having said that, Roman rule was quite different in its early days. The Roman Republic

was as rapacious and keen on collecting revenues from its subject
territories as any other expanding power. By the 2nd century BC,
the recklessness of Roman tax farmers, private entrepreneurs who
squeezed the provinces on behalf of the Roman state, was notorious
throughout the Mediterranean. The transformation of this rapacious
Republic into an empire that could be regarded at least as benevolent,
if not praiseworthy, was largely the achievement of one man: Augustus, the first Roman emperor. His sole rule (31 BC–AD 14) marked a
veritable watershed in Roman history and has duly been labelled the
'Augustan threshold'.

## The 'Augustan threshold': before and after

In his *Res Gestae*, the record of his accomplishments composed by the
first Roman emperor towards the end of his life, Augustus describes
the moment when the Roman Republic turned into a monarchy, and
he himself was transformed from Gaius Iulius Caesar (the name he
inherited from his adoptive father Julius Caesar), *divi filius*, 'the son of
a god', into *Augustus*, 'the venerable one', the sole ruler of the Roman
world. This was when, in his sixth and seventh consulships (the year
27 BC), he transferred his extraordinary powers back to the Senate and
the Roman people. In exchange, he received, among other honours,
the title of Augustus from the Senate.

> *'After that time I took precedence of all in rank [*auctoritas*],*
> *but of power I possessed no more than those who were my*
> *colleagues in any magistracy.'*

So he claimed. But who was this man who established the Roman
monarchy? Born as Gaius Octavius (but today commonly known as
Octavian), at the age of 18 he suddenly became a key figure in Roman
politics: in his will, the great Julius Caesar, murdered by Cassius and
Brutus on the Ides of March (15 March) 44 BC, had made Octavian his
principal heir and adoptive son. Once Caesar was deified, Octavian

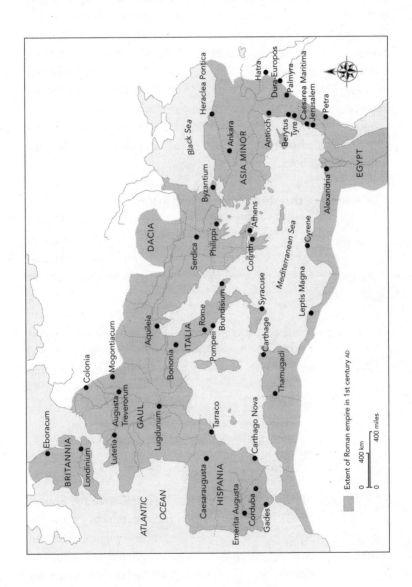

Extent of Roman empire in 1st century AD

became the son of a god and never used his name of birth again. Along with Caesar's name, young Octavian inherited the dictator's fortune and the loyalty of his legions. Thirteen long years of unrest with changing alliances followed: in 31 BC, Octavian defeated his former ally Mark Antony in a naval battle at Actium, and was now the sole survivor of a century-long struggle for power which had split the nobility, Rome's governing elite, for almost five centuries.

## KEY DATES

| | |
|---|---|
| 216 BC | Hannibal defeats Roman army at Cannae |
| 149–146 BC | Victory for Rome in third and final Punic war |
| 58–50 BC | Caesar's conquest of Gaul |
| 49–45 BC | Civil war: Caesar against Pompey and the Senate |
| 42 BC | Mark Antony and Octavian defeat Caesar's assassins at Philippi |
| 31 BC | Great naval victory for Octavian over Mark Antony and Cleopatra at Actium |
| 27 BC | Title 'Augustus' conferred by Senate on Octavian, who by now is effectively first emperor |
| AD 9 | Three legions destroyed in Teutoburg Forest |
| 43 | Claudian invasion of Britain |
| 66–71 | Jewish War |
| 69 | Civil war, Vespasian becomes emperor |
| 101–102/105–106 | Trajan's wars in Dacia (modern Romania) |
| 193–197 | Civil war, Septimius Severus gains power |
| 212 | Citizenship extended to whole free population of the empire |
| 284 | Diocletian divides empire into east and west, each with its own emperor |
| 378 | Defeat of Valens by Goths at battle of Adrianople |
| 410 | Sack of Rome by Goths |
| 439 | Vandals capture Carthage |
| 455 | Vandals sack Rome |
| 476 | Deposition of last Roman emperor, Romulus Augustulus |

But Rome was not yet ready for monarchy. Julius Caesar's obvious monarchic ambitions had cost him his life, and his adoptive son was determined not to make the same mistake. Despite internal upheaval that resulted in them splitting into factions, the members of the Roman senatorial aristocracy were united by a strong dislike of kingship. According to the foundation myth of the Republic, Brutus, a young Roman nobleman and supposed ancestor of Caesar's assassin of the same name, deposed the last Etruscan king – Tarquinius Superbus, whom the narratives unanimously depict as inept and cruel – in 509 BC. Brutus went down in history as a liberator, and kingship was discredited evermore: even in the 1st century BC, a revived monarchy would lack any legitimacy. For this reason, the form of government that Augustus adopted was not a monarchy in the proper sense. The old Republican institutions were not abolished, and the Principate, as it was called, was more than a monarchy in disguise: Augustus did not assume the offices themselves, but he did assume their responsibilities. And the visible honours which were conferred on him – the laurels, the golden *clipeus virtutis* ('shield of bravery') and the *corona civica* ('civic crown') fixed to the entrance of his house – were all rooted in Republican tradition. Instead of overtly creating a monarchy, Augustus claimed to have 'restored' the Republic. Indeed, by labelling himself *princeps* ('first man'), Augustus 'took precedence of all in rank' without possessing any more institutional power than his colleagues in the magistracies.

The Roman Republic was a political structure no less puzzling than the Principate. The historiographer Polybius (*c.* 200–140 BC), a Greek politician who had been deported to Rome, admired its mixed constitution, with its checks and balances between monarchic, aristocratic and democratic elements. Government was divided between the people (voting in various assemblies), the two consuls (who held the supreme command in times of war and presided over the Senate) and the Senate (the council in which former magistrates convened). In theory, any Roman citizen could rise through the ranks of the *cursus honorum* – the hierarchy of public offices – and become a senator. In practice, access was largely restricted to a few powerful families. Social mobility into the senatorial class was less open than it appeared at first sight.

The nobility's unity was reinforced by a number of institutions that were not part of any written constitution, but were effective nevertheless. Senators were tied to each other by mutual bonds of solidarity (*amicitia*, 'friendship') or aversion (*inimicita*, 'enmity'), which were handed down from one generation to the next. They had at their disposal large groups of followers who owed loyalty to the senators and in turn received protection (*patrocinium*). Powerful patrons could easily influence the crowds of their clients when it came to voting: candidates were supported both by their own clients and by those of their political allies. To increase the value of their patronage, aristocrats, whose economic basis was landed property, displayed overt pride in their ancestors, whose achievements would contribute to their own prestige. It was also every senator's mission to enhance his family's status through his own political and military achievements, and, by doing so, to accumulate *dignitas* ('dignity').

Even though the endemic strive for *dignitas* created a competitive social climate, the Roman nobility proved to be a surprisingly efficient political class. In little more than a century, between the First (264–241 BC) and the Third (149–146 BC) Punic wars, they turned the Republic into a truly imperial power and the Mediterranean into a *mare nostrum* ('our sea').

To understand this process, it is necessary to look back to Rome's early history, before the empire's growth began: in the 6th and 5th centuries BC, Rome was no more than a middle-sized city in central Italy which had cast off Etruscan dominance and maintained a close, albeit not always friendly, relationship to their kinsfolk in the towns in the hinterland of Latium. Just after they had eliminated their major regional rival, the Etruscan town of Veii (396 BC), the Romans lost a decisive battle against the Sennones, a migrating Gallic tribe, and Rome fell victim to the Gauls (387 BC). Only the Capitoline Hill withstood the siege, and the city itself was destroyed. The event was crucial for the Romans' political mentality – never again would an invader find Rome defenceless. Henceforth, the defeat and subjugation of potential enemies was the prime directive of Roman foreign policy.

By 300 BC, the Romans had tightened their grip on central Italy. They split the confederacy of Etruscan cities (357–353 BC), put down a revolt of the Latins (340–338 BC) and defended their sphere of influence against the Samnite League, a confederation of Sabellic tribes in southern Italy. In 280 BC, Rome suffocated the last pockets of Etruscan resistance. The city's dominance was briefly threatened in the same year, when Pyrrhus of Epirus, a Greek warlord called by the people of the south Italian town of Tarentum to lead them in their war against Rome, entered Italy with a large army and defeated the Romans in a series of battles. In the long term, however, Pyrrhus was unable to benefit from his military successes and had to retreat from Italy. The south of the peninsula with its large Greek population thus remained defenceless and was gradually conquered by Rome, which controlled Italy from the river Po to the Ionian Sea by 265 BC.

Rome was not the only bellicose, expansionist power in the Mediterranean in those years. What distinguished the Romans from their rivals was the unique cohesion of their elites which, in situations of strain, immediately resolved any dispute and clustered around their leaders. Perhaps even more important to their success was the relative generosity with which Rome enfranchised its citizenship. The Roman state was growing continuously, and consequently so was its military potential. When it had to face the other great powers, beginning with Carthage (from 264 BC onwards), then Macedon (215 BC) and finally the Seleucid empire (192 BC), Rome had not only one of the largest, but also one of the most experienced armies of the Mediterranean world. Roman legionaries had engaged in battle almost every year between 326 and 267 BC.

What the Republic lacked, however, was naval power. After the conquest of the Greek cities in southern Italy, overseas expansion was the next logical step. The nearest target beyond the Italian mainland was Sicily, an economically and strategically rewarding prize. Here, Rome's interests inevitably clashed with those of Carthage, the period's maritime superpower. In order to overcome the Punic city and its empire, the Romans had to build a fleet from scratch and adjust to naval tactics. Amazingly, they succeeded: in 241 BC, the Carthaginians sought for peace and ceded Sicily to Rome. The island became Rome's first province: the Latin term *provincia* meant the administrative district of a Roman magistrate.

## The harvest of war

The wars Rome waged overseas were prolific in terms of the establishment of new provinces: the islands of Corsica and Sardinia formed a province in 231 BC, northern Italy across the Po in 203 BC, Spain in 197 BC, Illyricum (former Yugoslavia and present-day Albania) in 167 BC, Macedonia and Africa (the territory of Carthage) in 146 BC, Asia Minor in 120 BC, and southern Gaul also in 120 BC. Defence and administration of the new provinces required an increasing number of soldiers and officials. By 133 BC, the Roman Republic had created an empire, but the impact that empire had on the Republic was ambivalent. Vast territories were annexed to the *ager publicus* (public land) and immediately occupied by members of the senatorial aristocracy, who accumulated enormous wealth by running large estates specializing in the production of crops destined for the market. At the same time, many smallholders, not least due to the length of military service, became impoverished, lost their plots of land and had to move to Rome, where they increased the population of the urban poor.

The social strata of Roman society drifted apart at an enormous speed. Individual aristocrats could no longer resist the temptation to take advantage of the distressed many for the sake of their own ambitions. Tiberius Gracchus, by descent one of the most prominent members of the nobility, reinvented himself as an advocate of the stranded crowds, demanding land distribution and a fair deal for the landless poor, thus pioneering a new, populist style of politics (133 BC). At first, senatorial class solidarity proved stronger than the demagogues: Tiberius and his brother Gaius, who also did not shy away from unconstitutional action, were slain by furious senators. But in the long term, the aristocrats could not prevent individual members from making their names at the nobility's expense.

Towards the end of the 2nd century BC, the situation was aggravated by the military reforms launched by Gaius Marius, a *homo novus* from a small town in Latium. For the first time, Marius admitted the landless crowds to the army, thus transforming Rome's previous militia – the civic army recruited mainly from the landowning middle classes – into a professional army of soldiers who made their living with warfare. For the new type of soldier, the general was far more than a military commander. The legionaries' hopes for booty and the golden handshake they expected when – usually after 20 years of service – they were discharged from the army rested upon their leader: a new, exceedingly strong bond of solidarity was created. In the long term it proved to be stronger than the Republic.

Domestic affairs and the expansion of empire became closely interwoven. Correspondingly, military prowess was crucial for the rise of the late Republic's influential men: Marius, Sulla, Pompey, Caesar – they all first led huge armies against external enemies and then into civil war against their Roman rivals. Caesar's strategy to obtain the Senate's mandate to conquer Gaul was exemplary, and then he used the mandate as his personal basis of power. The Gallic war (58–50 BC) welded together general and army and fostered allegiance. Caesar could firmly rely on his soldiery when he marched them across the river Rubicon in northern Italy (49 BC). The Rubicon marked the boundary of Italy, where returning armies were meant to lay down their arms and disband before entering Rome. Caesar entered the city and chased his opponents, Pompey in particular, throughout the Mediterranean in a bloody civil war.

The rise of military men like Caesar proved to be fatal for the Republic, but beneficial for the provincial populations. When Cicero, the conservative senator and famous orator, in a case against the corrupt Roman governor of Sicily, Gaius Verres, took the part of Verres' Sicilian victims (70 BC), this was an exceptional example of political impartiality. Generals such as Pompey and Caesar not only annexed large portions of territory to the empire, they also worked as brokers for the locals. By extending the genuinely Roman institutions of *patrocinium* and *amicitia* to the provinces, they created, for the first time in Roman history, a lobby for the periphery in the empire's heart.

Both innovations of the revolutionary period, the new military with its generals and the relationship of *patrocinium* between conqueror and conquered, were universalized by Augustus when he came to power. Before he set off eastwards to defeat his rival Mark Antony, Augustus demanded an oath of allegiance to be sworn by every single male inhabitant of the western provinces he controlled. This oath was later extended to the east, taken from the defeated Mark Antony, and formed the moral basis of the *auctoritas* Augustus refers to in his *Res Gestae*. He similarly inherited Caesar's veterans, to which he later added the surviving soldiery of the dictator's assassins, and still later Mark Antony's troops. His control of the army was Augustus' major asset when Rome's political structure was being reshuffled in the years following Actium. No senator could seriously compete with the man to whom all legionaries had personally sworn their oath of loyalty and whose image they bore on their legionary standards. Augustus also ensured loyalty by looking after the economic needs of his soldiers. He established no fewer than 28 military colonies in Italy alone, thus ensuring that the veterans received the arable land promised to them. (This practice was later abandoned and the soldiers received their discharge bonus in cash.) The Principate's heavy reliance on the army made it effectively a military dictatorship in disguise, illegitimate in the traditional and legal terms of the Republic. The new professional army was one of three decisive pressure-groups Augustus' successors had to reckon with.

## *Pax Romana*: ruling a world

In addition to the military, the senators (the representatives of the old Republic's ruling elite) and the *plebs urbana* (the crowds of the city of Rome) were decisive in the formation of the Principate. All three groups came to the emperor with their own particular concerns and expectations. The emperor on his part relied on the support and acceptance of each group. Failure to communicate with one or – worse – more of the three pressure groups inevitably resulted in serious consequences for the emperor: it meant in the final analysis his political – which in turn usually implied his physical – death.

The arena designed for communication with the Roman crowds was an arena in the most literal sense of the word: the amphitheatre. Gladiatorial games in Rome were far more than a bloody form of entertainment for the urban masses. The arena was a formidable stage where the emperor could engage with the people, and they with him. Here was where his public image was created, and where unity between the emperor and the various strata of Roman society (who all had their allocated seats in the auditorium) was celebrated. The arena, where prisoners met their death and where gladiators and animals staged bloodthirsty shows, was a savage place in the heart of Rome, whereas the gallery, where the spectators were seated according to their social rank, encapsulated everything that was Roman. In the amphitheatre, the Romans met outcasts representing an outlandish and alien world – the nemesis of order, peace and stability for which their empire stood. The crowd carefully watched how the emperor dealt with the strange, savage world they encountered in the arena. The crucial moment came when a gladiator was defeated and the emperor had to make the decision as to whether he would live or die. An unpopular choice invariably cost the emperor credit among the people.

Communication with the senators also required sensitive handling. The nobility, while it had ruled the Republic over the centuries, had nurtured a powerful feeling of superiority and exclusiveness. Augustus himself, when creating the Principate, had not dared to style himself as the senators' master (*dominus*) – a term closely related to the institution of slavery – but chose to be called *princeps* instead. From the point of view of the senatorial aristocracy, the emperor was one of their own. Senators expected the emperor to communicate with them on an equal footing. When the emperor Domitian (AD 81–96) believed he could dispose of such conventions and redesign the Principate as a proper monarchy, he also changed the style of the dinners with the senators. In the banquet halls of his newly built palace on the Palatine, Domitian – who was the first emperor to insist on the title *dominus* – separated himself physically from his guests, thus making visible the enormous social distance between himself and the senators. He did not survive long; in AD 96 he fell victim to a plot in which many courtiers and senators were involved. His successors hastened to undo Domitian's reforms.

Until 217, when the equestrian praetorian prefect Macrinus briefly became emperor, the Senate was the pool from which emperors were recruited. Since the dynastic principle was never firmly rooted in Rome, an emperor who lost acceptance could theoretically be challenged by any senator. Of particular importance in this game – and very dangerous for the ruling emperor – were those senators who commanded armies that were usually garrisoned along the distant frontiers. Once a ruling emperor had become unpopular with the soldiery, they would proclaim their own senatorial commander as rival-emperor. The pretender then usually marched on Rome and encountered his adversary on the battlefield. The first of a series of such usurpations happened when Nero's reign lay in ruins, in the Year of the Four Emperors (AD 69). Three generals from various areas of the empire tried to seize the imperial purple, but all failed. Only when Titus Flavius Vespasianus, Rome's successful supreme commander who put down the Jewish revolt in Palestine, appeared on the scene, did political stability return to Rome. Whereas the Principate had worked smoothly in the relatively calm 1st and 2nd centuries AD, its flaws – an inherent tendency towards usurpation and civil war – became apparent as soon as more troublesome times began for the empire.

In the late 2nd and early 3rd centuries, during which the Principate relied even more heavily on the military than previously, it was the senators who suffered. In relation to the other pressure groups the senatorial aristocracy lost substantial ground, being ousted from most of the administrative top jobs and military commands they previously had held. These positions were instead taken by members of the equestrian order, who were socially inferior to the senators but were more capable with regard to military affairs. Rome was increasingly being challenged by external enemies, so the emperors reacted by making the army larger and more efficient, but the improvement of Rome's military power was only available at a high price: an increase in numbers and pay weighed heavily on the budget. Furthermore, in a scenario with many theatres of war, the emperor as supreme commander could not be present at all the frontiers. This led to the appointment of professional officers to control large portions of these frontiers and armies in his stead. Those who were successful would then, in turn, direct their troops against the ruling emperor. All these factors contributed, directly or indirectly, to the weakening of the central government: the 50 years between the assassination of the emperor Severus Alexander (235) and Diocletian's accession (284) saw no less than 17 emperors coming and going, not including innumerable usurpers that were not recognized by the Senate.

## Military anarchy

These 'soldier emperors' fought a seemingly hopeless battle against migrating Germanic tribes, both along the Danube and the Rhine and also against the Sasanians in the East, who had replaced the far more defensive Parthians in 224. Neither the Sasanians nor the tribal groups had the potential to conquer Roman territory permanently, but they were able to overrun the frontier provinces, to raid and loot cities, and to disappear loaded with booty. It took Rome a generation to develop a strategy against the twofold threat that was in part a response to Roman expansion itself: the fall of the Parthian empire was largely a long-term consequence of repeated Roman aggression in the East, and the formation of new Germanic tribes that were much larger than the groups preceding them was at least to some extent a reaction to Roman campaigning, diplomacy and trade: the soaking of Roman commodities, concepts and know-how into Germany, combined with Germanic tribesmen joining the Roman auxiliary forces, changed social patterns across the Danube and the Rhine. What emerged from the change were compact, highly mobile groups that had personal allegiance to charismatic leaders and the belief in a commonly shared ancestry, and were far more dangerous to Rome than the petty chiefdoms that had dominated the scene in Caesar's day. By 260, Germanic tribes had repeatedly overrun Gaul and the Danube provinces, had crossed the Black Sea, devastated Greece and Asia Minor and some had even ravaged Italy, before the emperor Aurelian (270–275) had finally driven them out.

No less dangerous for Rome were the events in the East, where the Sasanians first took the stronghold of Hatra in present-day Iraq (240), and then repeatedly invaded the provinces of Mesopotamia and Syria, where they skirmished with the Romans but avoided a major battle. The direct clash between Rome and the Sasanians became unavoidable when the emperor Valerian (253–260) entered the eastern theatre with a large army in order to corner the Persian king Shapur (241–272). The consequent battle of Carrhae brought a disastrous defeat for the Romans – for the first time in Roman history, an emperor was captured by the enemy. Valerian's army was annihilated and the Roman eastern provinces became a power vacuum.

When Aurelian gained power in 270, the outlook seemed dismal for the new emperor. The situation along the Roman frontiers appeared bleak, with Germans raiding the Balkans, Greece, Asia Minor and even Italy, and separatist dominions had been established in Gaul and the East. It was only a question of time before another usurper would take on Aurelian. Public finances were in a perilous state. And yet the impression of a universal crisis may be illusory. The 'barbarian' invasions affected only relatively restricted areas and rarely fortified cities. The expansionism of the Sasanian empire had come to a halt. And the economic conditions in the provinces were by no means uniformly bleak. On the contrary: whereas some of the western heartlands of the empire – namely Italy and Gaul – may have been in gentle decline, the provinces in North Africa, Syria, Asia Minor and the Balkans were clearly flourishing.

## Becoming Roman: local and imperial traditions

All over the empire, 'romanization' had – by and large – been a success story. Roman material culture – with its luxury commodities, imperial and domestic architecture, water supply and drainage systems, roads and other means of communication, Roman citizenship, the sophisticated lifestyle of the elites – was sufficiently attractive to local populations, in particular the petty aristocracies of tribes and cities, to be adopted and adapted with enthusiasm. The urge for romanization came, therefore, from the periphery rather than the imperial centre: the locals themselves competed for the most convincing display of their Roman identity. Rome hardly had to impose its civilization upon its subjects. But becoming Roman did not mean that Greeks, Gauls, Syrians or North Africans had to abandon their own traditions, customs and convictions – or indeed their religious faith, which was usually incorporated into Roman religion. Roman tolerance allowed indigenous populations to insert their ancestral traditions into the wider imperial framework.

Local reflections of this cohabitation can be found everywhere from Roman Britain to Roman Egypt, mostly in the material culture, as literary evidence for the imperial periphery is generally scant; Tacitus' works on contemporary Britain and Germany are rare and precious exceptions. Artifacts such as statues of Apollo found in Gaul, in which the image of the Greco-Roman god combined with that of local deities, the representations on family tombs in the Libyan desert and the stunning wall paintings from several buildings in the Near Eastern town of Dura-Europos have been misinterpreted as abortive attempts to emulate Roman models. Recent scholarship tends to regard them as complex expressions of 'hybrid' cultures in which elements of both, the little and the great, traditions fused. But even this is questionable: the material culture of the Roman provinces seems to suggest that the periphery served as a middle ground in which numerous traditions met and made contact with each other, thus resembling perhaps the creole world of the Spanish Caribbean where something completely new emerged, than the proposed model of hybridization.

As a result, the empire became romanized, but not necessarily more homogenous than before. This was most apparent in the frontier zones in western Europe and the Near East. In general, the power and cultural appeal of empires do not simply finish at a boundary – though the Roman empire had a clear-cut border, the *limes* – but gradually fade out towards the periphery. One of the cultural mainstreams of the ancient Mediterranean, Hellenism, had struck roots throughout the Near East long before the Romans arrived: uncounted Greeks and Macedonians had settled in the vast area between the Mediterranean and the Indus since Alexander had subjugated the Achaemenid empire; still more locals had adopted the conquerors' lifestyle. In the twilight zone between east and west the various traditions existed side by side. Greek *poleis* – the *polis* was the fundamental model of an urban settlement governed by its own citizens, which the Greeks of the Archaic period (7th–6th centuries BC) had spread all over the Mediterranean – were built next to indigenous settlements, Greek was spoken along with Aramaic, western gods were worshipped along with eastern deities, Greek-style artifacts were produced together with native ones. From this, eastern Hellenism emerged, an idiosyncratic creole culture, neither 'western' nor 'eastern', but distinct and – despite obvious local variations – strikingly uniform in its appearance. This sphere of close interaction did not cease when the Romans arrived. Cross-border ties remained strong in the Partho-Roman Near East and they did not weaken when the Sasanians took over from the

Parthians. Phenomena such as the wall paintings from Dura-Europos, the stunning rise of the city of Palmyra – which made a short, but decisive appearance on the stage of world politics during the power vacuum that resulted from Valerian's defeat in 260 – and the puzzling religious complexity of places like Hatra can only be fully understood if the cultural ambiguity of the Syro-Mesopotamian steppe frontier is taken into account.

The frontiers seemed distant from Rome, but the inhabitants of the capital got a notion of what was happening on the periphery when Varius Bassianus Avitus, a youth from the Syrian town of Emesa, became emperor in 218. Avitus, an offspring of a local priestly dynasty, later became notorious under the name of his ancestral god: Elagabalus. Educated as a priest himself, he tried to introduce worship of the Syrian sun-god in Rome, where he met fierce resistance. His reign polarized the capital and provoked a cultural war which even divided the imperial palace. Elagabalus' attempt to turn Roman religion upside down was abortive, and the emperor was murdered after four years in power. But whereas most contemporaries tried to dismiss the revolution as just another mad emperor's fury, some observed the cultural rifts that had begun to split the empire. Elagabalus was unsuccessful, but he was the writing on the wall announcing that the great tradition of Greco-Roman, 'classical' elite culture was not the only expression of Roman imperial identity in these times. The Roman world was perhaps more than ever 'common to all', but it was no longer the 'single household' invoked by Aelius Aristides.

## Late Antiquity: the end of Rome?

The empire had begun to drift apart at specific points on the frontiers, where weaknesses were apparent and schisms inevitable: the imperial population was increasingly divided by religious, ethnic and cultural contrasts, and various parts of the empire slipped away from the central government's control for substantial periods of time. At first, however, this process was hardly visible. Aurelian had succeeded in eliminating the two renegade empires that had emerged at the empire's Gallic and Near Eastern fringes. When Diocletian came to power in 284, his first action was to change the Roman state's political and administrative layout. He appointed his fellow officer Maximian as 'Augustus' – now the title of the senior rulers – in 285, thus making him formally his co-emperor. In 293 two more emperors, Galerius and Constantius, were appointed, but remained inferior in rank. As 'Caesares' they were the designated successors of the two Augusti, who announced their abdication after their 20th year of rule, in 305. No matter whether the resulting tetrarchy (leadership of four men) was a master plan designed by Diocletian from the beginning or an ingenious piece of improvisation, the new array resolved two of Rome's most pressing problems: it integrated potential adversaries into Diocletian's camp and thus gave back urgently needed political stability to the empire, and it quadrupled the empire's military and administrative leadership, allowing emperors to be present where they were needed. Although laws issued by the tetrarchs were in principle still effective for all provinces, each emperor was in practice responsible for his own part.

Diocletian and his colleagues all shared the widespread belief that the problems of the empire were due to the deteriorating relationship between the Romans and their ancestral gods. In order to rectify this, the Augusti closely associated themselves with the Olympian gods by adopting the titles of *Iovius* (Diocletian) and *Herculius* (Maximian). It was their firm belief that common well-being could be restored by their subjects honouring the right gods. While religion had hardly been an imperial affair – it had traditionally been the business of the individual cities – faith now moved into the focus of the state's attention. For the first time in Roman history, Christians were systematically persecuted because of their faith.

Although the tetrarchs were successful in stabilizing the empire, their achievements did not survive long. After the abdication of Diocletian and Maximian and Constantius' death, the personal ambition of various pretenders overwhelmed the tetrarchy's sophisticated structure, causing the system to collapse and leading to another civil war. Furthermore, the traditional cults on which Diocletian and his co-emperors intended to base their rule were in rapid decline. The attempt to restore them through force was doomed to failure. Constantine, one of the pretenders, was acutely aware of that when he met his rival Maxentius, Maximian's son, at the Milvian Bridge, a few miles to the north of Rome, in 312. He reportedly received a vision before the battle – a message saying *in hoc signo vinces* ('in this sign, you shall conquer'). He saw the monogram of Christ (the Greek letters *chi* and *rho*) in the sky and immediately adopted it for his soldiers' legionary standards. This was politically a very opportune omen, as Christianity, which had gained numerous supporters during the preceding century, was now a force to be reckoned with. The battle was a triumph for Constantine, and Christianity turned from illegality to state religion almost overnight.

Constantine's move was shrewd. He re-integrated the Christians into Roman society and finally solved the problem of the Principate's inherent illegitimacy. By associating his fate with the Christians' almighty God he created a powerful, nearly inexhaustible source of authority for the ruling monarch. The emperor was now God's chief representative on earth. But Constantine and his successors were forced to realize that getting involved in the Church's affairs had its drawbacks. The early Church was divided over such theological issues as the relationship between God, his son and the Holy Spirit; to modern observers such niceties may appear trivial, but for contemporaries they were worth going to war for. Not accidentally, the trenches of the sectarian divide roughly resembled cultural schisms already visible in the 3rd century: the breaking away of various regional churches, mainly in the eastern provinces, became a major burden for the empire and prepared, indirectly and in the long run, for the defection of Syria and Mesopotamia – the sphere of eastern Hellenism – to the Muslim Arabs in the 7th century.

Under Constantine, the empire's centre of gravity moved irreversibly eastwards. In 326, a new capital was inaugurated which bore the emperor's name: Constantinople, ancient Byzantium, a Christian capital from the very beginning, home to its own Senate and magistrates. Here, the emperor and his court were closer to the resources of the wealthy East, and the city controlled the strategically important straits of the Dardanelles. After more than a millennium, Rome was rejected as the empire's political nerve centre. And so were the ancient traditions it stood for: the triumph of Christianity in its various denominations was almost complete, and paganism – even though there were a few minor pockets of resistance, most notably the old capital's senatorial aristocracy – was in agony. When he became sole emperor in 361, Constantine's nephew Julian tried to reform and restore paganism by overlaying it with the hierarchic structures of the Christian church, but soon he had to realize that he had tried to resuscitate a corpse. As a consequence, his attempt to roll back the wheel of history remained just a minor episode: the emperor was killed on a Persian campaign in 363, and his pagan 'Church' died with him. The over-hasty retreat from military action prompted by his successor led to a disgraceful defeat, and the Sasanians occupied the strategically important town of Nisibis in Mesopotamia.

The Persians, however, were not to remain the emperors' main concern for long. The menace of migrating tribes returned suddenly when a large group of Goths, fleeing the Huns, appeared on the Lower Danube and asked for permission to settle as Roman allies (*foederati*). Although the Romans usually turned down such requests when brought forward by entire tribal groups, they made an exception in this case. Soon, however, the situation spun out of control, not least because of the mismanagement of Roman officials. The Goths clashed with a numerically superior Roman army under the command of the emperor Valens near Adrianople in Thrace. For the empire, the battle ended in disaster: Valens was killed, an army of 20,000 men annihilated. The Roman legions never recovered fully from Adrianople; their ranks were filled with an increasing number of tribesmen who maintained, even as Roman soldiers, their allegiance to their leaders. Henceforth,

Roman armies and migrating Germanic tribes in arms were often hard to distinguish.

Following the death of the emperor Theodosius (379–395), the empire was divided between his two sons: Arcadius received the Greek East, Honorius the Latin West. The two sections irreversibly drifted apart. The stronger East managed to divert the bulk of the migrating tribes to the West, where their impact was devastating. Scholars are divided on the question whether the tribes encountered an empire in agony, crippled by internal strife and economic crisis, or whether Rome was, even at the turn from the 4th to the 5th century, a thriving polity, just accidentally swept away by hordes of marauding barbarians. Either way, the sheer facts are daunting: the Visigoths entered Italy (401); the Vandals, Suebi and Alans crossed the Rhine (406), from where Roman troops had been transferred to Italy the year before; Rome was captured and looted by the Visigoths (410); the Suebi, Burgunds, Visigoths and Vandals established de facto autonomous kingdoms in Gaul, Spain and North Africa (411–429); the Vandals captured and looted Rome (455). The long decline of the western empire ended in 476, when the Roman general Odoacer, of Germanic origin himself, deposed the last emperor Romulus ('Augustulus'), who, ironically, was named after the mythic founder of Rome.

Was this the end of Rome? In one sense, it was; in many other senses, clearly not. The western monarchy ceased in 476, but many of the institutions that made Rome did not. There were still the Senate, the consuls, praetorian prefects and numerous other officials. There was, physically, the city of Rome, the Eternal City which stands, manifold menaces notwithstanding, including various enemy attacks, traffic problems and incapable politicians, till the present day. There was also the Church, which had taken over many of the administrative duties in the towns and cities and which stood, with its learned higher clergy, for cultural and spiritual continuity. There was, of course, the second Rome, Constantinople, which became increasingly Greek in language and style, but strongly maintained the awareness of its Roman origin.

The eastern emperors, the rulers of the empire of the *rhomaioi*, as it was called in Greek, never really abandoned their claim to supremacy over the West, until Byzantium finally fell in 1453.

And there was, first and foremost, the idea into which the Roman empire had gradually been transformed. When Europe became fragmented, once more, into petty tribal kingdoms, the idea of empire proved powerful enough to survive and inspire the minds of ambitious rulers. The empire-turned-idea implied that empire was transferrable: *translatio imperii* was one of the dominant political ideologies in medieval and early modern Europe. It meant that the crown of empire was handed down from the Assyrians to the Babylonians and from them to the Persians, Greeks and finally Romans. The course of its onward journey depended on the observer's point of view: Otto of Freising, a German bishop of the 12th century, regarded Longobards, Franks and the Holy Roman empire as the Romans' natural heirs; the French poet Chrétien de Tours, a contemporary of Otto's, saw in France the logical continuation of the Roman empire; and Richard de Bury, an English intellectual, politician and cleric of the 14th century, believed that the English were the predestined caretakers for Rome's legacy. Constantinople was the 'second Rome', Moscow, its cultural and religious offspring, the 'third Rome' and Washington was – in the eyes of the founding fathers of God's chosen country – a 'fourth Rome'. Napoleon styled himself as a reincarnation of the Roman Caesars. And British thinkers, such as John Robert Seeley and Charles Dilke, the reformist politician, took Rome as a model for the British empire, which they emphatically advocated. The fascination with the Roman empire endures: is its fate the writing on the wall for imperial powers of later epochs, not least the United States? Its apparent relevance to the current situation may explain the persistent presence of ancient Rome in modern popular culture.

Did the year 476 then mean an end to Rome? Rather, when considering the enormous impact the empire had on European history since then, one is inclined to believe that it instead marked a new beginning.

# THE EARLY EMPIRES OF SOUTH ASIA

## 323 BC–AD 500

ROBIN CONINGHAM AND MARK MANUEL

When thinking of the mechanisms behind the term 'empire' in an Indian context, many consider the Anglo-Indian civil and military hierarchies which underpinned Britain's 'jewel in the crown' – the Raj – the exemplar. The nature of these hierarchies was reinforced at the coronation of each British ruler, none more explicitly so than when George V was proclaimed King-Emperor in the gateway of Delhi's Mughal fortress in front of an audience of 80,000 on 12 December 1911. As Kaisar-i-Hind, George became the master of 315 million subjects and over 5 million sq. km (1.9 million sq. miles), stretching from Persia in the west and China in the north to the eastern borders of Burma.

For all its apparent uniformity, the Raj was subdivided into a mosaic of directly administered provinces, tribal agencies largely run by elders, and over 500 princely states. Viceroys therefore had not only to contend with governors and nawabs, maharajas, nizams, mehtars, rajas, badshahs and a wali within each domain, but also with indistinct borders shared with a variety of other figures ranging from the Shah of Persia and the Emir of Afghanistan to the theocratic Dalai Lama of Tibet. The complexities of late 19th-century and early 20th-century India provide an extremely useful guide to the complexities of the region's first empires, which emerged at a time when historical records and inscriptions offer only partial coverage and need to be understood with reference to archaeology. The comparisons also display the difficulties of imposing imperial control over communities that inhabit different environmental settings, and that enjoy very different levels of social, economic and ideological integration with the centre.

The Raj's cadre of archaeologists and historians were keen to investigate their imperial antecedents, and viewed the earliest emergence of states in the Ganges valley and the northwest Indus region as the direct result of earlier waves of soldiers and administrators bringing imperial ideas and technology from the west. Sir John Marshall, Director-General of the Archaeological Survey of India between 1902 and 1928, saw clear evidence of Persian and Hellenistic imperial connections during his

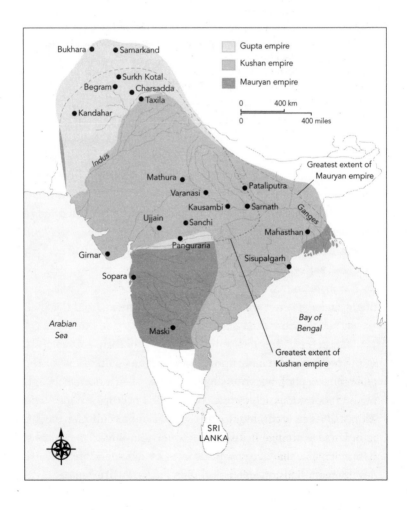

**KEY DATES**

| | |
|---|---|
| c. 550 BC | Annexation of Gandhara by Achaemenid empire |
| 326 BC | Conquest of Alexander the Great |
| 321 BC | Chandragupta Maurya founds the Mauryan dynasty |
| 272 BC | Asoka ascends to the Mauryan throne |
| 265 BC | Conquest of Kalinga, and Asoka's subsequent conversion to Buddhism |
| 185 BC | Collapse of Mauryan empire and emergence of Sunga dynasty |
| AD 60 | Kushan empire emerges in Bactria and Sogdiana |
| 105–127 | Kushan empire expands into Ganges basin under Vima Kadphises |
| 225 | Kushan empire collapses due to Sasanid pressure |
| 280 | Rise of the Gupta empire |
| 409 | Unifying campaigns of Chandragupta II |
| 530 | Invasions of north India by the Hephthalites and demise of Gupta's empire |

excavations of the city of Taxila in the Punjab. Sir Mortimer Wheeler, one of his successors as Director-General, sought and found similar evidence of an initial Persian foundation at the Bala Hisar or 'High Fort' of Charsadda in the vale of Peshawar. Not only did Wheeler suggest that such settlements were originally outposts of the Persian empire, he also suggested that the collapse of that empire under the onslaught of Alexander resulted in a migration of craftsmen to the east, providing the nascent states of the Ganges with the crafts of empire.

More recent scholars highlight the uniquely South Asian character of the region's states and empires and view the writings of Wheeler, and other earlier European scholars, as deliberately downplaying the region's indigenous achievements. Indeed, they suggest that ancient India and its early communities were classified as culturally stagnant in order to legitimize British rule. Whichever perception is correct, it is undeniable that two powerful forces have influenced South Asia's development – fusion and fission. This chapter will examine three of the earliest attempts to fuse distinct geo-political entities over large expanses of South Asia during its Early Historic period. Acknowledged by many as representing India's 'golden age', the successive Mauryan, Kushan and Gupta empires introduced key imperial characteristics which shaped the course of South Asian history for 2,000 years.

## The Mauryan empire

The Mauryan empire is frequently identified as the first example of a unified India, rising as it did from internecine fighting between kingdoms in the Ganges valley in the 4th century BC. Its founder, Chandragupta Maurya, exploited the power vacuum resulting from Alexander the Great's excursions into northwest India and seized control of the kingdom of Magadha, proclaiming himself king in 321 BC. Imposing hegemony from the Hindu Kush mountain range in the west to the Brahmaputra delta in the east, and from the foothills of the Himalayas in the north to the Deccan plateau in the south, Chandragupta Maurya fused together one of the largest empires witnessed in early South Asia.

### Mauryan literature, art and architecture

Our knowledge of the Mauryan empire comes from a limited number of textual sources – namely the *Arthasastra*, the writings of Megasthenes and the inscriptions of Asoka Maurya. The *Arthasastra* is a political treatise widely believed to have been compiled by Kautilya, Chandragupta Maurya's chief minister. Dating to the formative years of the Mauryan empire during the 4th century BC, it was never intended to be theoretical and the records of Megasthenes, Seleucid ambassador to Chandragupta Maurya's court, frequently corroborate its advice. Finally, many aspects of the empire's spatial, ethnic and administrative characteristics have been reconstructed from the rock and pillar edicts of Chandragupta's grandson, Asoka.

The *Arthasastra* details the idealized structure of a kingdom, providing us with an unparalleled insight into the philosophy of Mauryan political, military and economic strategy during the 4th century. Kautilya advised that all neighbouring kingdoms were enemies, but that distant lands were potential allies. Taking this categorization further, he considered strong kingdoms to be 'foes', weak kingdoms fit only to be 'exterminated' and kingdoms facing internal problems to be 'vulnerable'. This formative Mauryan philosophy dictated that it was the duty of prosperous kingdoms (like themselves) to extend their control over the weak through a combination of military campaigns and covert operations. Considering the rapid expansion of the Mauryans through northern India, it would appear that this was not merely a theoretical approach, but one which was actually realized. Once conquered, the *Arthasastra* also provided advice as to the organization and administration of a new province. It advocated the appointment of a prince or member of the royal family as governor but warned that princes may be a source of danger, and that competition between them could lead to wars of succession and the use of provincial forces against one another, as occurred with the bloody accession of Asoka in 272 BC.

Having removed fraternal threats to his new throne, Asoka planned the annexation of the last independent state of northern India, Kalinga. Trained for this task by governing Taxila as viceroy, Asoka led a brutal campaign and caused 100,000 deaths and 150,000 deportations. Appalled at the suffering that he had caused, Asoka revoked Kautilya's guidance and pursued a Buddhist-aligned philosophy of Dharma, which forsook violence. Far from being politically naive, the success of Asoka's new campaigns is illustrated by his bloodless expansion of hegemony over Sri Lanka, where his son converted the court to Buddhism. Asoka's edicts also record that he sent missionaries to his Hellenistic neighbours, but the spread of Buddhism into central and eastern Asia was only to occur later during Kushan times.

There is little extant Mauryan art or architecture, such monuments having been remodelled in later times, but the remnants suggest a centralized monumental style. Mirroring the iconoclasm of contemporary heterodoxical traditions, we have no images of the Mauryans themselves and the most striking survivals are Asoka's pillars which carried the emperor's edicts. Encapsulating his philosophy, these highly polished sandstone pillars were mostly quarried at Chunar on the Ganges and were surmounted by capitals bearing elephants, bulls, lions and horses. Reminiscent of Persian pillar styles, similarities may also be drawn between the Persian *apadana* (a pillared throne-room) and a rectangular pillared hall excavated in the precincts of the Mauryan capital, Pataliputra. This elite construction dwarfs the rectangular brick-built merchant houses of Bhita which comprised simple ranges of rooms set around a central courtyard. Much more remains of Mauryan Buddhist monuments, including Asoka's great stone stupas at Sanchi and Taxila. Built over relics of the Buddha and his disciples or at the scene of notable events, these solid 10-m (33-ft) high mounds represent clear imperial investment. Less well preserved are the smaller apsidal constructions that frequently accompany them, such as the shrine at Sarnath, where the Buddha first preached.

## Mauryan social and political structure

Asoka's rule witnessed the Mauryan empire at its zenith, as it fused much of the Indian subcontinent under a single political entity. Ancient historians have used the scant sources to suggest the presence of a highly centralized empire ruled from Pataliputra, modern Patna, through a council of ministers and imperially appointed provincial governors. Physically, this division is supported by the pre-eminent size of the capital Pataliputra (1350 ha, 336 acres) and the monumental nature of its timber defences. There was a second tier of fortified provincial capitals at Taxila, Ujjain, Tosali, Sisupulgarh, Maski, Mahasthan and Suvarnagiri, with further categories of sub-provincial cities like Bhita and then towns and villages. Administrative activities, such as markets and mints, may have been reserved for higher-order centres, while the lower-order settlements were purely agricultural.

Despite apparent corroboration between archaeology and the *Arthasastra*, a number of recent scholars have argued that Mauryan centralization is over-emphasized and note that there was little state investment in communication networks and that the provincial capitals were all already established before Mauryan hegemony. This is not to suggest that the Mauryans did not exercise control over large areas, but that their empire was not necessarily uniformly administered or that it was fully centralized. One scholar, for example, has suggested that the distribution of Asokan edicts indicates an ideological, rather than political, claim over the landscape and that the Mauryans co-ordinated a network of shared social, ritual and cultural ties rather than a centralized empire.

## The decline of the Mauryans and their legacy

The integration imposed by the Mauryan dynasty weakened in the 2nd century BC. Kingdoms that had succumbed to Mauryan domination began to reassert their identities and the Hellenistic rulers of Afghanistan expanded southwards. Events came to a climax when Pushyamitra Sunga, commander-in-chief of the Mauryan army, murdered Asoka's grandson and proclaimed himself the founder of a new dynasty. Cultural and ideological ties broken, the newly emergent Sunga state became increasingly restricted to the Gangetic heartland.

The Mauryan empire was the first recorded attempt to fuse the disparate populations of localized kingdoms into a conglomeration of kingdoms, chiefdoms and dynasties within a centralized polity. Whether the Mauryans developed an empire in the modern sense of the term is debatable, but their cultural influence was widely spread, particularly along key trade routes. Kautilya's formative strategy of brutal conquest was replaced in the 3rd century BC by Asoka who undertook conquest by Dharma. By twining central Mauryan hegemony with Buddhist proselytization of the peripheries, Asoka achieved a far greater influence in the region than his grandfather. His method of fusing disparate religions, languages and ethnic identities into a unity remains an ideal for South Asia's rulers, and it is no coincidence that when India achieved independence from the British empire, the new state chose one of Asoka's pillars as its national emblem.

## The Kushan empire

The rise of the Kushan empire marks a distinct shift in power from the Ganges valley to the Northwest. Central Asia and the Indian subcontinent were bound into a single political entity. This movement is also reflected in the emergence of a very different social, political and economic system. From territorial holdings in Central Asia in the 2nd century BC, the Kushan dynasty first asserted regional hegemony under Vima Kadphises in the 2nd century AD and remained in power until 375. A nomadic tribe, the Kushans were driven from their homelands and settled in Bactria in modern Afghanistan. Expanding into Kashmir, they found themselves acting as a buffer between the two ancient superpowers of the Romans and the Han by the 2nd century BC.

It was this unique vacuum between the ancient world's most powerful empires that allowed the Kushans to expand as they established control of the key trade route between the two states – the famed Silk Road. Constructing fortified strong-points at Dalverzin-tepe in Uzbekistan and Begram in Afghanistan, the Kushans were able to extract revenue from passing traders as reflected in the horde of Roman glass and metal and Chinese lacquer work recovered from a storeroom in the latter city. The presence of carved ivories from the Ganges in the hoard indicates the Kushan grip on the branch routes into South Asia, controlled from Mathura on the Jamuna river, Sirsukh in the Taxila valley and Peshawar at the gates of the Khyber pass.

### Kushan art, architecture and literature

For many years the chronology of the Kushan empire had been constructed from coins or oblique references within Chinese literature. This changed with the discovery of an inscription at Rabatak in Afghanistan in 1993, which revolutionized our knowledge. Written in the Bactrian language, the inscription provides a definitive king-list, as well as a list of the Kushans' provincial cities in northern India, including Kausambi and Pataliputra. The inscription is now supported by a number of documents and letters, discovered through the illegal looting of sites, which detail records of land-ownership across a large swath of the Silk Road from northern Pakistan to the Turfan Oasis in the west of China. This broad distribution and the common use of Bactrian script indicate the influence of the language which flourished under Kushan rule and provided a lingua franca for administrators and travelling traders alike.

Unlike the Mauryan use of existing cities, many of the Kushan strongholds had fresh foundations, such as the examples in the Taxila valley. Here, the old Hellenistic city of Sirkap was abandoned and a new site, Sirsukh, was created nearby. It enclosed an area of 1,370 x 1,000 m (4,510 x 3,280 ft) within a 5.5-m (18-ft) thick wall strengthened by a rounded berm. The layout of the city and the rounded stirrup bastions that punctuated the wall demonstrate strong links with the military architecture of Central Asia. The absence of thick occupation deposits within the enclosure suggests that Sirsukh may have housed a mobile force who could maintain control over a wide area, and similar plans have been identified at Begram and Dalverzin-tepe.

This investment in fortified strong-points reflects Kushan domination of a potentially hostile landscape and it can be assumed that speed and mobility allowed them to control key access points and regulate the trade networks that flowed along the Silk Road. There was a constant struggle between the Han, Central Asian princes, Romans and Parthians to establish control over this route. The Kushans established themselves as the dominant middle-men and this intercontinental trade network not only facilitated the movement of goods, but also the exchange of art, architecture, religion and philosophy.

Although the Kushans had a favoured style of military architecture, it is clear that they did not attempt to impose a single religious tradition on their empire but rather patronized key regional cults. Vima

Kadphises' son, Kanishka (127–147), thus dedicated a major ceremonial complex at Surkh Kotal in Afghanistan which combined dynastic statues with a fire-temple but also established a major Buddhist stupa at Shahji-Dheri, in Peshawar to the south. His coinage demonstrates similar plurality, and he was equally happy to be portrayed with the Hellenistic deity Helios, the Iranian divinity Adsho and the Buddha, whose identities were confirmed in Greek script. In particular, the reign of Kanishka is associated with a dramatic rise in the number of Buddhist monasteries, some newly established and some constructed at already significant sites.

This plurality of religious devotion and patronage is also evident in Kushan art. While the Mauryans were largely iconoclastic, Kushan art focused on the individual, and it is no coincidence that the Gandhara and Mathura schools of sculpture emerged at this time. Originally an important centre of Jainism, the Kushans established Buddhist shrines and stupas at Mathura when it became their southern capital. Well known for its production of Buddhas and Bodhisattvas, the Kushans commissioned their own images, including an outstanding life-size image of Kanishka carrying a sword and ceremonial mace. Even in the Buddhist heartland, however, the Kushans patronized less mainstream cults as indicated by the presence of a monumental naga, or snake shrine, at Sonkh, 22.5 km (14 miles) south of Mathura. Representing an attempt to incorporate a less centralized cult into their pantheon, it epitomizes the methods by which Kushan elites incorporated disparate regional populations into their empire.

## Kushan social and political structure

Although the Kushan were masters at utilizing regional cults and traditions, as in the case of Kajula Kadphises who depicted himself as Augustus on a curule chair, this makes our understanding of their social and political structure more difficult. The Mathura statue of his son, Kanishka, is inscribed with the title 'Great King, King of Kings, Son of God', and it has been suggested that this indicates the

Kushans adopted the South Asian concept of a universal ruler or Chakravartin. Son of God by title, the Rabatak inscription suggests that imperial administration was enforced by local officials, such as Nukunzuk the Ashtwalg and Shafar the Karalrang. It is also clear from Chinese records that client rulers were installed in peripheral areas like Kashgar, and that treaties were signed with petty rulers close to vulnerable passes such as with the rajas of Odi or Swat. Unlike the Mauryan system of a single imperial capital, the Kushan response to ruling an empire containing many different ethnicities, religions and languages stretching across two distinct regions was to operate from multiple capitals. With a summer capital in Begram, a winter capital in Mathura and a transitional capital in Peshawar, Kushan rulers were able to move annually between Central and South Asia. Moving the imperial powerbase from north to south ensured that the disparate parts of the empire were unified, and individual cities were governed by a mixture of princely viceroys and governors. Combining earlier Persian and Hellenistic traditions with concepts of divine kingship reinforced the operational flexibility of the Kushan emperors.

## The decline of the Kushans and their legacy

After the death of Vasudeva (191–225), the last of the Great Kushans, the empire was divided into eastern and western halves. At the same time as the rise of Ardashir, who had defeated the Parthian king and established the Sasanian dynasty in Persia, within 15 years the Sasanians had captured much of the western half of the Kushan empire. The major cities of Peshawar and Taxila were to fall to Ardashir's son Shapur I by 270 and their Gangetic territory was lost in the late 3rd century. The Kushan kings were left with a small territory in Central Asia, but were practically now no more than vassals of the newly emergent state. The dynasty held on until the 5th century when they were defeated by the Hephthalites who were to wreak havoc across much of northern India.

The Kushan empire successfully fused southern and Central Asia by respecting and patronizing regional traditions, while creating a central fortified line of communication from the Oxus to the Ganges. The Kushan methods of imperial rule were not revolutionary, indeed they copied and imitated previous Persian, Hellenistic and Indian rulers, but their choice of combinations was unique. Their coinage and religious patronage demonstrate these combinations, as does their ability to harness the newly emerged genre of iconic sculpture and to produce some of southern Asia's first imperial portraits. Fuelled by the luxury trade between east and west, they were also the first to establish formal winter and summer capitals, a feature which was to become an annual characteristic of later empires struggling to fuse the disparate communities of South Asia and its mountainous barriers to the north. Other than a distinct military and monastic architecture and iconic coinage, the Kushans' strategy of adopting regional customs and traditions had resulted in there being little linkage between the Kushans and modern South Asian communities who are greatly indebted to the Mauryans and Guptas. However, it was during Kushan hegemony that Buddhism began to spread along the Silk Road to Central Asia, China and beyond. This new branch of Buddhism, Mahayana, differed from the traditional Theravada Buddhism of South Asia, and was heavily influenced by Hellenistic and Persian ideas. The spread of Mahayana Buddhism was to have a huge impact upon the later development of east Asian ruling dynasties, which outlasted and superseded the Kushan empire from which it emerged.

### The Gupta empire

With the decline of Kushan power in the northwest, their Indian empire was fragmented into petty domains run by individuals who termed themselves maharajas and rajas. One such princeling was Chandragupta, who married a daughter of the Licchavi clan, and received the kingdom of Magadha as dowry. Reviving the Kushan title of 'Great King of Kings' or 'maharajadhiraja', Chandragupta and his son, Samudragupta (335–75), in the 4th century mounted a series of military campaigns and extended hegemony over the old kingdoms of the Ganges, exacting tribute or suzerainty from states to the south. Described by a descendant as 'the exterminator of all kings... whose fame was tasted by the waters of the four oceans', Samudragupta's direct control was restricted to the Ganges basin with a series of client-kingdoms extending down the eastern coast of India.

It was during the reign of Chandragupta II that the Gupta empire consolidated control of northern India from the Arabian Sea to the Bay of Bengal during a series of campaigns between 388 and 409. This military strategy was paralleled by a political one, when Chandragupta II's daughter married Rudrasena II, king of the Vakataka tribe, in a move that secured the southern borders. In order to consolidate his power in the west, Chandragupta II established a second capital at Ujjain and secured trade routes to the newly annexed Indian Ocean ports on the west coast. These ports, Broach, Chaul, Kalyan and Cambay, traded with the Mediterranean and western Asia and exported spices, peppers, sandalwood, pearls, semi-precious stone, indigo and herbs. In exchange they imported horses from Arabia, ivory from Ethiopia and goods from as far away as Madagascar and Zanzibar. On the east coast, ports such as Tamralipti, Ghantashala and Kadura were engaged in equally extensive trade with China and southeast Asia, allowing the Guptas access to the maritime Silk Road.

## Gupta art, architecture and literature

Ending the quest for the centralized socio-economic and religious integration of the Asokan ideal, the Gupta era is also referred to as the 'Classical Age of India' and is renowned for its commitment to art, architecture and Sanskrit poetry. Based at the old Mauryan imperial capital of Pataliputra, by the end of the Gupta reign northern India was transformed from a predominantly Buddhist landscape into one where Hindu cults were revived and where feudal land holdings were embedded. This revival was quite unlike that of the Kushan's use of Hindu gods on their coinage, as the Guptas established temples and patronized Brahmans by awarding them landholdings as well as re-establishing pre-Buddhist Vedic sacrifices, such as the Ashvamedha. This ancient rite allowed the king to release a sacrificial horse to wander for a year and then claim all the land through which it had travelled. Unifying imperial territory with Vedic sacrifices re-established the presence of a king of kings within South Asia and the court reinforced its precedence. The Vedic revival was paralleled by a revival in Sanskrit literature, and Chandragupta's court was revered for the presence of nine 'gems', or court poets. These included the dramatist Kalidasa, though another production of the era, the *Kama Sutra*, is rather more widely read today. Representing far more than simple titillation, it embodies the rigid norms of behaviour which governed the Gupta court. Finally, while textual sources record the establishment of Hindu temples throughout Gupta territories, few have survived though many of their Buddhist monuments still stand. The monuments range from the cave shrines and monasteries of their Vakataka sub-rulers at Ajanta, whose frescoes detail the lives of princes and paupers, to the great stupa at Sarnath and the state-sponsored University at Nalanda.

## Gupta social structure and decline

The Gupta emperors, or rather maharajadhirajas, ruled from their capital at Pataliputra and were surrounded by the members of the imperial court. Monumental inscriptions record the close presence of military and security advisers as well as court Brahmans and poets. Details concerning the social and political structure of the kingdom have survived in greater numbers. These records are not state archives but rather individual land-grants inscribed for prosperity on copper plates. From them it is possible to deduce that the core empire was divided into a number of territorial and administrative units, of which the largest was a *bhukti*, or province. The province was in turn subdivided into districts, or *pradesha*, and districts into villages and towns, where representative councils were involved in decision-making. As each copper plate represents the transfer of land from royal ownership to individual ownership, it is clear that the Guptas developed a

**XV** (above) Silver plate showing a Sasanian King of Kings hunting lions. The crown identifies him as Vahram V, also known as Vahram Gur (420–438), who was famous for his hunting exploits.

**XVI** (left) Sasanian plate with hunting scene from Iran, in silver with mercury gilding. The crown seems to identify the king as a 5th-century ruler, either Peroz or Kavad I.

**XVII** (right) Silver Sasanian drinking vessel from Iran, depicting the head of a horse that possibly reflects a hunting scene.

**XVIII** (above) A wall painting of a Roman villa, found in the House of Marcus Lucretius Fronto in Pompeii, preserved by the ash of Vesuvius for almost 2,000 years.

**XIX** (below) Roman material culture was eagerly adopted in the provinces. The Pont du Gard, a Roman aqueduct in southern Gaul (50 m high and 275 m long), was probably built in the 1st century AD to supply the city of Nemausus (Nîmes) with water.

**XX** A Gandharan ivory from the Kushan city of Begram, depicting two women standing below a balustrade, adorned with striped *dhotis* and wearing elaborate headdresses and jewelry. The great hoard of which this ivory formed a part demonstrates the wealth of goods flowing through the Kushan domain at the centre of trade between east and west.

**XXI** (opposite) When the First Qin Emperor died in 210 BC at the age of 49, he had already constructed a vast underground palace complex in which to enjoy the spirit world. Excavation of extensive pits at the site has uncovered thousands of life-size clay soldiers as well as civilian officials and servants – the Terracotta Army. This infantryman, mass produced but with individual features, is a typical example.

**XXII** (above) In 1980 archaeologists found exquisitely made half-sized gilt bronze models of two of the First Qin Emperor's personal vehicles. One was this light, fast chariot that may have been for the emperor to use on his posthumous hunting trips.

**XXIII** (below) The as-yet unexcavated man-made hill containing the mausoleum of the First Qin Emperor.

**XXIV** (above)  In 154 BC the Han emperor Jingdi installed some of his sons as rulers of his vassal kingdoms. One of these was Liu Sheng, king of Zhongshan until his death in 113 BC. Liu Sheng and his queen Dou Wan were buried with great splendour. This pair of tiny bronze leopards with gilded patterning and burning eyes of semi-precious stone were among the burial goods left with Dou Wan. Real leopards lived in the hills of Zhongshan.

**XXV** (below)  The body covering of Queen Dou Wan was made of 2,156 jade plaques held together with gold cord. Her husband Liu Sheng had an even more elaborate suit. Jade (nephrite) had long been valued above all other stone in China for its hardness and lustrous, fragile beauty.

**XXVI** (right) The gilt bronze oil lamp from Dou Wan's tomb in the form of a kneeling serving woman was as practical as it is elegant. The shade could be moved by the little handle to cast the light just where it was wanted, and the woman's wide right sleeve is a chimney to collect soot and reduce the risk of setting furnishings alight.

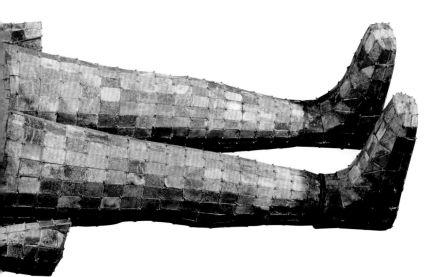

**XXVII** The Han kingdom of Changsha was ruled through the king's officials and vassals, headed by his hereditary chancellor, the Marquis of Dai. In the 1970s the tombs of the first marquis, his wife, and (likely) his son were opened at Mawangdui in today's Changsha. The body and burial goods – including food, textiles and lacquerware – of the marchioness were incredibly well preserved. Before it was replaced by fine porcelain after Han times lacquer was the preferred material for the eating and drinking vessels of the aristocracy. The tableware from the Mawangdui tombs includes this dish as well as a ewer from which water could be poured over diners' fingers.

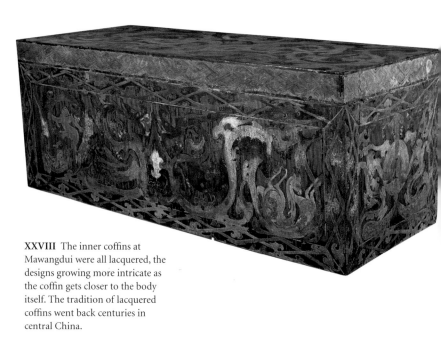

**XXVIII** The inner coffins at Mawangdui were all lacquered, the designs growing more intricate as the coffin gets closer to the body itself. The tradition of lacquered coffins went back centuries in central China.

strategy of permanent land alienation in return for religious, military and administrative services, creating a feudal link between crown and landlords.

Kumaragupta (414–454) was the last undisputed Gupta ruler, but even in his final years internal instability was apparent with the growing strength of the Pushyamitra clan. Such was their threat to the Ganges heartland that Kumaragupta's son, Skandagupta, was given the task of pacifying them. As recorded in his Bhitari inscription, Skandagupta undertook to 'restore the fallen fortunes of his family' and returned to Pataliputra victorious having used the vanquished king as his 'footstool'. On the death of his father, Skandagupta's accession was contested by his older brothers and, though victorious in 455, his authority was continually threatened. While his inscription on the Bhitari pillar merely relates that he 'joined in close conflict with the Huns', the Hephthalite threat to the stability of the Gupta state was very real. The protective ring of client rulers quickly capitulated within 30 years of Skandagupta's death in 467, and the Hephthalites penetrated into the Ganges basin itself. With collection of imperial revenues seriously disrupted and overland trade destabilized, the Gupta empire had collapsed by the middle of the 6th century and a mosaic of petty rulers rose to fill the vacuum. Chinese Buddhist pilgrims witnessed the resulting chaos, and the monk Xuanzang recorded that 'the towns and villages are deserted… and in ruins…. They are filled with wild shrubs and solitary to the last degree'. It would take the advent of Islam before the subcontinent would be united again.

While not as territorially expansive as the Mauryan or Kushan empires, the Gupta era represents a major shift in policy. When the Mauryan and Kushan attempts at centralization ended, a new model of client-kingdoms surrounding the imperial core run by governors was developed. As with the Kushans, they capitalized on the growing international trade routes and sought to maintain and revive earlier traditions by supporting not only Hindu institutions, but also Buddhist, Jain and other local traditions. This delicate political balance and freedom of religion ensured that art and literature from a wide variety of regions and backgrounds was able to prosper. While the Mauryan empire is regarded as the first unified empire of India and the origins of the modern state of India, the Gupta empire is portrayed as its zenith. Often referred to as a 'Golden Age', to many modern Indians the Gupta period was an era during which arts, literature, architecture, religion, music and poetry flourished under a single unified state, ruled by Hindus.

## The nature of early Indian empires

Here we have highlighted the unique nature of 'empires' within India. The phases of fusion and fission evident from the archaeological record testify to the continual quest for a uniform but sustainable pattern of political rule and religious patronage. The Mauryan empire was a decentralized one, its ideology of Dharma disseminated from a series of regional strongholds. The Kushans, remarkably tolerant of regional diversity, were adept at adopting pre-existing religious traditions within their borders. This tolerance, or perhaps astute political strategy, is best demonstrated on Kushan coinage where depictions of Hellenistic, Persian and South Asian deities can be found, often on opposing sides of the same coin. Finally, the Gupta empire is probably the closest of all three ancient dynasties to the modern definition of an empire. It was firmly built around a relationship between an imperial core and vassal states – a solution also followed by the Mughals. Yet it was not until the arrival of the British in the 18th century that the entirety of the subcontinent was brought under the rule of a single polity – and even then this was only brought about by the maintenance of a tenuous web of political alliances between maharajas, nawabs and tribal elders, and the occasional brutal repression of uncooperative elements.

The desire of early British scholars to portray the Raj as the natural successor to earlier Indian empires and post-Independence scholars to portray Indian history as one of unity and cohesion has created Indian empires with pervasive static or retrogressive characteristics. This chapter has demonstrated that the opposite is the case, and that the Early Historic empires of South Asia continually experimented with different combinations of ideology, religious practice and administrative organization to reach a point of territorial sustainability.

# THE EARLY EMPIRES OF CHINA

## 221 BC–AD 220

W. J. F. JENNER

The Qin and Han empires were big. Although their territories varied and were in places ill defined, they never covered less than 1,600 km (1,000 miles) from east to west and from north to south. They were populous: in AD 2 the Han government had nearly 60 million subjects on its books. With the exception of a few frontiers and inaccessible regions, these millions were closely governed by a centralized bureaucracy that imposed a single written language and a high culture and had more control over people's lives than any large state in Europe before the 18th century. In many areas of technology they were ahead of the Roman world. Qin and Han between them set the pattern for Chinese regimes for the next 2,000 years.

The Qin empire, founded in 221 BC, was meant to endure for ever, but actually lasted only 15 years, not long enough to impose any lasting changes on those parts of China that had not long been part of the kingdom of Qin. But the totalitarian bureaucratic dictatorship that had made the state of Qin so effective as a warfare state since the middle of the 4th century BC long survived the Qin empire. It gave Han, the regime that emerged from Qin's wreckage, the tools with which to make an empire that lasted for so long that, by the time it ended in AD 220, the pre-Han world was ancient history.

In 221 BC the king of Qin believed he had transformed the Chinese world. Over the previous nine years his armies – the real-life equivalents of the brigade of imposing terracotta soldiers buried to guard his tomb – had destroyed all the other states of China in a series of blitzkrieg wars. He had imposed unity after a period of over 500 years in which war and the threat of war between rival Chinese states were endemic, and now he wanted a more splendid title for himself than any Chinese ruler before him. He chose *huang di*, a term which implies not just 'emperor', its usual English translation, but also 'god'. He was the First Emperor, his successor would be the Second Emperor, and so it would go on till the Ten Thousandth Emperor. His permanent new order soon turned out to be as much of a delusion as the personal immortality to which he devoted his last years. Eleven years later he was dead, and after four more the Qin empire was gone.

Liu Bang, the Han dynasty's founder, joined the rebellions against Qin after the First Emperor's death as a minor local government official on the run. By skill and luck, he came out on top in the civil wars that followed the fall of Qin, becoming emperor in 202 BC. Far from having a grand plan to change the world, his whole career was one of improvising quick solutions to immediate problems. Yet he and his heirs managed in time to turn a precarious regime into a stable one. The Han empire, which both rejected and continued the Qin model of rule, lasted. After Wang Mang, an imperial in-law, replaced the Han with his own Xin (New) dynasty in AD 8 the most effective resistance to his rule came from peasant rebels; but those who put a new regime in place did so under the banner of Han. A new Han dynasty was created that continued for another 200 years.

## The rise and fall of Qin

Qin began as a poor and backward state on the edge of the Chinese world. Its chiefs had covered the flight from the Wei valley in 771 BC of the former supreme Chinese rulers, known as the Western Zhou, then taken most of the valley for themselves and been recognized as a Chinese state. The Wei valley was well protected by natural defences from rivals to the east, but for over 400 years Qin was a second-rank player in the wars to control China's core area, the north China plain, as it had no direct access to it. It lagged behind the transformation of the central Chinese states.

All this changed in the middle of the 4th century BC. Between 356 and 340 BC Duke Xiao of Qin enforced drastic reforms to strengthen his state and weaken society. These reforms were proposed and implemented by Shang Yang, a political consultant who had come to Qin from the east. Households were organized into groups of five and ten, with each member liable for crimes committed by any other member. Hereditary aristocracy was replaced by a system in which rank could be won only by serving the state in agriculture and war. Feudal relations gave way to direct rule by state officials. Idlers and traders would have their wives and children enslaved. Any comment on the reforms, even praise, was punished.

These and other changes gave the state direct control over its whole population and set it on the way to being a formidable military power. Qin used deliberately harsh measures to compel its subjects to obey it and serve its interests. Although Shang Yang's methods were somewhat relaxed after his death, the essentials were maintained. They worked. Qin grew stronger, pushing back its eastern neighbours and making bold moves to the south. In 316 BC Qin took the Sichuan basin, and in 278 BC the capital of the main Yangtze power, Chu. Diplomatic and military ruthlessness gave Qin strategic domination over the rich north China plain. In 260 BC the Qin army reportedly buried alive 400,000 soldiers who had surrendered. However, Qin ruthlessness was not reckless: it did not devour territory faster than the Qin dictatorship could absorb it.

This step-by-step approach changed after the future First Emperor came of age as king of Qin and took full power in 238 BC. Seventeen years later he had conquered the whole Chinese world and made himself emperor. His ambitions and his vanity knew no limits, as is clear from the inscriptions full of extravagant praise for his own achievements he had carved around the empire. After the conquests the harsh Qin dictatorship was forced upon a huge new population that resented it. The First Emperor used his power not just to impose unified laws, regulations, script, weights and measures on the whole empire, but also to make his new subjects work on vast projects. The

Xiongnu

Wuhuan

Zhongshan

Luoyang

Changsha

Lingqu Canal

South China Sea

Xianyang

Chang'an
(Xi'an)

Dunhuang

Yellow

Yangtze

Bay of Bengal

Jiaohe

Ferghana

Additional Han territory

Loosely held Han territory

Qin territory, later taken over by Han

Loosely held Qin territory

400 km

400 miles

0

0

biggest were war on the northern frontier and building, manning and supplying the Great Wall. This required huge numbers of conscripts from all over the empire. A network of highways was built from the capital Xianyang. Hundreds of thousands of families were forcibly resettled. Seven hundred thousand labourers were made to build his vast palaces and mausoleum. The severity of Qin rule eventually became self-defeating. In 209 BC rebellions spread all across the newly

### KEY DATES

| | |
|---|---|
| 247 BC | Ying Zheng, future First Emperor, becomes king of Qin |
| 221 BC | Shi Huang di proclaims himself First Qin Emperor after conquering other Chinese states |
| 209–206 BC | Widespread rebellions in conquered states end Qin |
| 202 BC | Liu Bang wins post-Qin civil wars, becomes Han emperor |
| 154 BC | Han vassal kings lose much power after failed rising |
| 127–119 BC | Massive Han offensives against Xiongnu on northern frontier |
| 108–90 BC | Han conquests in today's Xinjiang and Central Asia |
| 51 BC | Xiongnu shanyu (khan) accepts Han suzerainty |
| AD 8 | End of Western Han. Wang Mang makes himself emperor of Xin (New) dynasty |
| 17–23 | Risings bring down Wang Mang regime |
| 25 | Liu Xiu (Emperor Guangwudi) reestablishes Han dynasty (Eastern Han) |
| 91–101 | Han power in parts of Xinjiang restored |
| 107 | Beginning of resistance wars by Qiang people in west of empire |
| 166– | Bitter struggles between court eunuchs and regular officials |
| 175 | Definitive texts of five Confucian classics inscribed on stone in Luoyang |
| 184 | Yellow Turbans rebellion |
| 190 | Warlord Dong Zhuo destroys capital Luoyang |
| 220 | Last Han emperor deposed |

conquered territories, with locally recruited petty officials using their knowledge of the system to bring it down.

The Qin dictatorship had depended on an extraordinarily effective bureaucracy in which every post had its job description that the holder had to fulfil to the letter. No official, no matter how high or how low, had any security of tenure. He could be dismissed or punished for failure. Among the terracotta figures found in the First Emperor's huge burial complex are a few civilian officials. They do not look as impressive as the soldiers, but with their writing brushes they were as essential to state power within Qin as the armies were for dealing with external enemies. The officials kept detailed information on everyone so that no one could escape the demands of the state. They even reported how the rainfall was affecting the crops place by place and kept records of the girth of each draught ox each year so that their keepers could be rewarded or punished. The Qin information dictatorship was continued by Han.

A web of laws and regulations spelled out what officials and commoners must and must not do. If a criminal offence was committed legal officials had to find out exactly what had happened and then apply the correct punishments as specified in the code. There were regulations on how to investigate a crime, interrogate suspects, and write up the investigation. Oral statements had to be written down and put into the case file. If something in a statement seemed wrong the suspect had to be questioned again, and asked to explain any discrepancies. Torture was only to be used as a last resort because statements made under duress were unreliable, and its use had to be minuted in the file. Investigating officers could be punished for failing to get the truth. Qin legal culture was a formidable assertion of the state's determination to know everything. With modifications, Han continued to use Qin law.

## Improvising Han

Liu Bang joined the rebellions against Qin as a minor official and emerged from the seven years of chaos and civil war that followed to become the first emperor of a new dynasty, Han, in 202 BC. He rose from nowhere to obtain supreme power by knowing how to find a quick solution in a crisis. He was a fixer, even something of a trickster, and a clear-sighted political realist who knew how to get out of trouble and build coalitions. Although no soldier himself, he could use generals. When his armies took over the former Qin heartlands in 206 BC, he kept them in working order. His people seized Qin's military maps and central databases, and put the local bureaucracy into the service of his new local regime. The state machinery of pre-imperial Qin gave him a firm power base that enabled him to win the civil wars that followed the end of Qin and become Han emperor.

Beyond the firmly controlled Qin heartlands his empire was shaky from the outset. He did not have the resources to impose direct rule over the whole of China. He kept promises to allies in the civil wars to recognize them as vassal kings outside the Qin core area, and when they rose against him this justified crushing them. Replacing them as vassal kings with members of the Liu family also led to troubles for his successors when they in turn rebelled, but it bought time for Han to consolidate itself. None of the rebellions succeeded. Under his successors direct rule was extended over more of the empire and vassal kings and marquises lost most of their powers. One problem, however, that was never solved was that of the northern frontier.

## Emperors and officials

In theory the Han system was run by an all-powerful emperor. The founders of both Han dynasties understood the real world and could use power. They rose from obscurity in times of chaos and had to be realists to take the throne by force. Liu Bang's widow, Lü Zhi, had been his active and tough-minded partner throughout his dangerous career. From his death in 195 BC until her own 15 years later she ruled alone, first as regent for her son then, after his death, as reigning empress. This offended traditional views about a woman's place, but as a co-founder of the Han dynasty she was able to defy them. However, by trying to arrange a takeover of the Liu family regime by her own Lü family, she went too far. She made too many enemies, and the Lü were slaughtered once she died. After the founders few emperors made any impact. Many of them were chosen precisely because they were young children whose powers would be handled by regents.

Nearly all premodern Chinese historians of Qin and Han have given most of their attention to court politics, central government and the most powerful regional leaders. Their accounts show weaknesses in the dynastic system that one might think would have been fatal to it. There was no fixed rule, such as that of primogeniture, to determine succession. Another related weakness was that an emperor's wife did not necessarily have the same interests as the ruling house until he was dead and her son succeeded him. The higher-ranking wives of an adult emperor all wanted to produce a son and potential heir. This made for vicious struggles. There are plenty of stories of empresses trying to do away with rivals and their sons. Once a palace woman was mother of an emperor or potential emperor she would often use her position to advance her own blood relatives. An empress dowager could work with male relatives and trusted officials to have a son or a malleable young boy of the imperial clan chosen as emperor so as to allow them a long period of regency. The families and factions of rival palace women sometimes fought to the death in the streets or in the law courts. The highest point of imperial in-law power came in AD 8 when one of them, Wang Mang (45 BC–AD 23), replaced the Western Han dynasty with his own Xin (New) dynasty. His life and his regime both ended amid mass uprisings 15 years later. Yet despite all these problems at the centre the machinery of government generally continued to function in the capital and in the provinces.

The one Western Han emperor who was far from ineffectual was Liu Che, known as the emperor Wudi, who came to the throne in 141 BC as a boy of about 15 and ruled until his death in 87. His reign was by far the longest in both Han dynasties, and he was an active emperor who wanted to make progress. Under him men and resources were poured into wars with the Xiongnu, in Central Asia and in the south. However, regular tax and conscription were not enough to pay for these wars. The state had to establish monopolies in iron and salt, and levy duties on alcohol. His activism put intolerable strains on state and society. Weak emperors sometimes did less harm.

The next Han dynasty, later known as Eastern Han as it made its capital in Luoyang, presented itself as a restoration of the earlier or Western Han based in Chang'an. Although it was different from Western Han in some important ways, its emperors were also rather ineffective after the founder. The problem of overpowerful families of emperors' mothers continued. Another group who were more prominent than under the Western Han were palace eunuchs. They could be very useful to emperors and empresses who had been brought up under their influence. Unlike palace ladies and intact males, they could move between the harem and the outer world. Especially in the last century of Han rule there were frequent and at times bloody conflicts between the eunuchs and the regular bureaucracy.

All these problems mask the amazing achievement of the Han state in holding together so large an empire for so long, and in creating a Chinese identity that has lasted. Here the legacy of Qin administration proved to be lasting and effective. While rival cliques struggled for control of the palace and of key central government offices the provincial and local government machinery continued to function. Population registers were kept, tax and labour service levied, criminal laws enforced. The Han empire was a triumph of bureaucracy. The day-to-day administrative documents of Han frontier garrisons on the Great Wall that have been preserved in the dry sands of Gansu show government clerks keeping records of the soldiers, their performance in archery tests, their health, their movements and more. The amount of data recorded would tax a modern army's ability to process information. Until the middle of the Eastern Han men were conscripted for military service. The bureaucracy's efforts to keep records and an audit trail can be seen in the cemeteries for convicts who died when building the walls of the Eastern Han capital at Luoyang. With most bodies was a broken piece of brick on which the dead man's place of origin, criminal status, name and date of death were unceremoniously scratched, presumably so that the officials responsible could show where the men missing from their rolls had gone.

Even when magnates gained more control of local government by putting their nominees into jobs, the officials were still Han officials. Only in the final decades of the dynasty were forms of social organization outside the state's actual or nominal control allowed to develop, such as the Five Pecks of Rice cult in the southwest. And Han methods of bureaucratic rule were all continued under its successor states.

## Frontiers

The First Qin Emperor's domains in 221 BC were rather smaller than the ones over which the Eastern Han lost control over 400 years later. At the beginning of the Qin empire China – if we use the label to refer to regions under the rule of Qin or Han – extended in the north from southern Liaoning across to northern Shanxi and Shaanxi. At its northwest edge it included eastern Gansu but not today's Lanzhou. In the southwest direct rule was limited to the fertile Sichuan basin between Chengdu and Chongqing. Only some areas south of the Yangtze had been absorbed into the Chinese world, notably the river plains and lakes of its southern tributaries and the Nanjing, Suzhou and Hangzhou region. Qin opened up an inland route along rivers connected by the well-named Miraculous Canal (Ling Qu) near Guilin to today's Guangdong, but was able to establish no permanent Chinese presence so far south. The great majority of the Qin population lived on and around the north China plain and in the valleys of the Wei, Fen and Luo rivers that flowed into the Yellow river.

The northern frontier was a vital concern of the Qin and Han empires as the Xiongnu, mounted peoples of the grasslands to their north, posed a military threat to the whole of north China. Nomadic pastoralism – living primarily from the animals you keep and moving with them to find pasture – had developed on steppes across Eurasia in the 1st millennium BC. Some pastoralists moved huge distances and interacted along a belt of grasslands from the Black Sea to areas north of China. Well-preserved bodies in Xiongnu and pre-Xiongnu tombs in the Mongolian Republic and southern Siberia show both 'Mongoloid' and 'Caucasian' features.

In aggressive campaigns from 214 BC Qin drove the Xiongnu from the Ordos region (the area of today's Inner Mongolia inside the great northern bend of the Yellow river), and set up garrisons and settlers on both sides of the river. It built the first Great Wall from today's eastern Gansu to the coast, joining up the northern walls of earlier Chinese states. The immense human cost of Qin's forward policy contributed much to the hatred of the Qin regime by its own subjects. The policy was also a disaster for the Xiongnu, who reacted by making themselves a military power.

Being a Xiongnu meant belonging to a political-military confederacy under a leader called the shanyu. The confederacy was made up of many different ethnic or tribal groups, and was a political rather than an ethnic label. In 209 BC, when Qin was weakened by widespread rebellions, the Xiongnu recovered the Ordos region. Under Modun, the patricidal second shanyu, they took over their eastern neighbours and drove the Yuezhi, Indo-European speakers, from western Gansu. In 200 BC the Han founder barely escaped from encirclement by the Xiongnu inside the frontier, near today's Datong in northern Shanxi.

The absence of natural barriers along most of the frontier meant that the Xiongnu could choose where to concentrate their cavalry to push far into China proper. They lived both north and south of the belt of deserts, the Gobi, that divide the grasslands of Inner Mongolia from those in the Mongolian Republic. This gave them strategic depth, and enabled them to keep their families, flocks and herds far from the frontier and Chinese counter-attacks.

The Inner Mongolian grasslands posed a dilemma for the Qin and Han. If they pushed their defence line far enough north to prevent the

Xiongnu from occupying them they had to meet the astronomical cost of feeding garrisons at the end of long overland supply routes. But if Chinese defences were far enough south for convenient supply they were open to attacks by Xiongnu and others who were riding fresh horses that were well fed on the grasslands. Options open to Qin and Han included passive defence, or the Great Wall strategy; counter-attacks and pre-emptive strikes to destroy Xiongnu herds and families north of the desert belt; dividing the Xiongnu with big payments to clients; and a combination of two or more of these. All options were used, and all were expensive. The state had to be strong to make the people meet the costs.

For the first 60 years and more of the Han dynasty the Xiongnu dominated the north, raiding deep into China. Xiongnu power extended into Xinjiang and linked up with the Qiang people of what is now Qinghai, south Gansu and northwest Sichuan. Han tried and failed to buy the Xiongnu off until the reign of the emperor Wudi (140–87 BC).

Wudi launched a series of huge offensives from 127 to 117 BC. The most devastating of these campaigns in 121 BC and 119 BC were co-ordinated deep strikes from several points along the frontier into the northern heartlands of the Xiongnu, killing their people and animals. Han recreated the border defences and compelled settlers to occupy the disputed territories. These wars imposed intolerable losses on both sides. Exhaustion resulted in a comparatively peaceful period until in 101 BC Wudi began a new series of offensive wars that lasted until his death in 87 BC.

There is much first-hand evidence in documents found along the Great Wall on the organization and everyday life of frontier garrisons. With time Han developed a successful policy of dividing the Xiongnu against each other. The Eastern Han succeeded in bringing the Southern Xiongnu into supposed submission and in getting other steppe peoples to drive the Northern Xiongnu away. These policies were not quite the triumphs they seemed. The Southern Xiongnu were allowed to reoccupy the frontier grasslands, and Han power was pulled back from much of northern Shanxi and Shaanxi. The consequences were to be catastrophic. Generations of Southern Xiongnu learned how China worked from the inside. Within a century of the fall of Han they were to sack Luoyang and destroy a Chinese dynasty, the beginning of nearly three centuries in which north China was under barbarian rule. And the removal of the Northern Xiongnu only left a vacuum beyond the northern frontier into which Xianbei, Wuhuan and other steppe peoples moved, who were to cause trouble in the future.

Fears about the Xiongnu drove Han to extend its power and influence into Central Asia, Han's Western Regions. Under Wudi the first strategic move to the west against the Xiongnu was sending an envoy, Zhang Qian, on a dangerous mission far into Central Asia to contact the Xiongnu's old victims the Yuezhi, now resettled west of the Tianshan range, and establish a strategic alliance against the common enemy. Zhang returned around 126 BC, having spent ten years as a prisoner of the Xiongnu and having failed to win the Yuezhi alliance. But he could supply a lot of detailed intelligence about the settled and nomadic peoples of what is now Xinjiang and its western neighbours from Kazakhstan to Afghanistan. This informed Han's next moves. Han settled and walled the lands the Xiongnu had taken from the Yuezhi in the Gansu corridor as far as Dunhuang to 'cut off the Xiongnu's right arm' and stop them linking up with the Qiang of the Tibet-Qinghai highlands. This gave Han access to the Tarim basin. This huge region's inhabitants were mostly 'Caucasian'-featured speakers of Indo-European languages living in widely separated oases.

For the next 200 years and more Han and Xiongnu contended for mastery in Xinjiang. Western Han achieved some spectacular but short-lived military conquests beyond the Tianshan range, including Ferghana in today's Uzbekistan. The small oasis states of the Tarim basin, which controlled movement across a region that is mostly desert, came under direct or indirect Han domination for much of this time. However, those states maintained their own identities, adding Chinese elements to their cultures in which Iranian and Indian

influences were also strong. Their rulers used Han power and connections for their own purposes and were not absorbed into China.
In the end the Xiongnu were beaten and Han could not sustain the
costs of occupation. Contact with China did not end after Han had
left the area, however, and the trade with the Western Regions that
most influenced China was the importing of Buddhism.

Relations with Qiang and other peoples of the Eastern Tibet-
Qinghai plateau were no better than those with the Xiongnu, especially
in the Eastern Han period. The Qiang resisted Chinese rule and reoc-
cupied large areas of the northwest. To the northeast Han extended its
power into southern Liaoning and northern Korea as part of its grand
strategy of containing the Xiongnu.

The southern frontier offered fertile land and far more opportunities for expansion. The mountainous terrain south of the Yangtze river
divided the many peoples living in the valleys and the uplands. The
southern peoples could fight fiercely in defence of their own lands, as
they did right through to the 19th century, but they could not threaten
the existence of the empire.

The colonization of the south was begun by Qin, which established lines of communication to Guangdong, and in the southwest to
the lands south of Sichuan. Much more was done under Han. Wudi's
wars of expansion south of the Yangtze river significantly increased
the size of China. In some places local peoples were subdued, driven
back into the hills or, if they resisted, killed. Elsewhere they were
left alone. Some rulers appeared to have submitted to Han but in
fact maintained their independence. There were islands of Han rule
in today's southernmost provinces of China, as in parts of northern
Vietnam, though large areas were not controlled. Fujian was almost
untouched. Sometimes local cultures were destroyed and the people
uprooted, such as when defeated Yue peoples were forcibly moved to
north of the Yangtze.

By the end of Han the centre of gravity of the Chinese world had
shifted south. Much of the northern and western frontier regions

had in reality been lost to non-Chinese peoples. The Central Asian empire in Xinjiang and beyond, which had been repeatedly won and lost between about 110 BC and AD 150, was gone by the end of the dynasty. In the south, by contrast, the expansion of China along river valleys was to be permanent.

## Society and economy

The great majority of people lived off the land. The main food crops in the north were broomcorn and foxtail millet, which with their relatively low demand for water outside the summer rains were well suited to the unirrigated dry farming techniques that prevailed there. In the wetter climate of the south rice was the staple crop. Millets and rice had both been grown in China for at least 7,000 years before Qin and Han. Those who could afford it ate wheat.

In the 300 years before Han, farmers had swapped a largely Neolithic toolkit of wood, shell, stone and bone for iron-bladed tools, thus greatly increasing the output of food. Without that agricultural revolution there would not have been the grain to feed all the changes in the Chinese world from the 5th century BC on through the Han period, including the growth of population, state power, manufacturing, trade, cities and armies. Agricultural development continued under Han. Although it is impossible to quantify, there are signs of rising numbers of ox-drawn ploughs, seed-drills and other animal-powered equipment in the Han period, though most farming was probably still done with mattocks, hoes, sickles and other hand tools. Occasional indications of ratios of harvest to seed suggest that 10:1 was not unusual, a much higher yield than Roman farmers could expect.

Farmers also produced pulses, the main source of protein other than grain, and many kinds of fruit and vegetables. Meat was a privilege for the few. Dairy products were not part of the Chinese diet before the barbarian invasions that followed Han. While men grew the crops, women fed the silkworms with mulberry leaves, reeled the silk from the cocoons and spun it into thread. They also processed hemp, the main plant fibre for clothing in China before the later introduction of cotton, and wove hemp and silk cloth.

While some peasant families farmed their own land, others sold their labour as farm hands. There was a long-term trend through the Han period, and especially in the Eastern Han, for some families to become local magnates with large numbers of dependant tenants, serfs or slaves. The Qin and early Western Han policy of uprooting leading clans from their home districts and moving them to the area round the capital or the frontier was abandoned. Eastern Han tombs give lively images of the manorial economy and the way leading families wanted to go on living on their rural estates after death. Wall paintings and bas reliefs show all kinds of farm work as well as the pleasures of feasting, music and hunting. Ceramic models represent granaries, fishponds, grain-processing machinery and walled manor houses protected by high pagoda-like watchtowers, on some of which archers with crossbows keep guard.

More and more people farmed the fertile plains created by the silt carried down from the mountains by the Yellow and other north Chinese rivers over millions of years. Left to itself the Yellow river raises its own bed year by year until it changes course. From Han times onwards there were repeated efforts to contain the river within dykes, efforts that lifted the river above the plain and made the inevitable floods worse, most catastrophically in AD 11 when the river changed its route to the sea.

Except where communications were bad, agriculture was part of a commercial economy that continued to grow under Qin and Han. Walled cities and towns were primarily seats of state power, but they were also market centres linked in trade networks that enabled merchants and manufacturers to prosper when the empire was at peace. The greatest cities were Chang'an (Xi'an), the Western Han capital, and Luoyang that was rebuilt as the Eastern Han one. Most of Chang'an and much of Luoyang were taken up by huge palace complexes, but trade still flourished. A treatise on wealth creation written around 100 BC by Sima Qian celebrates the fortunes made by successful businessmen and women that enabled them to live like marquises and princes. He advocates a laissez-faire approach to the pursuit of self-interest. Although most trade was local, some high-value commodities repaid the cost of taking them to distant markets. Trade continued to let many people apart from primary producers prosper, but not all were pleased. Some 250 years after Sima Qian, the sour Confucian Wang Fu denounces what he sees in Luoyang: hordes of dealers making money as they live off the honest toil of the peasants. He takes the common Confucian view of the economy as a zero-sum game in which merchants are parasites. Merchants were expected to accept lower social status than officials, scholars and the landed classes. They had no legitimate political voice. Throughout the Qin and Han period high office was essential to social standing, and this applied even to the great rural magnates.

Commerce encouraged many developments in technology, from iron and steel for tools and weapons to grain-processing machinery and looms that could weave intricate brocades. Medicine made great progress. Fine lacquerware cups in early Han tombs are replaced by porcelain ones in late ones.

## Cultures and values under Qin and Han

Among the First Qin emperor's failures was his attempt to crush the open market in ideas of the 5th to 3rd centuries BC. Not content with imposing the Qin administrative order, in 214 BC he made it a criminal offence for anyone except a few state-appointed specialists to possess almost any books except practical manuals and Qin laws. The next year he also had some 460 scholars in the capital who had spoken against him buried alive. But in its few remaining years the Qin regime was not able to burn all the copies of banned books or kill all who had memorized them.

In the first century of Han rule the many pre-Qin schools of thought were revived, and there was lively competition between them.

As far back as records go the main concerns of thinkers in China had been politics and the ordering of society. The political theories known as Legalism that had underlain Qin rule – a strong state controlling the people through inescapable laws and taking much of their labour – continued to influence government. Although these principles were at first applied with a slightly lighter hand, the emperor Wudi reverted to harsh taxes and conscription to provide for his wars, while key ministers openly admired Legalism. The Qin system of criminal and administrative law continued to apply with only limited adjustments, and many Han officials made their careers enforcing the state's laws. Another tenet of Legalist thinking – a bureaucracy in which every official holds his job only at the ruler's pleasure and is rewarded or punished for how well he lives up to his job description – remained central to Han government.

Under the first Han rulers the methods of minimalist government associated with the mythical Yellow Emperor of remote antiquity and the more recent but shadowy Laozi were fashionable in ruling circles. Arguments that doing as little as possible was the way for the ruler to benefit the state and the people had much appeal in an empire that needed to be left alone to recover from decades of destructive war. Another approach to politics that revived for a while under Han but had no appeal to the state was that of the Mohists, a sect that had long been against the extravagance of rulers. Although they were at a court conference on frontier policy in 81 BC, they disappear from the record soon afterwards.

Great efforts were made to recover and put in order pre-Qin books of all kinds in Han times. Apart from a few early texts found by archaeologists in recent decades, all the surviving books from pre-Qin China are as handed down by Han editors. Sima Qian, whose universal history has for over 2,000 years been hugely influential in fixing our images of the pre-Qin, Qin and early Han world, was a great anthologist as well as a brilliant writer. After being penally castrated in 99 BC he devoted himself to completing the great history of China and the world known to China from remote antiquity to his own times, a project begun by his father. *Shiji, Records of the Astronomer/Historian* – the office he held combined both functions – reflects the intellectual diversity and liveliness of the early Han. In its pages he presents many different views, letting his subjects use their own words where possible. He adopts a variety of formats. One set of chapters summarizes official records of events in annalistic form. Some topics are dealt with in thematic monographs. Reference material is put in tables that can be skipped when not needed. Most of the book consists of lively accounts of representative figures of their times from sages to gangsters and of foreign nations. Where other texts of his sources survive we can see that he presents them fairly. Some of his best stories must have come by word of mouth. He does not impose a unified narrative or an overriding ideology to the book. Shiji represents Han written culture at its best. Although its form was copied by later historians, its energy and multiplicity of views was never matched.

The school of thought that triumphed under Han traced its roots back to Confucius (*c.* 551–479 BC), a Ru scholar. Ru used the texts of the Zhou past to educate the sons of the aristocracy and gentry. Confucius had been so charismatic and persuasive a teacher and interpreter of the classics that his students and their later followers made the Ru school 'Confucian'. Few Ru scholars had seemed of practical use to rulers desperate to strengthen their states in the cut-throat international competition of the 4th and 3rd centuries BC. Qin had been hostile to them long before the First Emperor ruled the state of Qin, and he had persecuted them. After Qin its hostility to them became an asset to Confucians, who evidently enjoyed taking the moral high ground in denouncing Qin.

Once the Han empire was securely established Confucians had even more in their favour. Given that Han had the practical benefits of Legalist bureaucratic dictatorship and laws, an astute ruler saw advantages in cushioning this with the Confucian model of an ordered, family-based society in which everyone knew their place. Through the

Han centuries education mainly meant learning the classics. The classics as interpreted by Confucians taught people how to behave. They also inculcated into future officials a sense of duty to their superiors and to those under them. A good Confucian official was not only moved by the hope of reward and the fear of punishment. He was also expected to have a conscience and do the right thing for its own sake. Being a gentleman – the goal of all good Confucians – was a matter of how one acted, not just of birth. As parvenus the early Han emperors were also susceptible to Confucianists' advice on how to locate themselves in a great tradition of Chinese kingship going back thousands of years, even when they were really the heirs of Qin.

The emperor Wudi, who in most of his actions was a Qin-style Legalist, did more than any of his predecessors to promote Confucianism as something approaching a state ideology. Many of his officials were selected on the strength of their knowledge of the classics or their supposed Confucian behaviour. Wang Mang justified many of his policies by appealing to Confucian classics. Under the Eastern Han the classics were so important to the state that definitive texts of them all were carved in stone and displayed in Luoyang so that there could be no doubt about the authoritative wording. The text of some of the classics was deeply contested. Some scholars traced their preferred texts back to versions in old, pre-Qin, script. Others preferred texts written down from memory in the new Han script. Old-texters and new-texters accused each other of corrupting the text for political purposes. Such issues aside, the Confucian tradition served on the whole to justify a moderate conservatism that ensured social order and the basic welfare of the common people. It also discouraged original thinking.

The capital Luoyang was also the site of the Eastern Han imperial university, the successor to a smaller, Western Han university founded by Wudi. In it specialists in each of the classics taught thousands of students from across the empire who saw a classical education as the key to an official career. In the bitter struggles that pitted some career officials against imperial in-laws and eunuchs in the 2nd century AD, students sided with Confucian-minded officials and were involved in some of the earliest mass student protests in history. The close association between the state, Confucian values and office-holding that was formed in Han times was to continue for the rest of dynastic Chinese history.

Although Confucian traditions required certain rituals which were valuable for symbolizing the social and natural order, including sacrifices to heaven and to ancestors, Confucianism was not a numinous religion; nor did it offer personal connections with a deity. Yet there were other belief systems in Han times offering the help of deities in securing a good afterlife, as can be seen from the decorations and furnishings of Han tombs in which they look after the deceased. One cult was that of the immortality-giving Queen Mother of the West. There was widespread excitement across China early in 3 BC when her devotees prepared for her coming, only to be disappointed. One group of beliefs and practices that sought to obtain magical powers, culminating in becoming an immortal, was associated with Daoism. The Daoist pursuit of immortality included physical exercises for correct breathing – a silk chart of exercises was found in a tomb of the 2nd century BC – as well as sexual techniques to build up the life force in the body. But did this amount to a religion?

One undoubtedly religious cult that fatally weakened the Eastern Han was that of the Way of Great Peace, which offered forgiveness of sins, social support and the promise of a new world for the saved. This highly organized sect prepared coordinated uprisings across eastern China in 184. The rebels were called Yellow Turbans because their headcloths were the colour of the new heaven that was to take over the world. Han's own armies could not defeat them, so local magnates did so with their private armies then went on to fight among themselves for the empire. From then till the formal end of the dynasty in 220, Han emperors were only puppets of warlords.

One religion that reached China by the 1st century AD, probably as a result of contact with central, western and southern Asia following

Han intervention in Xinjiang, was Buddhism. The few mentions of it in accounts of Eastern Han suggest a private minority cult. It would await the disorder that followed the fall of Han to transform the Chinese mental world.

Two changes that Qin and Han made to the written culture they inherited were the imposition of a unified script and the invention of paper. As a great empire could only be governed through written documents, it was essential that they should all be in the same writing. Qin insisted that its Chinese script replace the multiplicity of scripts in the various pre-Qin states. The Han standard script was much closer to modern Chinese writing. Once the technique of turning a pulp of vegetable fibres into sheets of light, flexible writing material had been developed in Eastern Han times, paper proved to be much more convenient than the bundles of wooden or bamboo strips used previously. Paper made the physical process of writing quicker and easier. The writing brush's freedom of movement on paper made possible China's supreme visual art form, calligraphy. By the end of the Eastern Han China was becoming a paper culture.

# RULERS AND LEADERS

## PHARAOHS OF NEW KINGDOM EGYPT

*18th Dynasty*

| | |
|---|---|
| 1539–1514 BC | Ahmose I |
| 1514–1493 BC | Amenhotep I |
| 1493–1481 BC | Thutmose I |
| 1481–1479 BC | Thutmose II |
| 1479–1425 BC | Thutmose III |
| (1473–1458 BC | Hatshepsut) |
| 1426–1400 BC | Amenhotep II |
| 1400–1390 BC | Thutmose IV |
| 1390–1353 BC | Amenhotep III |
| 1353–1336 BC | Akhenaten |
| 1336–1332 BC | Smenkhkara |
| 1332–1322 BC | Tutankhamun |
| 1322–1319 BC | Ay |
| 1319–1292 BC | Horemheb |

*19th Dynasty*

| | |
|---|---|
| 1292–1290 BC | Ramesses I |
| 1290–1279 BC | Sety I |
| 1279–1213 BC | Ramesses II |
| 1213–1204 BC | Merenptah |
| 1204–1198 BC | Sety II |
| (1202–1200 BC | Amenmesse) |
| 1198–1193 BC | Siptah |
| 1198–1190 BC | Twosret |

*20th Dynasty*

| | |
|---|---|
| 1190–1187 BC | Sethnakhte |
| 1187–1156 BC | Ramesses III |
| 1156–1150 BC | Ramesses IV |
| 1150–1145 BC | Ramesses V |
| 1145–1137 BC | Ramesses VI |
| 1137–1129 BC | Ramesses VII |
| 1129–1126 BC | Ramesses VIII |
| 1126–1108 BC | Ramesses IX |
| 1108–1099 BC | Ramesses X |
| 1099–1069 BC | Ramesses XI |

## HITTITE KINGS

| | |
|---|---|
| ?–1650 BC | Labarna |
| 1650–1620 BC | Hattusili I |
| 1620–1590 BC | Mursili I |
| 1590–1560 BC | Hantili I |
| between 1560 and 1525 BC | Zidanta I |
| | Ammuna |
| | Huzziya |
| 1525–1500 BC | Telipinu |
| between 1500 and 1400 BC | Alluwamna |
| | Tahurwaili |
| | Hantili II |
| | Zidanta II |
| | Huzziya II |
| | Muwatalli I |
| between 1400 and 1350 BC | Tudhaliya I/II |
| | Arnuwanda I |
| | Hattusili II |
| | Tudhaliya III |
| 1350–1322 BC | Suppiluliuma I |
| 1322–1321 BC | Arnuwanda II |
| 1321–1295 BC | Mursili II |
| 1295–1272 BC | Muwatalli II |
| 1272–1267 BC | Urhi-Teshub |

| | | | |
|---|---|---|---|
| 1267–1237 BC | Hattusili III | 1209–1207 BC | Arnuwanda III |
| 1237–1209 BC | Tudhaliya IV | 1207–? BC | Suppiluliuma II |

## ASSYRIAN AND BABYLONIAN KINGS

| *Assyria* | | 680–669 BC | Esarhaddon |
|---|---|---|---|
| 911–891 BC | Adad-nirari II | 668–627 BC | Assurbanipal |
| 890–884 BC | Tukulti-Ninurta II | 627–623 BC | Assur-etel-ilani |
| 883–859 BC | Assurnasirpal II | 622–612 BC | Sin-shar-ishkun |
| 858–824 BC | Shalmaneser III | | |
| 823–811 BC | Shamshi-Adad V | *Babylonia* | |
| 810–783 BC | Adad-nirari III | 625–605 BC | Nabopolassar |
| 782–773 BC | Shalmaneser IV | 604–562 BC | Nebuchadnezzar |
| 772–755 BC | Assur-dan III | 561–560 BC | Amel-Marduk |
| 754–745 BC | Assur-nirari V | 559–556 BC | Nergal-Shar-Usur |
| 744–727 BC | Tiglath-Pileser III | 556 BC | Labashi-Marduk |
| 726–722 BC | Shalmaneser V | 555–539 BC | Nabonidus |
| 721–705 BC | Sargon II | | |
| 704–681 BC | Sennacherib | | |

## ACHAEMENID KINGS OF THE PERSIAN EMPIRE

| 559–530 BC | Cyrus II (the Great) | 424 BC | Sogdianus |
|---|---|---|---|
| 530–522 BC | Cambyses II | 424–405 BC | Darius II |
| 522 BC | Bardiya (Smerdis) | 405–359 BC | Artaxerxes II |
| 521–486 BC | Darius I (the Great) | 359–338 BC | Artaxerxes III |
| 486–465 BC | Xerxes I | 338–336 BC | Artaxerxes IV |
| 465–425 BC | Artaxerxes I | 336–330 BC | Darius III |
| 425–424 BC | Xerxes II | | |

## PROMINENT ATHENIAN POLITICIANS

| late 6th century BC: enacted reforms 508 BC | Cleisthenes | died 422 BC | Cleon |
|---|---|---|---|
| | | 451–404 BC | Alcibiades |
| | | died 388 BC | Thrasybulus |
| c. 524–459 BC | Themistocles | late 5th century BC to late 350s BC: played key role in foundation of second Athenian confederacy | Timotheus |
| died c. 467 BC | Aristides | | |
| died late 450s BC | Cimon | | |
| early 5th century BC: responsible for democratic reforms 462 BC, murdered shortly after | Ephialtes | | |
| | | c. 405–335 BC | Eubulus |
| | | c. 390–325 BC | Lycurgus |
| c. 495–429 BC | Pericles | 384–322 BC | Demosthenes |

## ALEXANDER AND HIS SUCCESSORS

| | | | |
|---|---|---|---|
| 338–323 BC | Alexander | 121–96 BC | Antiochus VIII Grypus |
| | | 115–95 BC | Antiochus IX Cyzicenus |
| *Antigonids of Macedon* | | 96–95 BC | Seleucus VI Epiphanes Nicanor |
| 306–301 BC | Antigonus I Monophthalmus | | |
| 306–283 BC | Demetrius I Poliorcetes | 95–88 BC | Demetrius III Philopator |
| 283–239 BC | Antigonus II Gonatas | 95–83 BC | Antiochus X Eusebes |
| 239–229 BC | Demetrius II | 95 BC | Antiochus XI Philadelphus |
| 229–221 BC | Antigonus III Doson | 94–84 BC | Philip I Philadelphus |
| 221–179 BC | Philip V | 87 BC | Antiochus XII Dionysus |
| 179–168 BC | Perseus | 83–69 BC | (Tigranes of Armenia) |
| *Seleucids* | | 69–64 BC | Antiochus XIII Asiaticus |
| 305–281 BC | Seleucus I Nicator | 65–64 BC | Philip II |
| 281–261 BC | Antiochus I Soter | | |
| 261–246 BC | Antiochus II Theos | *Attalids of Pergamum* | |
| 246–225 BC | Seleucus II Callinicus | 283–263 BC | Philetaerus |
| 225–223 BC | Seleucus III Soter | 263–241 BC | Eumenes I |
| 223–187 BC | Antiochus III the Great | 241–197 BC | Attalus I Soter |
| | | 197–159 BC | Eumenes II Soter |
| 187–175 BC | Seleucus IV Philopater | 159–138 BC | Attalus II |
| 175–164 BC | Antiochus IV Epiphanes | 138–133 BC | Attalus III |
| 163–162 BC | Antiochus V Eupator | | |
| 162–150 BC | Demetrius I Soter | *Ptolemies* | |
| 150–145 BC | Alexander Balas | 305–283 BC | Ptolemy I Soter |
| 145–142 BC | Antiochus VI Epiphanes | 283–246 BC | Ptolemy II Philadelphus |
| 138–129 BC | Antiochus VII Sidetes | 246–222 BC | Ptolemy III Euergetes I |
| 129–125 BC | Demetrius II NIcator | 222–204 BC | Ptolemy IV Philopator |
| 126 BC | Cleopatra Thea | 204–180 BC | Ptolemy V Epiphanes |
| 125–121 BC | Cleopatra Thea and Antiochus VIII Grypus | 180–145 BC | Ptolemy VI Philometor |
| 125 BC | Seleucus V | | |

| | | | |
|---|---|---|---|
| 145–144 BC | Ptolemy VII Neos Philopator | 88–81 BC | Ptolemy IX |
| 145–116 BC | Ptolemy VIII Euergetes II Physcon | 80 BC | Ptolemy XI Alexander II |
| | | 80–58 BC | Ptolemy XII Neos Dionysus |
| 139–101 BC | Cleopatra III | 58–55 BC | Berenice IV |
| 116–107 BC | Ptolemy IX Soter II | 55–51 BC | Ptolemy XII |
| | | 51–47 BC | Ptolemy XIII |
| 107–88 BC | Ptolemy X Alexander | 51–30 BC | Cleopatra VII Philopator |
| 101–88 BC | Cleopatra Berenice | 47–44 BC | Ptolemy XIV |
| | | 36–30 BC | Ptolemy XV |

## PARTHIAN AND EARLY SASANIAN KINGS

| *Parthian* | | 55–58 | Vardanes II |
|---|---|---|---|
| 238–211 BC | Arsaces I | 78–105 | Pakoros II |
| 211–191 BC | Arsaces II | 80–90 | Artabanus III |
| 191–176 BC | Priapatios | 105–147 | Vologases III |
| 176–171 BC | Phraates I | 109–129 | Osroes I |
| 171–138 BC | Mithridates I | 116 | Parthamaspates |
| 138–127 BC | Phraates II | 140 | Mithridates IV |
| 127–124 BC | Artabanus I | 147–191 | Vologases IV |
| 123–88 BC | Mithridates II | 190 | Osroes II |
| 95–87 BC | Gotarzes I | 191–208 | Vologases V |
| 90–77 BC | Orodes I | 208–228 | Vologases VI |
| 77–70 BC | Sinatruces | 216–224 | Artabanus IV |
| 70–57 BC | Phraates III | | |
| 57–54 BC | Mithridates III | *Sasanian* | |
| 57–38 BC | Orodes II | 224–241 | Ardashir I |
| 38–2 BC | Phraates IV | 241–272 | Shapur I |
| 2 BC–AD 4 | Phraatakes | 272–273 | Hormizd I |
| 8–12 | Vonones I | 273–276 | Vahram I |
| 10–38 | Artabanus II | 276–293 | Vahram II |
| 40–45 | Vardanes I | 293 | Vahram III |
| 40–51 | Gotarzes II | 293–303 | Narseh |
| 51 | Vonones II | | |
| 51–78 | Vologases I | | |

## ROMAN EMPERORS

| *Julio-Claudian Dynasty* | | 37–41 | Caligula |
|---|---|---|---|
| 31 BC–AD 14 | Augustus | 41–54 | Claudius |
| 14–37 | Tiberius | 54–68 | Nero |

*Civil War of 69*

| | |
|---|---|
| 68–69 | Galba |
| 69 | Otho |
| 69 | Vitellius |

*Flavian Dynasty*

| | |
|---|---|
| 69–79 | Vespasian |
| 79–81 | Titus |
| 81–96 | Domitian |

*Adoptive Emperors and the Antonine Dynasty*

| | |
|---|---|
| 96–98 | Nerva |
| 98–117 | Trajan |
| 117–38 | Hadrian |
| 138–61 | Antoninus Pius |
| 161–180 | Marcus Aurelius |
| (161–69 | and Lucius Verus) |
| 180–92 | Commodus |

*Civil War of 193*

| | |
|---|---|
| 193 | Pertinax |
| 193 | Didius Julianus |

*Severan Dynasty*

| | |
|---|---|
| 193–211 | Septimius Severus |
| 211 | Geta |
| 211–17 | Caracalla |
| 217–18 | Macrinus |
| 218–22 | Elagabalus |
| 222–35 | Alexander Severus |

*Third-century Crisis*

| | |
|---|---|
| 235–38 | Maximinus Thrax |
| 238 | Gordian I |
| 238 | Gordian II |
| 238 | Pupienus and Balbinus |
| 238–44 | Gordian II |
| 244–49 | Philip the Arab |
| 249–51 | Decius |
| 251–53 | Trebonianus Gallus |
| 253 | Aemilius Aemilianus |
| 253–60 | Valerian |
| 253–268 | Gallienus |

| | |
|---|---|
| 268–270 | Claudius II |
| 270 | Quintillus |
| 270–75 | Aurelian |
| 275–76 | Tacitus |
| 276 | Florianus |
| 276–82 | Probus |
| 282–83 | Carus |
| 283–84 | Numerian |
| 283–85 | Carinus |
| 260–69 | Postumus |
| 269 | Laelianus |
| 269 | Marius |
| 268–71 | Victorinus |
| 271–74 | Tetricus |

*Later Roman Empire*

| | |
|---|---|
| 284–305 | Diocletian |
| (286–305 | Maximian) |
| 305–6 | Constantius I |
| 305–11 | Galerius |
| 306–7 | Severus II |
| 306–12 | Maxentius |
| 310–13 | Maximinus Daia |
| 307–37 | Constantine |
| (308–24 | Licinius) |
| 337–40 | Constantine II |
| 337–50 | Constans I |
| 337–61 | Constantius II |
| 360–63 | Julian |
| 363–364 | Jovian |

*House of Valentinian*

| | |
|---|---|
| 364–78 | Valens |
| /364–75 | Valentinian |
| 367–83 | Gratian |
| 375–92 | Valentinian II |
| 392–94 | Eugenius |

*Theodosian Dynasty*

| | |
|---|---|
| 379–95 | Theodosius I |
| 395–408 | Arcadius |
| /395–423 | Honorius |
| 408–50 | Theodosius II |
| /423–25 | Johannes |
| /425–55 | Valentinian III |

*The Final Emperors*

| | | | |
|---|---|---|---|
| 455 | Petronius Maximus | 467–72 | Anthemius |
| 455–56 | Avitus | 472 | Olybrius |
| 456–61 | Majorian | 473–74 | Glycerius |
| 461–65 | Severus III | 474–75 | Julius Nepos |
| | | 475–76 | Romulus Augustulus |

## RULERS OF EARLY SOUTH ASIAN EMPIRES

| *Mauryan rulers* | | 105–127 | Vima Kadphises |
|---|---|---|---|
| 321–297 BC | Chandragupta Maurya | 127–147 | Kanishka |
| | | 140–183 | Huvishka |
| 297–272 BC | Bindusara | 191–225 | Vasudeva |
| 272–235 BC | Asoka | | |
| 235–221 BC | Dasaratha | *Gupta emperors* | |
| 221–185 BC | Brihadratha | 319–335 | Chandragupta |
| | | 335–375 | Samudragupta |
| *Kushan emperors* | | 380–413 | Chandragupta II |
| 30–80 | Kujula Kadphises | 414–454 | Kumaragupta |
| 80–105 | Vima Taktu | 455–467 | Skandagupta |

## QIN AND HAN EMPERORS OF CHINA

*This list follows the Chinese convention of dating reigns from the first new year after the death of the previous emperor. Very short reigns have been omitted.*

| *Qin* | | 86–74 BC | Zhaodi |
|---|---|---|---|
| 221–210 BC | Qin Shi Huang di, First Qin Emperor | 73–49 BC | Xuandi |
| | | 48–33 BC | Yuandi |
| 209–207 BC | Qin Er Huang di, Second Qin Emperor | 32–7 BC | Chengdi |
| | | 6–1 BC | Aidi |
| | | AD 1–5 | Pingdi |
| *Western or Earlier Han* | | *Xin* | |
| 206/2–195 BC | Gaozu or Gaodi (Liu Bang) | 9–23 | Wang Mang |
| | | *Eastern or Later Han* | |
| | | 25–57 | Guangwudi |
| 194–188 BC | Huidi | 58–75 | Mingdi |
| 187–180 BC | Empress Lü | 76–88 | Zhangdi |
| 179–157 BC | Wendi | 89–105 | Hedi |
| 156–141 BC | Jingdi | 107–125 | Andi |
| 140–87 BC | Wudi | 126–144 | Shundi |
| | | 147–167 | Huandi |
| | | 168–189 | Lingdi |
| | | 190–220 | Xiandi |

# CONTRIBUTORS

**Alastair Blanshard** is the Paul Eliadis Chair of Classics and Ancient History at the University of Queensland, Australia. His publications include *Sex: Vice and Love from Antiquity to Modernity* (2010) and *Classical World: All That Matters* (2015).

**Trevor Bryce** is a Near Eastern historian and Honorary Professor in Classics at the University of Queensland. He has been awarded an Australian Centenary Medal for Service to Australian Society and the Humanities in the Study of History. His publications include *The World of the Neo-Hittite Kingdoms* (2012) and *Ancient Syria: A Three Thousand Year History* (2014).

**Robin Coningham** is UNESCO Professor in the Department of Archaeology at Durham University. He has conducted fieldwork in Bangladesh, India, Nepal, Pakistan and Sri Lanka. He is the author of *The Archaeology of South Asia: From the Indus to Asoka* c. 6500 BCE – 200 CE (2015) (with Ruth Young) and editor of *Archaeology, Cultural Heritage Protection and Community Engagement in South Asia* (2019) (with Nick Lewer).

**W. J. F. Jenner** has been writing on Chinese history and culture for over 50 years. His books include *Memories of Loyang* (1981) and *The Tyranny of History: The Roots of China's Crisis* (1992).

**Ted Kaizer** is Professor in Roman Culture and History at Durham University. His main research interest is the social and religious history of the Near East in the Late Hellenistic and Roman periods. He is the author of *The Religious Life of Palmyra* (2002) and editor of *Religion, Society and Culture at Dura-Europos* (2016).

**Lloyd Llewellyn-Jones** is Professor in Ancient History at Cardiff University, specializing in the history, culture and society of Greece and Achaemenid Iran. His publications include *King and Court in Ancient Persia 559 to 331 BCE* (2013) and *Designs on the Past: How Hollywood Created the Ancient World* (2018).

**Bill Manley** is Honorary President of Egyptology Scotland and a tutor in Egyptology and Coptic at the University of Glasgow Centre for Open Studies. His books include *Egyptian Hieroglyphs for Complete Beginners* (2012) and *Egyptian Art* (2017).

**Mark Manuel** is a Research Fellow in the Department of Archaeology at Durham University, focusing on South Asian landscape archaeology. He works primarily at the World Heritage Sites of Lumbini and Tilaurakot in Nepal, Anuradhapura and Polonnaruwa in Sri Lanka and Champaner-Pavagadh in India.

**Michael Sommer** is Professor of Ancient History at the Carl von Ossietzky University of Oldenburg, Germany. He has published extensively on Phoenician history, economy and culture as well as the Roman empire.

**Marc Van De Mieroop** is Professor of Ancient Near Eastern History at Columbia University, New York City, and founding editor of the *Journal of Ancient Near Eastern History.* He is the author of *Philosophy before the Greeks: The Pursuit of Truth in Ancient Babylonia* (2015) and *A History of the Ancient Near East, ca. 3000–323 BC* (3rd edition 2016).

# FURTHER READING

## GENERAL

Alcock, S. E., T. N. D'Altroy, K. D.
Morrison and C. M. Sinopoli (eds),
*Empires: Perspectives from Archaeology
and History* (Cambridge, 2001).

Baring, E., *Ancient and Modern
Imperialism* (London, 1910).

Hardt, M. and A. Negri, *Empire*
(Cambridge, MA, 2001).

Howe, S., *Empire: A Very Short
Introduction* (Oxford, 2002).

Said, E., *Culture and Imperialism* (London
& New York, 1993).

## EGYPT

Baines, J. E. and J. Malek, *Cultural Atlas
of Ancient Egypt* (Oxford, 2004).

Dodson, A. M. and D. Hilton, *The
Complete Royal Families of Ancient
Egypt* (London & New York, 2004).

Gardiner, A. H., *The Kadesh Inscriptions
of Ramesses II* (Oxford, 1960).

Grimal, N., *A History of Ancient Egypt*
(Oxford, 1992).

Häsel, M., *Domination and Resistance:
Egyptian Military Activity in the Southern
Levant, c. 1300–1185 BC* (Leiden, 1998).

Kemp, B. J., *Ancient Egypt: Anatomy of a
Civilisation* (London, 1989).

Kitchen, K. A., *Pharaoh Triumphant: The
Life and Times of Ramesses II, King of
Egypt* (Warminster, 1983).

Kozloff, A. and B. M. Bryan, *Egypt's
Dazzling Sun: Amenhotep III and his
World* (Cleveland, 1992).

Leahy, M. A., *Libya and Egypt, c. 1300–
750 BC* (London, 1990).

Manley, W. P., *The Penguin Historical
Atlas of Ancient Egypt* (London, 1996).

Manley, W. P., *The Seventy Great
Mysteries of Ancient Egypt* (London
& New York, 2003).

Moran, W. L., *The Amarna Letters*
(Baltimore & London, 1992).

Morkot, R. G., *The Black Pharaohs:
Egypt's Nubian Rulers* (London,
2000).

Murnane, W., *The Road to Kadesh:
A Historical Interpretation of the Battle
Reliefs of King Sety I at Karnak* (rev.
ed., Chicago, 1990).

Mysliwiec, K., *The Twilight of Ancient
Egypt* (New York, 2000).

O'Connor, D., *Ancient Nubia: Egypt's
Rival in Africa* (Philadelphia, 1993).

Redford, D. B., *Egypt, Canaan and Israel
in Ancient Times* (Princeton, 1992).

Reeves, C. N., *The Complete
Tutankhamun* (rev. ed., London &
New York, 2006).

Romer, J., *Ancient Lives. The Story of
the Pharaohs' Tombmakers* (London,
1984/2003).

Sandars, N., *The Sea Peoples: Warriors of
the Eastern Mediterranean* (rev. ed.,
London & New York, 1985).

Shaw, I. M. E., *The Oxford History of
Ancient Egypt* (Oxford, 2000).

Wilkinson, R. H., *The Complete Temples
of Ancient Egypt* (London & New
York, 2000).

## HITTITES

Akurgal, E., *The Art of the Hittites*
(London, 1962).

Beal, R. H., *The Organisation of the Hittite Military* (Heidelberg, 1992).

Beckman, G. M., *Hittite Diplomatic Texts* (2nd ed., Atlanta, 1999).

Beckman, G. M., R. Beal, and G. McMahon (eds), *Hittites Studies in Honor of Harry A. Hoffner Jr* (Winona Lake, IN, 2003).

Bryce, T. R., *Life and Society in the Hittite World* (Oxford, 2002).

Bryce, T. R., *Letters of the Great Kings of the Ancient Near East* (London & New York, 2003).

Bryce, T. R., *The Kingdom of the Hittites* (new ed., Oxford, 2005).

Chavalas, M. W. (ed.), *The Ancient Near East* (Oxford, 2006).

Freu, J. and M. Mayozer, *Des origines à la fin de l'ancien royaume hittite: Les Hittites et leur histoire* (Paris, 2007).

Gurney, O. R., 'The Hittite Empire', in M. T. Larsen (ed.), *Power and Propaganda* (Copenhagen, 1979), 151–65.

Gurney, O. R., *The Hittites* (London, 1990).

Hoffner, H. A., *The Laws of the Hittites: A Critical Edition* (Leiden & New York, 1997).

Hoffner, H. A. and G. M. Beckman (eds), *Kaniššuwar: A Tribute to Hans Güterbock on his Seventy-Fifth Birthday* (Chicago, 1986).

Kitchen, K. A., *Pharaoh Triumphant: The Life and Times of Ramesses II* (Warminster, 1983).

Klengel, H., *Geschichte des Hethitischen Reiches* (Leiden, 1999).

Klock-Fontanille, I., *Les Hittites* (Paris, 1998).

Macqueen, J. G., *The Hittites and their Contemporaries in Asia Minor* (rev. ed., London & New York, 1986).

Macqueen, J. G., 'The History of Anatolia and of the Hittite Empire: An Overview', in J. M. Sasson (ed.), *Civilizations of the Ancient Near East* (vol. 2, New York, 1995), 1085–1105.

Singer, I., 'New Evidence on the End of the Hittite Empire', in E. D. Oren (ed.), *The Sea Peoples and their World: A Reassessment* (Philadelphia, 2000), 21–33.

Van den Hout, T., 'Khattushili III, King of the Hittites', in J. M. Sasson (ed.), *Civilizations of the Ancient Near East* (vol. 2, New York, 1995), 1107–20.

Yener, K. A. and H. A. Hoffner (eds), *Recent Developments in Hittite Archaeology and History, Papers in Memory of Hans G. Güterbock* (Winona Lake, IN, 2002).

## ASSYRIA AND BABYLONIA

Bahrani, Z., *Rituals of War: The Body and Violence in Mesopotamia* (Cambridge, MA, 2008).

Boardman, J. (ed.), *The Assyrian and Babylonian Empires and other States of the Near East (Cambridge Ancient History*, 2nd ed.: vol. 3, pt 2) (Cambridge & New York, 1991).

Curtis, J. E. and J. E. Reade (eds), *Art and Empire: Treasures from Assyria in the British Museum* (New York, 1995).

Finkel, I. L. and M. J. Seymour, *Babylon: Myth and Reality* (London, 2008).

Joannès, F., *The Age of Empires: Mesopotamia in the First Millennium* (Edinburgh, 2004).

Kuhrt, A., *The Ancient Near East* (vol. 2, London & New York, 2005).

Larsen, M. T. (ed.), *Power and Propaganda* (Copenhagen, 1979).

Oates, J. *Babylon* (rev. ed., London & New York, 2008).

Parpola, S. and R. M. Whiting (eds), *Assyria 1995* (Helsinki, 1997).

Porter, B. N., *Images, Power, and Politics: Figurative Aspects of Esarhaddon's Babylonian Policy* (Philadephia, 1993).

Reade, J., *Assyrian Sculpture* (Cambridge, MA, 1999).

Saggs, H. W. F., *The Might that was Assyria* (London, 1984).

Van De Mieroop, M., *A History of the Ancient Near East, ca. 3000–323 BC* (2nd ed., Oxford, 2007).

Wiseman, D. J., *Nebuchadnezzar and Babylon* (Oxford & New York, 1985).

## PERSIA

Allen, L., *The Persian Empire* (London, 2005).

Boardman, J., *Persia and the West. An Archaeological Investigation of the Genesis of Achaemenid Art* (London, 2000).

Briant, P., *From Cyrus to Alexander. A History of the Persian Empire* (Winona Lake, 2002).

Brosius, P., *The Persian Empire from Cyrus II to Artaxerxes I* (Lactor 16, Cambridge, 2000).

Cawkwell, G., *The Greek Wars: The Failure of Persia* (Oxford, 2005).

Cook, J. M., *The Persian Empire* (London, 1983).

Curtis, J. and N. Tallis (eds), *Forgotten Empire: The World of Ancient Persia* (London, 2005).

Dandamayev, M. A., *A Political History of the Achaemenid Empire* (Leiden, 1989).

Dandamayev, M. A. and V. G. Lukonin, *The Culture and Social Institutions of Ancient Iran* (Cambridge, 1989).

Drews, R., *The Greek Accounts of Eastern History* (Cambridge, MA, 1973).

Farrokh, K., *Shadows in the Desert: Ancient Persia at War* (Oxford, 2007).

Fried, L. S., *The Priest and the Great King: Temple–Palace Relations in the Persian Empire* (Winona Lake, IN, 2004).

Frye, R. N., *The Heritage of Persia* (London, 1962).

Gershevitch, I., *The Cambridge History of Iran, vol 2. The Median and Achaemenian Periods* (Cambridge, 1985).

Hall, E., *Inventing the Barbarian: Greek Self-Definition through Tragedy* (Oxford, 1989).

Harper, P. O., J. Aruz, and F. Tallon (eds), *The Royal City of Susa: Ancient Near Eastern Treasures in the Louvre* (New York, 1992).

Harrison, T., *Greeks and Barbarians* (Edinburgh, 2002).

Kuhrt, A., *The Persian Empire: A Corpus of Sources from the Achaemenid Period* (2 vols, London, 2007).

Mackey, S., *The Iranians: Persia, Islam and the Soul of a Nation* (New York, 1996).

Malkin, I., *Ancient Perceptions of Greek Ethnicity* (Cambridge, MA, 2001).

Matheson, S. A., *Persia: An Archaeological Guide* (London, 1972).

Miller, M., *Athens and Persia in the Fifth Century BC: A Study in Cultural Reciprocity* (Cambridge, 1997).

Olmstead, A. T., *History of the Persian Empire* (Chicago, 1948).

Roisman, J., *Brill's Companion to Alexander the Great* (Leiden, 2003).

Root, M. C., *The King and Kingship in Achaemenid Art: Essays on the Creation of an Iconography of Empire* (Leiden, 1979).

Sancisi-Weerdenburg, H., 'The Fifth Oriental Monarchy and Hellenocentrism', in H. Sancisi-Weerdenburg and A. Kuhrt (eds), *Achaemenid History, vol. 2. The Greek Sources* (Leiden, 1987), 117–31.

Tuplin, C. (ed.), *Persian Responses: Political and Cultural Interaction with(in) the Achaemenid Empire* (Swansea, 2007).

Wiesehöfer, J., *Ancient Persia from 550 BC to 650 AD* (London & New York, 1996).

Wilber, D. N., *Persepolis: The Archaeology of Parsa, Seat of the Persian Kings* (Princeton, 1969).

## ATHENS

Boedeker, D. and K. A. Raaflaub (eds), *Democracy, Empire and the Arts in Fifth-Century Athens* (Cambridge, MA, 1998).

Camp, J., *The Athenian Agora* (rev. ed., London & New York, 1998).

Cargill, J., *The Second Athenian League* (Berkeley & Los Angeles, 1981).

Finley, M. I., 'The Fifth-Century Athenian Empire: A Balance Sheet', in P. D. A. Garnsey and C. R. Whittaker (eds), *Imperialism in the Ancient World* (Cambridge, 1978).

Hornblower, S., *The Greek World, 479–323 BC* (3rd ed., London, 2002).

Hurwit, J. M., *The Athenian Acropolis: History, Mythology and Archaeology from the Neolithic Era to the Present* (Cambridge, 1998).

Kagan, D., *The Peloponnesian War* (New York, 2003).

Low, P., *Interstate Relations in Classical Greece* (Cambridge, 2007).

Meiggs, R., *The Athenian Empire* (Oxford, 1972).

Neils, J., *The Parthenon: From Antiquity to the Present* (Cambridge, 2005).

Parker, R., *Athenian Religion: A History* (Oxford, 1996).

Samons, L. J., *Empire of the Owl: Athenian Imperial Finance* (Stuttgart, 2000).

## ALEXANDER AND HIS SUCCESSORS

Austin, M. M., *The Hellenistic World from Alexander to the Roman Conquest.* (Cambridge, 2006).

Bowman, A. K., *Egypt after the Pharaohs, 332 BC–AD 642: From Alexander to the Arab Conquest* (2nd ed., Berkeley, 1996).

Bugh, G. R., *The Cambridge Companion to the Hellenistic World* (Cambridge, 2006).

Cartledge, P., *Alexander the Great: The Hunt for a New Past* (Woodstock, 2004).

Chamoux, F., *Hellenistic Civilisation* (Oxford, 2003).

Erskine, A. (ed.), *A Companion to the Hellenistic World* ( Oxford & Malden, MA, 2003).

Gehrke, H-J., *Geschichte des Hellenismus* (2nd ed., Munich, 1995).

Gruen. E. S., *The Hellenistic World and the Coming of Rome* (Berkeley, 1984).

Kuhrt, A. and S. Sherwin-White, *Hellenism in the East* (London, 1987).

Préaux, C., *Le monde hellénistique: La Grèce et l'Orient de la mort d'Alexandre à la conquête romaine de la Grèce (323–146 av. J.-C.)* (Paris, 1978).

Sherwin-White, S. M. and A. Kuhrt, *From Samarkhand to Sardis: A New Approach to the Seleucid Empire* (London, 1993).

Shipley, G., *The Greek World after Alexander 323–30 BC* (London, 2000).

Walbank, F. W., *The Hellenistic World* (3rd ed., London, 1992).

Weber, G. (ed.), *Kulturgeschichte des Hellenismus: Von Alexander dem Großen bis Kleopatra* (Stuttgart, 2007).

## PARTHIA AND SASANIA

Butcher, K., *Roman Syria and the Near East* (London, 2003).

Colledge, M., *The Parthians* (London, 1967).

Colledge, M., *Parthian Art* (London, 1977).

Curtis, J. E. (ed.), *Mesopotamia and Iran in the Parthian and Sassanian Periods* (London, 2000).

Dąbrowa, E. (ed.), *Ancient Iran and the Mediterranean World: Proceedings of an International Conference in Honour of Professor Józef Wolski* (Krakow, 1998).

Dignas, B. and E. Winter, *Rome and Persia in Late Antiquity: Neighbours and Rivals* (Cambridge, 2007).

Dirven, L., 'The Palmyrenes of Dura-Europos: A Study of Religious Interaction in Roman Syria', in M. H. Dodgeon and S. N. C. Lieu (eds), *The Roman Eastern Frontier and the Persian Wars (AD 226–363)* (Leiden, 1991).

Edwell, P., *Between Rome and Persia: The Middle Euphrates, Mesopotamia and Palmyra under Roman Control* (London, 2007).

Errington, E. and V. S. Curtis, *From Persepolis to the Punjab: Exploring Ancient Iran* (London, 2007).

Hopkins, C., *The Discovery of Dura-Europos*, ed. B. Goldman (New Haven & London, 1979).

Isaac, B., *The Limits of Empire: The Roman Army in the East* (rev. ed., Oxford, 1992).

Kennedy, D. and D. Riley, *Rome's Desert Frontier from the Air* (London, 1990).

Lepper, F. A., *Trajan's Parthian War* (London, 1948).

Lerouge, C., *L'image des Parthes dans le monde gréco-romain* (Stuttgart, 2007).

Millar, F., *The Roman Near East, 31 BC–AD 337* (Cambridge, MA, 1993).

Sarkhosh Curtis, V. and S. Stewart (eds), *The Age of the Parthians* (London, 2007).

Sartre, M., *The Middle East under Rome* (Cambridge, MA, 2005).

Wiesehöfer, J. (ed.), *Das Partherreich und seine Zeugnisse* (Stuttgart, 1998).

Wiesehöfer, J, *Ancient Persia from 550 BC to AD 650* (London, 2001).

Wolski, J., *L'empire des Arsacides* (Lovanni, 1993).

Yarshater, E. (ed.), *The Cambridge History of Iran: The Seleucid, Parthian and Sasanid Periods* (vol. 3, pts 1–2 Cambridge, 1983).

## ROME

Cameron, A., *The Later Roman Empire, AD 284–430* (Cambridge, MA, 1993).

Eck, W., *The Age of Augustus* (Oxford, 2003).

Goodman, M., *The Roman World, 44 BC–AD 180* (London, 1997).

Gruen, E. S., *The Hellenistic World and the Coming of Rome* (Berkeley, 1984).

Harris, W. V., *War and Imperialism in Republican Rome: 327–70 BC* (Oxford, 1979).

Heather, P. J., *The Fall of the Roman Empire: A New History* (London, 2006).

Jones, A. H. M., *The Greek City from Alexander to Justinian* (Oxford, 1940).

Millar, F., *The Emperor in the Roman World (31 BC–AD 337)* (New York, 1977).

Millar, F., *The Roman Near East: 31 BC–AD 337* (Cambridge, MA, 1993).

Potter, D. S., *The Roman Empire at Bay, AD 80–395* (London, 2004).

Potter, D. S., *Rome in the Ancient World* (London & New York, 2009).

Scott, S. and J. Webster (eds), *Roman Imperialism and Provincial Art* (Cambridge, 2003).

Sherwin-White, A. N., *Roman Citizenship* (2nd ed., Oxford, 1973).

Sommer, M., *Römische Geschichte II: Rom und sein Imperium in der Kaiserzeit* (Stuttgart, 2009).

Treggiari, S., *Roman Social History* (London, 2002).

Ward-Perkins, J. B., *The Fall of Rome and the End of Civilization* (Oxford, 2005).

Wells, C. M., *The Roman Empire* (2nd ed., London, 1992).

Woolf, G., *Becoming Roman: The Origins of Provincial Civilization in Gaul* (Cambridge, 1998).

## INDIA

Agrawal, D. P., *The Archaeology of India* (London, 1982).

Allchin, F. R. (ed.), *The Archaeology of Early Historic South Asia: The Emergence of Cities and States* (Cambridge, 1995).

Coningham, R. A. E., 'The Archaeology of Buddhism', in T. Insoll (ed.), *Archaeology and World Religion* (London, 2001), 61–95.

Coningham, R. A. E., 'South Asia: From Early Villages to Buddhism', in C. Scarre (ed.), *The Human Past* (London & New York, 2006), 518–551.

Coningham, R. A. E. and I. Ali (eds), *Charsadda: The British-Pakistani Excavations at the Bala Hisar* (Oxford, 2007).

Coningham, R. A. E. et al., 'The State of Theocracy: Defining an Early Medieval Hinterland in Sri Lanka', *Antiquity* 81: 1–21.

Coningham, R. A. E. and M. J. Manuel, 'Warfare in Ancient South Asia', in P. de Souza (ed.), *The Ancient World at War* (London & New York, 2008), 229–242.

Dani, A. H. and V. M. Masson (eds), *History of Civilisations of Central Asia, vol 1. The Dawn of Civilisation: Earliest Times to 700 BC* (Paris, 1992).

Harmatta, J., B. N. Puri and G. F. Etemadi, *History of Civilisations of Central Asia, vol 2. The Development of Sedentary and Nomadic Civilisations: 700 BC to 250 AD* (Paris, 1994).

Kulke, H. and D. Rothermund, *History of India* (London, 1992).

Marshall, J. H., *Taxila: An Illustrated Account of Archaeological Excavations* (Cambridge, 1951).

Morrison, K. D., 'Trade, Urbanism and Agricultural Expansion: Buddhist Monastic Institutions and the State in the Early Historic Western Deccan', *World Archaeology* 27: 203–221.

Rangarajan, L. N. (trans.), *Kautilya, The Arthasastra* (New Delhi, 1992).

Raychaudri, H., *Political History of Ancient India* (Calcutta, 1972).

Seneviratne, S., 'The Mauryan State', in H. J. M. Claessen and P. Skalnik (eds), *The Early State* (The Hague, 1978).

Thapar, R., *Asoka and the Decline of the Mauryas* (New Delhi, 1963).

Trautmann, T. R., *Kautilya and the Arthasastra: A Statistical Investigation of the Authorship and Evolution of the Text* (Leiden, 1971).

Wheeler, R. E. M., *Charsada: A Metropolis of the North-West Frontier:* (London, 1962).

## CHINA

Balazs, E., 'Political Philosophy and Social Crisis at the End of the Han Dynasty', in Arthur F. Wright (ed.), *Chinese Civilization and Bureaucracy: Variations on a Theme* (trans. H. M. Wright) (New Haven, 1964).

Bodde, D., *China's First Unifier: A study of the Ch'in Dynasty as seen in the Life of Li Ssu* (Leiden, 1938/1967).

de Bary, W. T. and I. Bloom (eds), *Sources of Chinese Tradition* (2nd ed., vol 1, New York, 1999), 225–374.

de Crespigny, R., *Northern Frontier: The Policies and Strategy of the Later Han Empire* (Canberra, 1984).

Di Cosmo, N., *Ancient China and its Enemies: The Rise of Nomadic Power in East Asian History* (Cambridge & New York, 2002).

Hulsewé, A. F. P., *Remnants of Ch'in Law: An Annotated Translation of the Ch'in Legal and Administrative Rules of the 3rd century BC, discovered in Yün-meng Prefecture, Hu-pei Province, in 1975* (Leiden, 1985).

Hulsewé, A. F. P., with an introduction by M. A. N. Loewe, *China in Central Asia, the Early Stage, 125 BC–AD 23: An Annotated Translation of Chapters 61 and 96 of the History of the Former Han Dynasty* (Leiden, 1979).

Lewis, M. E., *The Early Chinese Empires: Qin and Han* (Cambridge, MA, 2007).

Loewe, M., *A Biographical Dictionary of the Qin, Former Han and Xin Periods (221 BC–AD 24)* (Leiden, 2000).

Loewe, M., *Crisis and Conflict in Han China, 104 BC to AD 9* (London, 1974, reissued 2005).

Loewe, M., *Everyday Life in Early Imperial China during the Han Period, 202 BC–AD 220* (London & New York, 1968).

Loewe, M., *Records of Han Administration* (Cambridge, 1967).

Portal, J. (ed.), *The First Emperor: China's Terracotta Army* (London, 2007).

Twitchett, D. and M. Loewe (eds), *The Cambridge History of China*, vol. 1, *The Ch'in and Han Empires, 221 BC–AD 220* (Cambridge, 1986).

Wang Zhongshu, *Han Civilization*, trans. Chang Kwang-chih and others (New Haven & London, 1982).

Watson, B. (trans.), *Records of the Grand Historian: Qin Dynasty* by Sima Qian (Hong Kong & New York, 1993).

Watson, B. (trans.), *Records of the Grand Historian: Han Dynasty* by Sima Qian, 2 vol. (Hong Kong & New York, 1993).

Yang Hsienyi and G. Yang (trans.), *Selections from Records of the Historian* by Szuma Ch'ien (Beijing, 1979).

# PICTURE CREDITS

# INDEX